Rhetorical Grammar: Grammatical Choices, Rhetorical Effects

SECOND EDITION

Martha Kolln
THE PENNSYLVANIA STATE UNIVERSITY

Allyn and Bacon
Boston London Toronto Sydney Tokyo Singapore

Vice President: Eben W. Ludlow
Series Editorial Assistant: Morgan Lance
Marketing Manager: Lisa Kimball
Manufacturing buyer: Aloka Rathnam
Cover Administrator: Suzanne Harbison
Editorial-Production Service: Electronic Publishing Services Inc.

Simon & Schuster/A Viacom Company
Needham Heights, Massachusetts 02194

Library of Congress Cataloging-in-Publication Data

Kolln, Martha.
Rhetorical grammar: grammatical choices, rhetorical effects/
Martha Kolln.—2nd ed.
p. cm.
Includes index.
ISBN 0-02-365871-1
1. English Language–Rhetoric 2. English Language–Grammar.
I. Title.
PE1408.K696 1996
808'.042—dc20 95-8300
CIP

10 9 8 7 6 5 4 3 2 1 00 99 98 97 96 95

Printed in the United States of America

Contents

Preface

In the preface to the first edition of *Rhetorical Grammar: Grammatical Choices, Rhetorical Effects*, I posed two questions:

> Is there a place for grammar in composition courses?
> Can we justify spending time on grammar when our goal is to teach writing?

I firmly believed that the answer to both was "yes"—that not only does grammar have a place, but that we as writing teachers have an obligation to include language study in our classes.

The success of the first edition—and the responses to it from students and teachers—certainly confirmed those beliefs. In classes for both freshmen and advanced writers, in classes for teacher training, readers of *Rhetorical Grammar* have discovered that understanding the structure of language in a conscious way can, indeed, help students develop as writers.

And is there time for grammar in a syllabus that is already crowded with prewriting, drafting, and revising and with reading what others have written? You are probably already spending time on grammar. When you work on sentence combining; when you discuss coherence and transition; when you explain in a conference why a particular structure is misplaced or awkward; when you help students understand the effects of certain words on the reader; when you suggest that an idea be subordinated; when you point out redundancy; when you praise gems of precision—these are principles of grammar that are now part of your writing class. This book will help you teach these and many more such principles—and it will do so in a systematic way.

You'll discover that the lessons in this book are not the definitions and categories and rules of traditional grammar that your students encountered back in junior high. Rather, *Rhetorical Grammar* brings together the insights of composition researchers and linguists; it makes the connection between writing and grammar that has been missing from our classrooms. It also avoids the prescriptive rules of handbooks, offering instead explanations of the rhetorical choices that are available. And, perhaps what is most important, it gives students confidence in their own language ability by helping them recognize the intuitive grammar expertise that all human beings share.

This difference in the purpose of *Rhetorical Grammar* is especially important. Too often the grammar lessons that manage to find their way into the writing classroom are introduced for remedial purposes: to fix comma splices and misplaced modifiers and agreement errors and such. As a consequence, the study of grammar has come to have strictly negative, remedial associations—a band-aid for weak and inexperienced writers, rather than a rhetorical tool that all writers should understand and control.

This book, then, substitutes for that negative association of grammar a positive and functional point of view—a rhetorical view: that an understanding of grammar is an important tool for the writer; that it can be taught and learned successfully if it is done in the right way and in the right place, in connection with composition. The book can also stimulate class discussion on such issues as sentence focus and rhythm, cohesion, reader expectation, paraphrase, diction, revision—discussions of rhetorical and stylistic issues that will be meaningful throughout the writing process. And the students will learn to apply these grammar concepts to their own writing.

Readers familiar with the first edition of *Rhetorical Grammar* will notice several substantial changes in this edition. Most obvious are the two new chapters: The formerly brief section on cohesion has become Chapter 2, with expanded discussions emphasizing the connection between grammar and reader expectation, the known–new contract, parallelism, and repetition. Chapter 11, "The Rhetoric of Punctuation," added at the request of reviewers, summarizes the punctuation principles found throughout the book with both discussion and a glossary. Other major changes include a substantial revision of Chapter 1, making the description of sentence structure more accessible, and, throughout the chapters, the addition of exercises designed for class or small-group discussion. The self-instructional quality of the first edition has been retained, with the inclusion of answers to the odd-numbered items in the exercises.

Depending on the goals of your course, you may find that *Rhetorical Grammar* is the only text your students need; on the other hand, it can certainly work well in conjunction with a reader or rhetoric. In either case, you'll discover that class time can be used much more efficiently when your students come to class with the shared background that the text provides. *The Instructors Manual* includes answers to the even-numbered items in the exercises, further explanations of grammatical principles, and suggestions for class activities.

Acknowledgments

When we launched the first edition of *Rhetorical Grammar* in 1991, we weren't sure that a writing text devoted to language structure (especially one with the G word in the title!) would fly. But it did. So my thanks go to the writing teachers who believed that their students could profit from such instruction. And I'm certainly grateful to those who have written and called with their comments and suggestions.

I would also like to acknowledge the following individuals who gave me so much help with their reviews of the book: Avon Crismore, Ph.D., Indiana University-Purdue University-Fort Wayne, Nancy C. De Joy, Ph.D., Nazareth College, Cynthia Haynes-Burton, University of Texas at Arlington, and Michael W. Munley, Ball State University. And thanks to James Murphy, Carroll College who reviewed the entire manuscript. I'm sure these reviewers will be able to see their influence in this edition.

I reserve special thanks for the support and encouragement and goodwill that continue to come my way from the folks at Allyn and Bacon—especially Eben Ludlow, editor extraordinaire and friend.

Finally, I acknowledge the love and support of a wonderful family, which, since the first edition, has expanded to include Shelley, Devon, Riley, Dennis, and, most recently, Jenny.

Martha Kolln

Chapter 1

Grammar and the Rhetoric of Sentences

A weasel is wild. Who knows what he thinks? He sleeps in his underground den, his tail draped over his nose. Sometimes he lives in his den for two days without leaving. Outside, he stalks rabbits, mice, muskrats, and birds, killing more bodies than he can eat warm, and often dragging the carcasses home. Obedient to instinct, he bites his prey at the neck, either splitting the jugular vein at the throat or crunching the brain at the base of the skull, and he does not let go. One naturalist refused to kill a weasel who was socketed into his hand deeply as a rattlesnake. The man could in no way pry the tiny weasel off, and he had to walk half a mile to water, the weasel dangling from his palm, and soak him off like a stubborn label.

—Annie Dillard, *Teaching a Stone to Talk*

U.S. mileage standards are another scandal. In 1975, during the oil crisis, the U.S. government gave American automakers ten years to improve their cars' mileage rate from 14 miles per gallon to 27.5 miles per gallon. When oil prices came back down in the 1980s, the government relaxed the standard again. Transportation experts at the E.P.A. argue that the mileage requirement might reasonably be raised to 40 miles per gallon. Meanwhile, every time we turn the key in a car's ignition, we turn up the planet's thermostat.

—Jonathan Weiner, *The Next One Hundred Years*

Management as a practice is very old. The most successful executive in all history was surely that Egyptian who, 4,500 years or more ago, first conceived the pyramid, without any precedent, designed it, and built it, and did so in an astonishingly short time. That first pyramid still stands. But as a discipline, management is barely fifty years old. It was first dimly perceived around the time of the First World War. It did not emerge until the Second World War, and then did so primarily in the United States. Since then it has been the fastest-growing new function, and the study of it the fastest-growing new discipline. No function in history has emerged as quickly as has management in the past fifty or sixty years, and surely none has had such worldwide sweep in such a short period.

—Peter F. Drucker, "The Age of Social Transformation," *The Atlantic Monthly* (November 1994)

The three paragraphs you just read, while written by different authors on different topics, have a number of common traits. Perhaps the most conspicuous is the structure, in each case, of the first sentence. Read the three as a list, and you'll see—and hear—the similarity:

A weasel is wild.
U.S. mileage standards are another scandal.
Management as a practice is very old.

You probably noticed that in all three the main verb is a form of *be* (*is*, *are*), which serves as a link between the subject and a description or characteristic of the subject. This use of *be* as a linking verb—"something is something"—is a common **sentence pattern**[1] in English. You won't have to read far in most modern essays (or in this textbook) to find this "something is something" pattern. In fact, you will find three in the paragraph you are reading now.

You've had years of experience with the linking-*be* pattern. It is one of a handful of patterns that underlie the structure of all our sentences. These skeletal structures and our system for fleshing them out constitute the grammar of English.

In this book you will look at these patterns and their expansions from a rhetorical point of view—that is, from the view of a writer with a particular purpose and audience. You will learn about the choices available to you and the effect those choices have on your reader.

Thinking about grammar in this way—as a tool for the writer—may be new to you. The definition of the word *grammar* that we are using here may be new as well: Here *grammar* refers to the underlying system of rules that enables people to speak their native language. Every human being has such a system—an innate language ability that somehow, in some miraculous way, develops into speech at an early age.

You were little more than a year old when you began to demonstrate your grammar ability by naming things around you; within a few months you were putting together two- and three-word strings, and before long your language took on the features of adult sentences. No one taught you. You didn't have language lessons. You learned all by yourself, from hearing the language spoken around you—and you did so unconsciously.

[1]Words in boldface are explained in the Glossary of Terms, beginning on page 235.

Linguists tell us that this process of language development is universal; that is, it occurs across cultures, and it occurs in every child with normal physical and mental development. No matter what your native language is, you have internalized its grammar system. By the time you were five or six years old, you were an expert at telling stories, at asking questions, at describing people and places, probably at arguing. The internalized system of rules that accounts for this language ability of yours is our definition of *grammar*.

It's important that you recognize that expertise. Why? The answer is simple, based on plain old common sense. If you have confidence in your language ability, perhaps that confidence will carry over into your writing. Confidence breeds enthusiasm. And every teacher knows—students know, too—the importance of enthusiasm to success in any venture.

Those of you whose mother tongue is not English will bring varying degrees of grammar expertise to your writing. And, unlike the subconscious expertise you have in your native language, your knowledge of the grammar of English is likely to be conscious knowledge—rules about sentence structure that you learned in English classes or conclusions that you reached on the basis of experience, perhaps when you compared the rules of English to those of your native language.

Writing, of course, requires much more conscious knowledge than does speech: For starters, there's the alphabet to learn, the skills of handwriting and spelling and punctuation to master, all of which you began to do as soon as you started school. You've also learned that the written language is not simply written-down speech. Depending on the rhetorical situation—the purpose and audience—the vocabulary you use in writing may be more formal and the sentence structure more elaborate than that of the spoken language. Our conversations include slang and sentence fragments that are often inappropriate in writing.

Your conscious understanding of grammar comes into play most noticeably when you are rethinking what you have just written—when you are revising. And it's important to recognize that revising is not simply a step that you carry out somewhere toward the end of the writing process; it's not a coat of polish you apply before turning in your paper. Revising is itself a process—a recursive, back-and-forth rereading and listening and rethinking and selecting process that goes on in your head and on your paper, beginning with the first paragraph of the first draft. Writing involves grammatical choices from beginning to end.

The study of rhetorical grammar, then, is essentially a matter of consciousness raising, of learning to use the tools that our writing system has available. Understanding the structure of language in a conscious way will enable you to manipulate sentences, to use the tools, with genuine control.

The Structure of Sentences

The linking-*be* pattern provides a good illustration of both our subconscious grammar ability and the importance of rhetorical awareness. As native speakers, we learn to use *be*, with its irregular past tense forms (*was*, *were*) and its three present tense forms (*am*, *are*, and *is*) without even realizing they are related to *be*, the infinitive form. Nonnative speakers, of course, must spend a great deal of conscious effort on the uses of *be* in English, just as native English speakers must do when confronted with the equivalent of *be* in studying a foreign language. On the other hand, as your composition teachers may have warned you, it's very easy to overuse *be*. That first paragraph of discussion at the opening of this chapter, with its three linking-*be* sentences, may, in fact, illustrate such overuse. We'll come back to this subject in the discussion on "Choosing Verbs" (Chapter 6).

Meanwhile, the linking-*be* pattern can help illuminate the underlying structure of our sentence patterns.

Before looking at all of the separate slots in the **sentence,** we will examine their two-part structure: the **subject** and the **predicate.**

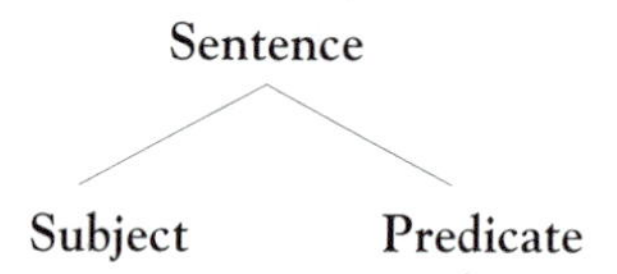

You probably know these labels from your study of grammar in junior high or high school. They name the functions of the two parts of every sentence. The **subject,** as its name implies, is the topic of the sentence, the something or a someone that the sentence is about; the **predicate** is the point that is made about that topic.

In the linking-*be* sentences we've been looking at, the first "something," of course, is the subject. In the following sentences, you'll find a "something" or "someone" occupying the subject slot, so you will probably have no trouble recognizing the dividing line between the two basic parts:

A weasel is wild.
U.S. mileage standards are a scandal.
Tomatoes give me hives.
Linda's sister graduated from nursing school.
Gino's father flew helicopters in Vietnam.
Management as a practice is very old.

If you divided the sentences like this,

A weasel / is wild.
U.S. mileage standards / are a scandal.
Tomatoes / give me hives.
Linda's sister / graduated from nursing school.
Gino's father / flew helicopters in Vietnam.
Management as a practice / is very old.

—and chances are good that you did—then you have recognized the two basic units of every sentence.

This two-part structure underlies all of our sentences in English, even those in which the two parts may not be apparent at first glance. In many questions, for example, the subject is buried in the predicate half of the sentence; to discover the two parts, you have to recast the question in the form of a **declarative sentence,** or statement:

Question: Which chapters will our test cover?

Statement: Our test / will cover which chapters.

In the **command,** or **imperative sentence,** one of the parts may be deleted altogether, with the subject "understood":

(You) Hold the onions!
(You) Sit down.
(You) Come with me to the concert.

Another way to describe the sentence slots, the subject and the predicate, is according to the form of the structures that fill them:

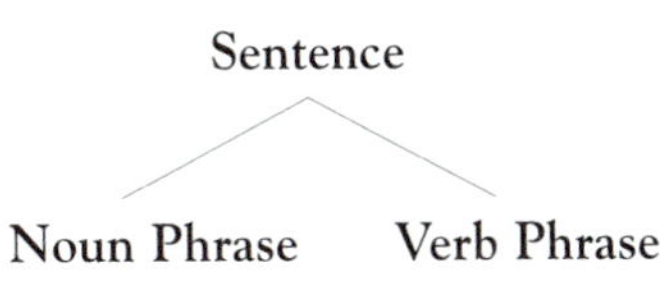

The subject slot is generally filled by a **noun phrase,** and that's exactly what these six subjects are:

A *weasel*

U.S. mileage *standards*

Tomatoes

Linda's *sister*

Gino's *father*

Management as a practice

The term *phrase* refers to a group of words that acts as a unit. A noun phrase consists of a headword noun with all of the words and phrases that modify it. In the preceding list of noun phrases, the headwords are in italics.

In each of the six sample sentences, the predicate is a **verb phrase** in form, as the predicate always is. Like the noun phrase, the verb phrase is a unit with a headword, in this case, a verb. In the following verb phrases, the verbs are in italics:

is wild.

are a scandal.

give me hives.

graduated from nursing school

flew helicopters in Vietnam.

is very old.

Remember that the term *predicate* refers to the whole verb phrase and *subject* to the whole noun phrase—not to just their headwords.

You were probably able to make the divisions between the subjects and predicates on the basis of meaning, by identifying what was being said about something or someone. But if you're not sure, you can use your grammar expertise to double check: Simply substitute a **pronoun** for the subject. That pronoun, you will discover, stands in for the entire noun phrase:

He	is wild. (*It* can also be used for animals.)
They	are a scandal.
They	give me hives.
She	graduated from nursing school.
He	flew helicopters in Vietnam.
It	is very old.

Pronoun expertise is a good example of a native speaker's intuitive system of grammar. We use pronouns automatically, usually at the second mention of a noun or noun phrase:

A weasel is wild. Who knows what he thinks?

Linda's sister graduated from nursing school. She's starting a job at our local hospital next week.

In Chapter 5 we will look further at pronouns, including the tricky ones that writers sometimes have problems with.

EXERCISE 1

Draw a line to separate the subject and predicate in each of the following sentences. Remember the trick of substituting a pronoun to discover where the subject ends.

1. The government relaxed mileage standards in the 1980s.
2. Transportation experts at the E.P.A. have argued for stricter standards.
3. When will oil prices go up again?
4. How many different chimes does this grandfather clock have?
5. Bill Clinton, the governor of Arkansas, was elected president in 1992.

6. The president's wife, Hillary Rodham Clinton, headed the task force on health care.
7. Why was the health-care issue so complicated?
8. Don't forget to vote on Tuesday.
9. My uncle from Laramie, my dad, and I are going to hike the Appalachian Trail next summer.
10. The long trail, extending from Maine to Georgia, is maintained by the Appalachian Trail Commission.
11. My roommate and I became friends right away.
12. What do weasels think?
13. My son's kindergarten teacher is teaching the children Spanish.
14. The images and information gathered by the Space Shuttle *Challenger* will add a great deal to our knowledge of weather patterns.
15. One of the *Challenger*'s objectives was to help scientists study volcanoes.

Sentence Patterns

Unlike the subject, which occupies one slot in the sentence, the predicate can be divided into more than one. You'll recall that in the linking-*be* pattern we've looked at, the predicate has two slots:

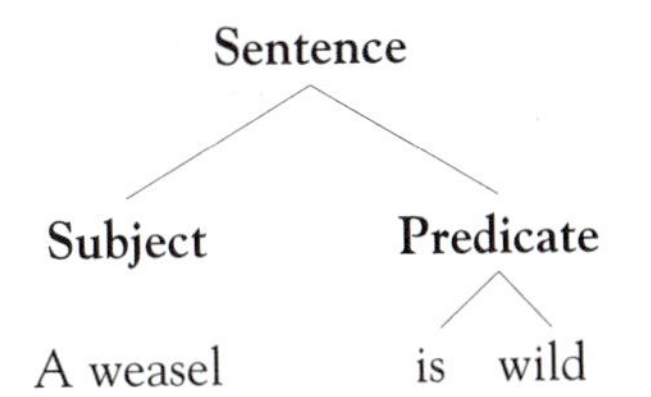

In this pattern the slot following *be* is called a **subjective complement,** because it says something about the subject. Most transitive verbs also have a single slot following the verb, but that one functions as a **direct object**; some transitive verbs have two slots. And one class of verbs, the intransitives, have no required slots in the predicate other than the verb itself.

Because these variations among the patterns are in the predicates, we group sentences into classes on the basis of their verbs. The labels for these verb classes—*be*, **linking, intransitive, and transitive**—are probably familiar to you, even though the concept of sentence patterns may be new.

The following description of the four groups, then, emphasizes the sentence as a series of slots rather than simply a string of words. All of the slots are labeled according to their functions. As you will learn in later chapters, the great versatility of our sentences derives in part from the variety of structures that can fill the slots and from our ability to expand them with modifiers.

Because the variations in sentences are determined by their predicates, we could actually call the sentence patterns "predicate patterns." But another, even more accurate—and useful—label would be "**clause** patterns." The words ***clause*** and ***sentence*** are close in meaning: All sentences are made up of one or more clauses. But a clause need not be a whole sentence. A clause can function as a modifier within another sentence or as a required slot, such as subject or direct object. For example, we could use our linking-*be* sentence as a direct object, following a verb like *say:*

Annie Dillard says that *the weasel is wild.*

Here the whole clause takes the place of a noun phrase, and while it's still a clause, it has lost its status as a sentence. We could also use it as a subordinate clause, added onto a complete sentence:

Because the weasel is wild, it should be approached with great caution.

Again, although it has lost its status as a sentence, it is still a clause.

The Be Patterns

It shouldn't surprise you to learn that the linking-*be* pattern is our most common use of *be* in its role as main verb.* But because that is not its only pattern, we are putting *be* into a group separate from that of the linking verbs. In the first pattern, you will see that the slot following *be* is filled not by a noun phrase or an adjective that describes the subject but rather by an **adverbial,** a word or phrase, in this case, that tells where or when. This pattern is not generally considered the *linking* use of *be*.

Pattern 1:

Subject	Be	Adverbial
My friends	*are*	*in the library.*
The rehearsal	*is*	*tomorrow.*

The linking-*be* examples that opened this chapter included two different structures as subjective complements: an **adjective** (A weasel is *wild*) and a **noun phrase** (U.S. mileage standards are *another scandal*). Those are the two you'll also see in the sample sentences for Pattern 2 that follow:

Pattern 2:

Subject	Be	Subjective Complement	
Gino's father	*was*	*a pilot.*	(noun phrase)
This soup	*is*	*salty.*	(adjective)

*Be has an important role in our grammar other than that of main verb, the role we are discussing here. It also serves as an auxiliary to express the progressive aspect of verbs (*were eating, am studying, should be going, has been helping*) and to form the passive voice (*was baked, is being announced*).

The Linking Verb Pattern

The term *linking verb* applies to all verbs other than *be* completed by a subjective complement—the adjective or noun phrase that describes or identifies the subject. Among the common linking verbs are the verbs of the senses—*taste, smell, feel, sound,* and *look*—which often link an adjective to the subject. *Become* and *remain* are the two most common that connect a noun or noun phrase. Other common linking verbs are *seem, appear,* and *prove.*

Pattern 3:	Subject	Linking Verb	Subjective Complement
	My roommate and I	*became*	*good friends.*
	This soup	*tastes*	*salty.*

The Intransitive Verb Pattern

The intransitive pattern is the only one in which the predicate consists of the verb alone.

Pattern 4:	Subject	Intransitive Verb
	The whole class	*complained.*
	The baby	*is sleeping.*

As you know, such skeletal sentences are fairly rare in actual writing. The point here is that they are grammatical: They require no complement to be complete sentences. In the next section, "The Optional Slot," you will read about adverbial modifiers, which are commonly added to all the sentence patterns, including this one. However, adding a modifier does not change the basic pattern. For example,

The whole class complained *bitterly*
and
The baby is sleeping *upstairs in the guest room*

remain Pattern 4 sentences.

The Transitive Verb Patterns

Unlike the intransitive verbs, all transitive verbs take one or more **complements.** The transitive patterns are classified in three groups on the basis of those complements. All transitive verbs have one complement in common: the direct object. Pattern 5, which has only that one complement, can be thought of as the basic transitive verb pattern.

Pattern 5:	Subject	Transitive Verb	Direct Object
	My roommate	*baked*	*this apple pie.*

At first glance, you might mistake this sentence for a Pattern 3, given the fact that the slot following the verb is occupied by a noun phrase. The distinction lies in the relationship between that noun phrase and the subject. In Pattern 3 (*My roommate and I became good friends*), the two noun phrases have the same **referent:** *My roommate and I* and *good friends* refer to the same people. We could, in fact, say

My roommate and I *are* good friends,

using the linking *be*. On the other hand, in Pattern 5 the subject slot and the direct object slot have different referents. We obviously cannot say, with any degree of seriousness,

My roommate *is* an apple pie.

In Chapter 6, which discusses verbs in more detail, you will discover another distinguishing feature of transitive verbs, one that provides a test of sorts: A transitive verb can almost always be transformed into the **passive voice**:

This apple pie was baked by my roommate.

Pattern 6:	**Subject**	**Transitive Verb**	**Indirect Object**	**Direct Object**
	Marie	*gave*	*Ramon*	*a birthday gift.*

In this pattern, two noun phrases follow the verb, and here all three—the subject, the direct object, and the **indirect object**—have different referents: *Marie*, *Ramon*, and *a birthday gift* all refer to different people or things. We traditionally define *indirect object* as the recipient of the direct object or the person to whom or for whom the action is performed. In most cases this definition applies accurately. A Pattern 6 verb—and this is a limited group—usually has a meaning like "give," and the indirect object usually names a person who is the receiver of whatever the subject gives.

An important characteristic of the Pattern 6 sentence is the option we have of shifting the indirect object to a position following the direct object, where it will become the object of a preposition—in other words, switching the two object slots:

Marie gave a birthday gift to Ramon.

You might choose this order if, for example, you want to put the main emphasis, or focus, on Ramon, or if you want to add a modifier. This long modifier fits the end of the sentence much more smoothly than it would fit in the middle. Compare the two:

Marie gave a birthday gift to Ramon, *a friend from her old neighborhood in Pasadena.*
Marie gave Ramon, *a friend from her old neighborhood in Pasadena,* a birthday gift.

The original order will be more effective if it's the direct object you wish to emphasize or expand:

> Marie gave Ramon a birthday gift, *a necktie she had made herself.*

You'll discover, if you read the sentence aloud, that the end position in this pattern will receive the greatest stress. You will learn more about sentence stress and focus in Chapters 2 and 3.

Pattern 7:	**Subject**	**Transitive Verb**	**Direct Object**	**Objective Complement**
	The class	*considered*	*the homework*	*a real drag.*
	The teacher	*called*	*the students*	*lazy.*

In this pattern the direct object is followed by a second complement, called an **objective complement**—a noun phrase or an adjective that describes the direct object. Note that the relationship between these two complement slots is the same as the relationship between the subject and the subjective complement in Patterns 2 and 3. In fact, we could easily turn these two slots into a pattern 2 sentence:

> The homework is a real drag.
> The students are lazy.

It's obvious that this linking-*be* version of the relationship has changed the meaning: To call the students lazy, as in Pattern 7, does not mean that they really are lazy.

In the passive voice, the Pattern 7 sentence with a verb like *call* or *consider* or *label* offers the writer a way of suggesting laziness without attributing the opinion. This is the passive we often hear in the political arena:

> The welfare recipients were called lazy.
> The senator's proposal was labeled anti-business.

Here the writer or speaker can associate the label—"lazy," "anti-business"—with the subject without coming right and saying so, as would happen with the linking-*be*. You'll read more about this rhetorical strategy in Chapter 6.

In the sample sentence with *consider*, an alternative structure uses the infinitive *to be* with the objective complement:

> The class considered the homework *to be a real drag.*

This version has the identical meaning of the original; in fact, the *to be* is really "understood" in that first version. The only differences are in the length of the sentence and in its rhythm. Sometimes you may want the extra beat of rhythm that the infinitive *to be* provides. If you read both versions aloud, you'll hear a slightly greater emphasis on *homework* when the infinitive is included; in other words, both *homework* and *drag* get emphasis.

Another fairly common structure that's closely related to Pattern 7 is a sentence with a verb like *think* or *find* followed by a whole clause as the direct object:

> I think (*that*) *the price of movie tickets is ridiculous*.

This is actually a Pattern 5 sentence: It has only one slot, the direct object, following the verb. But it would be easy to revise this sentence into a straight Pattern 7:

> I consider the price of movie tickets ridiculous.

In both versions, *ridiculous* is a complement of the noun phrase *movie tickets*—in one case a subjective complement (because *movie tickets* is the subject of the embedded clause) and in the other an objective complement (because *movie tickets* is the object). Note, too, that in the sentence with *think* the word that signals the clause—*that*—is optional. We often leave it out for the sake of brevity and tightness. You'll discover, however, that sometimes you'll want to leave it in to signal that a clause is coming.

These kinds of options that are available to you as a writer illustrate the versatility of the language. In English you can be sure that there's always more than one way to express a thought.

A Word about Wordiness

It may be time to bring up the concept of wordiness, a label that generally carries negative connotations. You're probably accustomed to hearing praise for conciseness and brevity in prose, for leanness, so you might be tempted to delete the optional *that* in the previous example or the *to be* in the Pattern 7 sentence on the grounds of wordiness, of superfluous fat. Think again. "Lean" may be an important goal in headlines and telegrams and postcards and résumés, but in essays other goals take precedence. Clarity, of course, is one of them. And, yes, sometimes clarity calls for brevity, for a lean version of a sentence. But rhythm and focus and readability—considerations of the reader—are much more important. Think about the way the reader will comprehend what you have written. Help the reader all you can to read your words with the meaning that you intended.

We'll look more closely at this important concept in the study of cohesion in Chapter 2 and of sentence rhythm in Chapter 3. And in Chapter 9 we'll examine some good reasons for writing short, lean sentences.

The Optional Slot

There's another important slot to add to the discussion, as mentioned in connection with the intransitive pattern: the optional **adverbial.** We regularly add information about time and place and manner and reason and so on. In fact, the reason most of our written sentences are longer than the bare skeletal patterns is that we commonly add one or more adverbial structures.

1. During the Vietnam War, Gino's dad was a pilot.
2. Because weasels are wild, they should be approached with great caution.
3. Yesterday the teacher called the students lazy when they complained about their assignment.
4. I got up early to study for my Spanish test.

The term *adverbial* refers to any grammatical structure that adds what we think of as "adverbial information"—that is, information about time, place, manner, reason, and the like. It adds the kind of information that **adverbs** add, and adverbs, you may recall from your grammar classes of old, are modifiers of verbs. In the first and second examples, you'll see **prepositional phrases**: *During the Vietnam War* tells "when"; *with great caution* tells "how." The second and third sentences include **subordinate clauses**: The *because* clause tells "why"; the *when* clause, of course, tells "when." The third and fourth include adverbs of time, *yesterday* and *early*. And sentence four also has an **infinitive phrase**, *to study for my Spanish test*, that tells "why."

It's important to recognize that when we use the word *optional*, we are referring only to grammaticality, not to the importance of the adverbial information. If you remove those underlined adverbials from the four sentences, you are left with grammatical, albeit skeletal, sentences. However, even though the sentence is grammatical in its skeletal form, many times the adverbial information is the very reason for the sentence—the main focus. For example, if you tell someone,

> I got up early to study for my Spanish test,

you're probably doing so in order to explain when or why about your morning schedule; the adverbials are the important information. The adverb, *early*, tells when and the infinitive verb phrase, *to study for my Spanish test*, tells why. The main clause—the fact that you got up—goes without saying!

In Chapter 7 these various adverbial structures are discussed in detail.

EXERCISE 2

Underline each of the adverbial structures in the following sentences; identify each according to the kind of information it provides (time, place, reason, manner, etc.) and according to its form (adverb, prepositional phrase, verb phrase, clause). Time adverbials include not only points in time but also spans of time, duration, and frequency. Now identify the sentence patterns.

1. Sometimes a weasel lives in his den for two days without leaving.
2. The weasel bites his prey at the neck.
3. During the oil crisis, motorists waited in long lines at the gas station.
4. After oil prices fell in the 1980s, the government relaxed the standards again.

5. In which locker did you put your backpack?
6. That first pyramid still stands.
7. In 1992, we elected Bill Clinton president.
8. The state of the economy was the big political issue during the 1992 election campaign.
9. I save money by walking to work.
10. My bike disappeared from the bike rack when I rode it to work last summer.
11. Everyone smiles in the same language.
12. Mickey worked steadily in the lab throughout the night to finish her project before the Monday deadline.
13. My roommate gave me a bad time because I used her computer without permission.
14. Wash your hands thoroughly after handling chemicals.
15. In Chapter 7 you will study adverbials in detail.

Punctuation and the Sentence Patterns

There's an important punctuation lesson to be learned from the sentence patterns with their two or three or four slots:

> Do not mark boundaries of the required slots with punctuation.
>
> That is, never separate
> - the subject from the verb.
> - the direct object from the objective complement.
> - the indirect object from the direct object.
> - the verb from the subjective complement.
>
> And, with one exception, never separate
> - the verb from the direct object.

The one exception to this rule occurs when the direct object is a direct quotation following a verb like *say:*

He said, "I love you."

Here the punctuation convention calls for a comma before the quoted words, but in the following sentences there is simply no place for commas:

The images and information sent back by *Voyager 2* have given our space scientists here on Earth enough information about four of our distant planets to keep them busy for years to come.

All of the discussion groups I took part in during Orientation Week were extremely helpful for the incoming freshmen.
The sportswriters considered the game between the Aggies and the Longhorns one the truly great games of the current season.

Even though the structures that fill the slots may be long—they may even require a pause for breath—the slot boundaries are never marked by commas. In Chapter 8, where we examine ways of adding modifiers to the noun phrase, we will encounter sentences in which punctuation is called for *within* a slot—for example, within a noun phrase—but even in those situations the rule still applies: no commas *between* slots.

EXERCISE 3

Draw vertical lines between the slots of the following sentences, then identify their sentence patterns. You might want to begin by locating the verb. And don't forget the trick of discovering where a noun phrase slot begins and ends by substituting a pronoun. This trick will work for all of the noun phrase slots—not just the subject. Remember, too, that optional adverbial information can occupy the opening and/or closing slots in the sentence.

1. In 1747 a physician in the British navy conducted an experiment to discover a cure for scurvy.
2. Scurvy was a serious problem for men at sea.
3. Dr. James Lind fed six groups of scurvy victims six different remedies.
4. The men who ate oranges and lemons every day recovered miraculously.
5. Although it took fifty years for the British Admiralty Office to recognize Lind's findings, it finally ordered a daily dose of fresh lemon juice for every British seaman.
6. Interestingly, Lind's discovery also affected the English language.
7. The British called lemons "limes" in the eighteenth century.
8. Because of that navy diet, people call British sailors "limeys."

For Group Discussion

1. Here the sentences in each pair or group look alike. Use your knowledge of sentence patterns to explain how their meanings differ. Think about the function of the slots.

   The teacher made the test hard.
   The batter hit the ball hard.

My husband made me a chocolate cake.
My husband made me a happy woman.

The singer appeared tired at the concert.
Black clouds appeared suddenly on the horizon.

Farmers in Illinois grow a lot of corn.
The corn grows fast in July.
We grew weary in the hot sun.

2. Sentences that we have been calling "linking-*be*" sentences are called "Categorical Propositions" (CPs) by logicians and rhetoricians. The CP makes an assertion—it states a proposition—about a particular subject. The following linking-*be* sentences illustrate the three basic kinds of CPs:

   A. Chocolate is *Ben & Jerry's* most delicious flavor.
   B. New York City is the largest city in the United States.
   C. Television is the cause of a great many social problems.

Although all three sentences look alike, in that all three conform to the "something is something" pattern, they are actually quite different. And although they may resemble the linking-*be* topic sentences that opened this chapter, only one has the potential for being an effective topic sentence. In other words, not all CPs can hold their own as topic sentences.

The best kind of CP is an arguable proposition. It sets up a response in the reader, a response that says "Prove it." And in so doing, it sets up expectations in the reader. Let's look at the responses the typical reader might make to the three sentences here:

A. Says who? It isn't nearly as tasty as their French Vanilla, in my opinion.

This categorical proposition in (A) is simply a matter of personal taste—not arguable.

B. I know that. Doesn't everyone? Why are you telling me this?

The CP in (B) is a fact, a statement that can be verified. It's not uncommon to see facts as paragraph openers, but they tend to be weak ones—especially well-known facts—because they give no clue as to their purpose. Try to predict what a paragraph with this opening sentence is about.

C. I disagree. Prove it.

Like sentence (A), the third also states an opinion, but it's one that's open to debate—an arguable proposition. Because it deals with probability, you can bring evidence to support your side. The reader can infer where this paragraph is going.

Decide which of the following CPs would make good topic sentences. You'll want to think about the way in which a reader would respond:

(1) Florida is the ideal place to retire.
(2) It is wrong to use animals for testing cosmetics.
(3) Jogging is boring.
(4) Jogging is a popular sport.
(5) Italy is the world's largest producer of wine.
(6) The lemur, a shrewlike creature, is at home both on the ground and in the trees.
(7) Reading comic books is a complete waste of time.
(8) Movie popcorn is always too salty.
(9) A weasel is wild.
(10) U.S. mileage standards are a scandal.

Now rewrite the weak topic sentences to improve them, if possible. Also try your hand at revising them to avoid using the linking-*be*.

PUNCTUATION REMINDER

Do not mark boundaries of the required slots with punctuation.

Chapter 2

Cohesion

Unlike Chapter 1, where we looked at the internal structure of the sentence and the relationship of its parts, the study of **cohesion** concerns the connection of sentences to one another, to the "flow" of a text, to the ways in which a paragraph of separate sentences becomes a unified whole.

The word *cohesion* generally calls to mind that familiar list of connective words that signal relationships between sentences—such words and phrases as *however, on the other hand, in addition to, first, second,* and so on.[1] These connective devices are important, of course; they help to make the meaning clear. And in some cases they are absolutely necessary—for example, when a sentence offers a contrast, when it takes the reader on an unexpected path. But these connective devices are certainly not the most common source of cohesion in the language. The grammar itself provides the usual—and the strongest—cohesive glue.

Here is the opening of the "weasel" paragraph we read in Chapter 1:

> A weasel is wild. Who knows what he thinks? He sleeps in his underground den, his tail draped over his nose. Sometimes he lives in his den for two days without leaving. Outside, he stalks rabbits. . . .

The pronoun *he* connects the second sentence to the first—only that one word, but clearly a strong grammatical tie. The next sentence is loaded with ties: not only the

[1]The words *cohesion* and *coherence* are sometimes used interchangeably. More often, however, *coherence* includes also the global features of the work that make it a unified whole: the overall arrangement of paragraphs and, in books, chapters; in certain scholarly works, the inclusion of an abstract, of footnotes, bibliography, and index; the accurate presentation of statistics; and other standard features for particular writing situations.

repeated *he* in the subject slot but also specific nouns you would expect to read in connection with an animal—*sleep, underground den, tail, nose*. The third sentence repeats both *he* and *den*, along with *his*. The fourth, which you can read in Chapter 1 in its entirety, details the weasel's hunting ability, and begins again with *he*. Its first word, *outside*, contrasts with the "inside" designation *in his underground den* of sentence three.

Vocabulary ties such as these—pronouns, repeated words, words that co-occur, that is, words from the same domain or category—are crucial elements in defining a group of sentences as a cohesive text. Working together with these ties are three other important aspects of cohesion, all of which you will want to consider, especially while revising. We will take them up in this chapter: **reader expectation,** the **known-new contract,** and **parallelism.**

Reader Expectation

Have you ever come across a teacher's "awk" noted in the margin of a written assignment, or have you yourself ever judged a piece of writing as awkward? Perhaps in reading a composition of your own or that of your classmate you have felt that something was amiss—but you couldn't quite put your finger on the something. Such problems can sometimes be traced to thwarted expectations.

Both our reading and our conversations are loaded with expectations; we have a sense of direction about language. Although we may not know exactly what's coming next, when we hear it—or read it—we recognize if it's appropriate. It's when the ideas take an unexpected turn that the "awk" response can set in, when a passage fails to fit that expectation, that sense of appropriateness: "I didn't know exactly what was coming next—but I certainly didn't expect *that!*"

In conversation, we can call a halt to the speaker: "Wait! What was that you just said?" But as readers, of course, we don't have that option. Instead, we find ourselves thinking, "Why am I reading this now?" Even though it's only a fleeting thought, it doesn't take many such interruptions—the pause, the second thought, the backtracking—to obstruct the cohesive flow of a piece of writing.

Where do a reader's expectations come from? Obviously, from what has gone before, from the prior text, or, in the case of an opening paragraph, from the title or, possibly, from the author's reputation. Within a paragraph, reader expectation begins with the opening sentence. The writer, of course, has all manner of possibilities for setting up that expectation. The first sentence of this paragraph, because it is a question, sets up the expectation of an answer—or perhaps a second question.

Following is the opening sentence from a paragraph in an article about the "most glamorous sweepstakes in sports"—the Triple Crown of Thoroughbred racing. This paragraph follows the article's opening section discussing the eleven horses that have successfully swept the three races of the Triple Crown since its inception in 1914, the most recent being Affirmed in 1978. The paragraph is preceded by a heading: "Three races become the ultimate test."

> The sweep is so rare and difficult because each race has unique demands and the series as a whole requires unusual ruggedness.

This opening sentence has no doubt set up an expectation in you, the reader, about what is coming next. It's certainly a well-written sentence. Its most important words are those that get the loudest stress: *difficult, unique demands, unusual ruggedness*. As a reader, you have every right to expect the next sentence to in some way discuss the difficulties, demands, and/or ruggedness of the Triple Crown sweep.

Now read the complete paragraph:

> The sweep is so rare and difficult because each race has unique demands and the series as a whole requires unusual ruggedness. Racehorses usually do best with about a month between races. In the Triple Crown they must race three times in 36 days, over three different tracks, and at three different distances, all longer than most have ever tried before.
>
> —Steven Crist, "High Stakes," *USAir Magazine* (May 1994)

That second sentence is surely a letdown, however momentary. Not that it's unimportant: We need to understand why the demands are unique. But we were expecting something else here.

Remember that, as with many other facets of language, a reader's expectations are not necessarily conscious thoughts. A thwarted expectation may constitute only a fleeting break in concentration, a momentary blip in the flow. But remember, too, it's that blip that produces the "awk."

Active readers do more than simply process the words and meanings of a particular sentence as they are reading it. They also fit the ideas of the current sentence into what they already know: knowledge garnered both from previous sentences and from their own experience. At the same time, they are developing further expectations.

To become aware of the reader's expectations means to put yourself in the reader's shoes—or head. It requires the ability to read your own ideas objectively, to see and hear your own words as someone else might. This is one more step on the way to consciousness raising about the written language.

For Group Discussion

1. Look again at the weasel paragraph at the opening of Chapter 1. Delete the second sentence, the question. Discuss how that deletion has altered reader expectation. In what way does the presence of the question change the expectation set up by the opening sentence? Compose an alternative second sentence in the form of a statement, rather than a question. Compare your version to Dillard's in terms of its effect on a reader's expectation.

2. Revise the second sentence of the Triple Crown paragraph to eliminate that blip of awkwardness. In other words, prepare the reader for the information about the time between races; prepare the reader to expect it.
3. Write down (or read aloud to your group) a partial paragraph from your current essay assignment. Then ask the other members of the group to predict what's coming next.

The Known–New Contract

Seeing the sentence as a series of slots, as we did in Chapter 1, will help you understand another important aspect of cohesion called the **known–new contract,** one that is closely bound up with reader expectation.

In the opening of this chapter, we saw examples from the weasel paragraph of pronouns as cohesive ties. We noted especially the pronoun *he* in the subject slot, referring, of course, to the weasel. Sometimes the pronoun functions as a determiner, a noun signaler, as in the following passage. Here you'll see *its* as the determiner in the second sentence of the first paragraph and in both sentences following the topic sentence of the second paragraph:

> Portland, sixty miles from the Pacific Ocean, is by no means immune to the suburbanization that has sapped the vitality from many cities. Its suburbs now contain about two thirds of the area's 1.4 million residents and about half of the area's jobs. Yet as the suburbs have grown, the downtown has become more attractive and popular than ever.
>
> Downtown Portland has distinct edges. Its eastern border is the deep, navigable Willamette River, lined for more than a mile by Tom McCall Waterfront Park, a grassy, mostly level expanse suited to events that draw thousands such as the Rose Festival (Portland calls itself the "City of Roses"), a blues festival, and a summer symphony series. Its western border is the steep West Hills, which contain Washington Park, home of the International Rose Test Gardens, where more than 400 varieties of roses are cultivated, and Forest Park, whose 4,800 acres of Douglas fir, alder, and maple constitute one of the largest nature preserves and hiking areas in any American city.
>
> —Philip Langdon, "How Portland Does It," *The Atlantic Monthly* (November 1992)

In the weasel paragraph, *he* constitutes the entire subject; in the Portland paragraph, in all three cases, *its* stands for the possessive noun *Portland's* and acts as a signal for the headwords: *suburbs*, *eastern border*, and *western border*. But no matter how it functions—whether it fills the whole slot or acts as a determiner—the pronoun always has an **antecedent,** a previously mentioned nominal, or noun-like, structure that it stands for. For that reason a pronoun represents "known information." It is this known information that helps provide the cohesive tie between sentences. The three *its* sentences here are typical, with the known information in the subject slot, the new information in the predicate.

Linguists have found this "known–new" sequence to be so pervasive a feature of prose that it has come to be called a contract. The writer has an obligation, a contract of sorts, to fulfill expectations in the reader—to keep the reader on familiar ground. The reader has every right to expect each sentence to be connected to what has gone before, to include that known element.

Part of the problem in the second sentence of the Triple Crown paragraph is the subject *racehorses*. We were probably expecting *they* as the subject, referring to races. Obviously racehorses are part of the picture—the most important part, of course—but they are not the topic under discussion in the opening sentence. Here the author has broken the known–new contract by not putting known (in this case *expected* might be the more accurate label) information in the subject slot.

You might think, at first glance, that in the Portland paragraphs the *its* determiners are the only parts of the subjects that qualify as known. But look again. The headword *suburbs*, following the first *its*, echoes the noun *suburbanization* in the opening sentence. The ties in the second paragraph are equally explicit. The main idea of the opening sentence is the presence of the downtown's distinct edges. Because the word *borders* is a synonym for *edges*, *borders* constitutes known information. Even *eastern* and *western* qualify as known, given that an area's borders are commonly described in terms of compass points. In other words, in all three appearances of *its*, the subject noun phrases constitute known information; as expected, the predicates introduce new ideas.

The ties between sentences are often less obvious than the pronouns and cognate words and synonyms in the Portland passage. For example, in the sentence after the following paragraph opener, you might expect to find *he* (the president) or *it* (the message) as the subject:

> The president delivered his State of the Union message to a joint session of Congress last night.

If so, you might be surprised to read,

> Every seat in the gallery was full. The Cabinet secretaries and the Joint Chiefs of Staff occupied seats of honor in the front row.

As you see, these two sentences contain no repeated information; however, they do continue the theme stated in the first sentence, with details that should carry no surprise for the reader. In this case the known information is the common knowledge about presidential addresses to joint sessions of Congress—information that the reader can be presumed to know.

The cohesion provided by shared knowledge does have its pitfalls, however: It's not always as strong a tie as the pronoun or noun phrase that clearly points back. For example, even though the reader of the previous paragraph is not likely to say "Seats? Gallery? I wonder why I'm reading about full galleries," that new topic may nevertheless have been something of a surprise; it may have thwarted—at least momentarily—the expectations of someone who had been expecting details of the president's message. And, as you read earlier, all it takes is one moment of hesitation to produce a sense of awkwardness.

One way to strengthen the tie between the second sentence—the one about the gallery—and its predecessor is to drop a hint in that opening sentence about what the reader can expect next, to suggest a direction. As it now reads, the first sentence is no more than a statement of fact. You can often strengthen this kind of topic sentence by including an opinion, by making it an arguable proposition. Sometimes just a word or two will do the job:

> The president delivered his *much anticipated* State of the Union message to a joint session of Congress last night.

"Much anticipated" goes beyond the facts of who, when, where, and why. It's an opinion. Now the reader is inclined to respond with "Who says?" or "Anticipated for what reason?" And it carries the suggestion of the audience and what they are thinking, so the sentence about the filled gallery comes as no surprise—it fits more easily into the category of what's known.

The issues of reader expectation and the known–new contract revealed a problem with cohesion in the following passage, part of a student's first draft of an essay about laying a carpet. The paragraph before this one explained how to place the tack stripping:

> After the tack stripping has been placed correctly, the room is ready for padding. The pad, made of urethane, comes in rolls that are six feet wide and 120 feet long. The customer has his choice of what thickness he wants. There is regular padding, three quarters of an inch thick, and heavy padding, one inch thick. The pad is rolled out from wall to wall. . . .
>
> —Todd Lindberg

There is no problem with the general topic sentence. The opening clause ties the paragraph to the previous one. And the second sentence is tied to the first by the known information in the subject: *the pad*. The reader expects *the pad* or *padding* or *it* to be the subject. The third sentence introduces the idea of thickness, which is new information. But notice that the subject of the third sentence—the customer—is also new information. The reader probably didn't expect that change of topic. The lack of old information should signal the writer of a possible trouble spot, a weakness in cohesion.

Sometimes in paragraphs filled with factual details, such as the dimensions of the carpet pad, you may be tempted to add variety by introducing a completely new idea. In this essay the idea of the customer is certainly relevant, because it is the customer who chooses the carpet and hires the mechanic to install it; the fact of customers for carpeting is within the shared knowledge of writer and reader. But this is probably not the best place to introduce the customer—not if it adds nothing important and at the same time detracts from the reader's expectations.

How can the known–new principle of cohesion help you as a writer? Are you supposed to stop after every sentence and estimate the cohesive power of your next subject? No, of course not. That's not the way writers work. But when you are revising—and remember, revising goes on all the time, even during the first draft—you will want to keep in mind the issues of reader expectation and the known–new contract, to put yourself in your reader's shoes to see if you've kept your part of the bargain.

EXERCISE 4

Examine the following student paragraphs, paying particular attention to the cohesive ties of old and new information. Have the writers fulfilled the known–new contract?

1. Public and private literacy programs combined have helped only about four million American adults. These results are linked to the special problems literacy programs have to overcome. One such problem is irregular class attendance. If an adult has small children or must hold down two jobs, class attendance becomes difficult. On the large scale, though, a problem of policy focus exists. Should public policy focus on improving the suggested source of illiteracy—elementary and secondary education? Or should public policy gear itself toward teaching the present illiterate population to become literate?

   —Karen Way

2. Created by Congress in 1980, the 17.9 million acre Arctic National Wildlife Refuge (ANWR) lies in the northeast corner of Alaska, bordered by Canada's Yukon Territory and the Arctic Ocean. The refuge was founded about ten years after the massive oil find at Prudhoe Bay, west of the refuge. Geologists suspected there was oil on the Coastal Plain of the ANWR as well. Quickly an environmental conflict was born. Pro-development forces, noting that the country had just gone through tripled gas prices, argued the country needed the deposits to reduce dependence on foreign imports. Conservationists countered that the wildlife and habitat of the Arctic represented a resource just as precious as petroleum.

   —David Hamburger

EXERCISE 5

Revise the following passages to improve their cohesion. Think especially about reader expectation and the known–new contract.

1. The Gateway Arch at the edge of the Mississippi River in St. Louis is the world's tallest monument. Eero Saarinen designed the stainless steel structure that commemorates the Westward Movement.
2. Psychologists believe that color conveys emotional messages. Advertisers routinely manipulate consumers using color psychology. The pure white backgrounds and bold primary colors of detergent boxes are thought to influence buyers. Cleanliness and strength are associated with those colors.
3. The relentless heat of California's great Central Valley makes the summer almost unbearable at times. Over 110° is not an unusual temperature reading from June through September. Bakersfield often records the hottest temperature in the valley.
4. Getting chilled or getting your feet wet won't cause a cold. Weather is not the culprit that causes the common cold. Viruses are to blame.
5. The space program had no women astronauts until 1983. Sally Ride teamed up with a crew of four men on the Space Shuttle *Challenger* that year.
6. In the summer of 1993, floods in the Midwest wiped out farmlands and homes. They caused $15 billion to $20 billion in damage. Almost 70,000 people were left homeless by the floods. The Mississippi and Missouri River and their feeder rivers and streams overflowed their banks. More than 15 percent of the contiguous states (the lower 48) were affected by the floods. Two months of heavy rain brought on the floods. Roads, bridges, and other infrastructure across ten states were damaged or completely wiped out by the overflowing rivers. It is being called the "great flood of 1993." The National Weather Service describes it as the most devastating flood in modern U.S. History.

Parallelism

In Chapters 9 and 10 you will read about parallel structures *within* the sentence, a kind of repetition you may be familiar with. For example, when Lincoln in his Gettysburg Address used the phrases "of the people, by the people, and for the people," he was using parallelism to dramatize his point. President Kennedy's parallel verb phrases, "pay any price, bear any burden, meet any hardship, support any friend, oppose any foe," have a similar dramatic effect. **Parallelism** refers to repeated similar structures.

Some of the cohesive devices that we mentioned at the opening of this chapter provide opportunities to include parallelism within a paragraph. Words like *first, second,* and *third;* phrases like *on the one hand* and *on the other hand* invite sentences that repeat words or phrases, that have common, parallel structures. The more carefully you construct such sentences, the more they will add to the cohesiveness of your prose.

But even more opportunities exist for other kinds of parallel structures: the repetition of words and phrases and rhythms that tie sentences and paragraphs together—that is, *between* sentences and paragraphs—in the same way that the Lincoln and

Kennedy repetitions work *within* sentences. We saw a simple parallel tie in the passage about Portland: When we read *The western border* in the third sentence, we immediately recognized the connection to the second, which began with *The eastern border*.

Besides its cohesive power, parallelism can add drama to a paragraph, just as it does in presidential speeches. The repetitions in the following paragraphs have obviously been included for their dramatic effect:

> That knowledge has become the key resource means that there is a world economy, and that the world economy, rather than the national economy, is in control. Every country, every industry, and every business will be in an increasingly competitive environment. Every country, every industry, and every business will, in its decisions, have to consider its competitive standing in the world economy and the competitiveness of its knowledge competencies.
>
> —Peter F. Drucker, "The Age of Social Transformation," *The Atlantic Monthly* (November 1994)

> Why imagine that specific genes for aggression, dominance, or spite have any importance when we know that the brain's enormous flexibility permits us to be aggressive or peaceful, dominant or submissive, spiteful or generous? Violence, sexism, and general nastiness are biological since they represent one subset of a possible range of behaviors. But peacefulness, equality, and kindness are just as biological—and we may see their influence increase if we can create social structures that permit them to flourish.
>
> —Stephen Jay Gould, *Ever Since Darwin*

It's fairly common to find the added drama of parallelism used in conclusions, as we see in the following, the final paragraph of an article about two people who follow storms across the Midwest:

> Corso and Dorr will drive on for another two weeks, perpetrating horseplay. They will follow warm fronts across the plains, hunting for the dry line and the triple point. They will listen to brain-killing rock music and consume lethal quantities of deep-fat-fried chicken. They will stand on top of their car to photograph supercells. They will cover about 10,000 miles, their eyes on the clouds, slowly turning the inside of their car into a landfill of empty tortilla chip bags and cola bottles, hoping for a tornado. Where next? I ask. "We'll see how the fronts shape up," Corso says. "But I'm thinking maybe we'll buzz over to New Mexico—we could catch some good lightning!"
>
> —Richard Wolkomir, "Squalls Ahead, East or West, These Storm Chasers Never Rest," *Smithsonian* (October 1994)

Besides the drama of parallelism in this last passage, you'll notice that the author has used another structure commonly found in conclusions—the catchy quotation. Both are strategies you might want to experiment with in the conclusions of your own essays.

Repetition vs. Redundancy

Rather than commending these three authors for effective parallelism, you may be tempted to accuse them of unnecessary repetition, a problem that goes by the label *redundancy*. How do we distinguish between them? How do we tell the difference between good repetition and bad?

Parallelism of the kind we see here—parallelism as a stylistic device—invariably calls attention to itself. Did these authors intend to do that, to call attention to these structures? Clearly, the answer is "Yes—and for good reason." In all three passages, the use of repetition has added a dramatic dimension to the prose.

The use of repetition as a stylistic device is discussed further in Chapter 10, "The Grammar of Style."

For Group Discussion

---

1. In the following paragraph, from an article on charter schools, the writer achieves parallelism in the discussion of pedagogical principles by means of sentence structure. What, specifically, has she used here to achieve that parallelism? How does the sentence structure affect the known–new contract?

It is too early to measure the success of charter schools. But for all their diversity, it is interesting to note that many seem to be embracing a very similar set of pedagogical principles. First, reduce class size. Make sure parents are heavily involved. (Contracts with parents are a common feature.) Just as important, keep school size small, particularly in the inner city, where kids desperately need a sense of family and personal commitment from adults. Encourage active hands-on learning, in part through the intelligent use of technology. For older kids, drop the traditional switching of gears and classrooms from math to social studies to biology every 45 minutes and substitute lengthier classes that teach across disciplines.

—Claudia Wallis, "A Class of Their Own," *Time* (October 31, 1994)

2. Check an essay of your own or that of a classmate to identify places where parallel repetitions will enhance the cohesiveness of a paragraph. You may find one possibility for revision where you have used pronouns in subject position, as Wolkomir did in the passage about Corso and Dorr—either repeating the subject–verb sequence as he did or by repeating noun phrases instead of substituting pronouns. Another possibility is the repetition of introductory adverbial phrases. Check your concluding paragraph, too, as a potential spot for the added drama of parallelism. But remember that such parallel structures do call attention to themselves, so you'll want to use that kind of repetition only when the passage deserves the added attention.

RHETORICAL REMINDERS

Have I anticipated my reader's expectations?

Is the known information in the beginning of the sentence, where it can provide a cohesive tie to the previous sentence, with the new information in the predicate?

Have I taken advantage of parallelism as a cohesive device?

Chapter 3

A Sense of Rhythm

One of the most important aspects of your expertise with sentences is your sense of rhythm. (And that holds true even if you can't carry a tune!) Our language has a rhythm just as surely as music does—a regular beat. For example, if you read the opening sentence in this paragraph out loud, you'll hear yourself saying "one of the most" in almost a monotone; you probably don't hear a stressed syllable, a beat, until you get to *important:*

one of the most imPORTant

And you probably rush through those first four words so fast that you pronounce "of" without the *f*, making "one of" sound like the first two words in "won a prize."

The rhythm of sentences, what we call the **intonation pattern,** can be described as valleys and peaks, where the loudest syllables, those with stress, are represented by peaks:

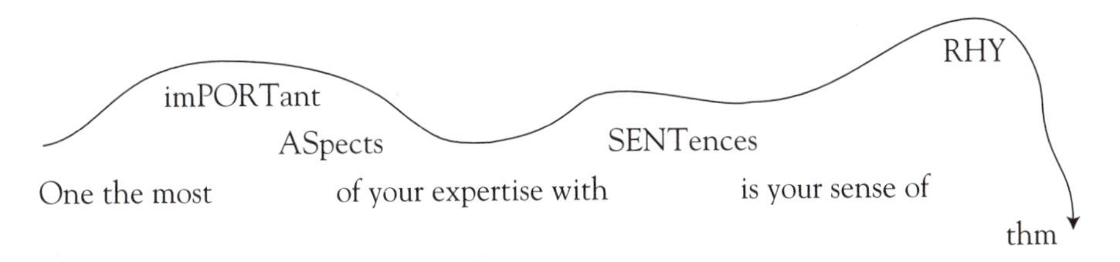

Not all the peaks are of the same height—we have different degrees of stress—but they do tend to come at fairly regular intervals. As listeners we pay attention to the peaks; that's where we'll hear the information that the speaker is focusing on. And as speakers we manipulate those peaks and valleys to coincide with our message, reserving the loudest stress, the highest peak, for the new information, which will be our main point of focus.

Such sentence manipulation is not something we ordinarily think about, nor is it a skill we were taught; for native speakers it's automatic, part of our native language ability. On the other hand, if you're not a native speaker of English, mastering the rhythm of sentences may be difficult, especially if the sentence rhythm of your native language does not have a regular beat like English. Certainly, a dominant feature of some "foreign accents" is the absence of that rhythm, with peaks and valleys in unexpected places or missing altogether.

But even for you who are not native speakers, recognizing the relationship between the rhythm of sentences and the message, as we will examine in this chapter, will be helpful to you as writers. You will also find it helpful in practicing your own listening skills to focus on sentence rhythm, with its peaks and valleys.

Sentence rhythm is a feature of all modes of language, not just speech. The peaks and valleys are there when we read silently, and they are there when we write, as we think of the words and phrases while moving our pen or punching the keyboard. Although philosophers may debate about whether it's possible to think in the absence of language, we are certainly conscious of doing our own thinking in words. In fact, we often "write" mental lists; we hold silent conversations with ourselves; we scold ourselves; we rehearse what we plan to say to others and what we wish we had said but didn't. And that interior language, the sentences and fragments of our inner voice, has all the peaks and valleys that our spoken language has.

But unlike speaking and listening and thinking, reading and writing are not intuitive behaviors; they are learned. And as with all learned behaviors, people vary widely in their ability to perform them. So when people read, there are undoubtedly differences in the intonation of their inner voices as well, variations in the degree to which their intonation interprets the writer's intention. We have no way of testing this assumption, of course; we can't record a reader's inner voice. But it seems safe to assume that an inexperienced or unskilled reader, one who struggles with the words, will surely miss a great deal of the meaning that sentence rhythm contributes. And the child who is just learning to read, who gives equal emphasis to nearly every syllable, is clearly not hearing the nuances of the writer's rhythm. It's obvious, too, that writers vary in their ability to use sentence rhythm to their best advantage—or, rather, to the reader's advantage. The writer who does not understand the rhythm, or who disregards it, who simply gives no thought to the peaks and valleys, will not be in complete control of the message the reader gets.

End Focus

The rhythm of sentences is closely tied to their binary structure (discussed in Chapter 1), as well as to the known–new contract (discussed in Chapter 2). The sentence topic, stated in the subject, will usually be a valley or a low peak in the intonation contour; the prominent peak of stress will occur in the predicate, on the new information, generally on the last or next-to-the-last slot in the sentence. Linguists describe this common rhythm pattern as **end focus.**

The contrast between the valleys and peaks of rhythm is easy to demonstrate in short sentences. As you read the following, listen for the syllable that gets main stress:

> The common cold is caused by a virus.
> My chemistry books cost over sixty dollars.
> Barbara wrecked her motorcycle.
> Sentence rhythm is related to the known–new contract.

We normally don't read sentences in lists, of course; we read them in context. And as readers we count on the context, on the meaning, to guide the reading, to help us put the emphasis where it belongs. Our job as writers, then, is clear: If we want readers to understand our intentions and to focus on the new information, we must help them by taking sentence rhythm into account. The following passages provide a simple lesson on the way in which end focus and sentence rhythm work together:

> Dennis told me that Barbara had an accident this morning on her way to work. But I think he got his facts wrong. Barbara wrecked her motorcycle yesterday.
>
> Dennis told me that Barbara had an accident this morning on her way to work. But I think he got his facts wrong. Yesterday Barbara wrecked her motorcycle.

As you probably noticed, the only difference between the two passages is in the rhythm pattern of the last sentence. You probably stressed the adverb *yesterday*, the new information, in both cases—even in the second passage, when *yesterday* appears in an unexpected place, the opening slot. However, by putting the new information in the opening, the writer has simply disregarded the reader's expectation that the new, important information in the sentence will be at the end. That placement for *yesterday* is the kind of unnatural rhythm that is likely to elicit a writing teacher's "awkward" in the margin.

In case you're tempted to do that kind of switching—opening the sentence with an adverbial just for variety's sake, to relieve the monotony of starting every sentence with the subject—think again! If what you're planning to switch to the opening position is the new information—don't do it! Remember the known–new contract and the principle of end focus. Save the new information for the end of the sentence, the point of main stress.

For Group Discussion

You saw the following pair of sentences in Chapter 1, where it was used to illustrate the movability of the indirect object, in this case *Ramon:*

Marie gave Ramon a gift.
Marie gave a gift to Ramon.

The two versions of the sentence obviously mean the same thing; the only difference lies in their focus. But that difference creates different expectations in the reader. You'll recall from the discussion of cohesion in Chapter 2 that the cohesive "flow" the reader experiences can be interrupted when those expectations are not met.

Imagine each of these sentences as the opening of a paragraph and think about what you, as the reader, expect to read next. You might even try predicting the subject of the second sentence. Here are three possibilities for the paragraph's second sentence:

It was a wool scarf she had knit herself.
She had shopped for days before finding the perfect necktie.
He wondered who had told her it was his birthday.

Decide which follow-up sentence has the most cohesive force. In other words, which one would you, as a reader, expect to follow each of the openers? Why?

EXERCISE 6

Read the following passages, listening carefully to the intonation contour of each sentence. Indicate the words (or syllables) that get main stress. Compare your reading with that of your classmates.

1. Never invest in something you don't understand or in the dream of an artful salesperson. Be a buyer, not a sellee. Figure out what you want (be it life insurance, mutual funds or a vacuum cleaner) and then shop for a good buy. Don't let someone else tell you what you need—at least not if he happens to be selling it.

—Andrew Tobias (*Parade*)

2. Plaque has almost become a household word. It is certainly a household problem. But even though everyone is affected by it, few people really understand the seriousness of plaque or the importance of controlling it. Plaque is an almost invisible sticky film of bacteria that continuously forms on the teeth. Plaque germs are constantly multiplying and building up. Any dentist will tell you that controlling plaque is the single most important step to better oral health.

—advertisement of the American Dental Association

3. Punitive notions of disease have a long history, and such notions are particularly active with cancer. There is the "fight" or "crusade" against cancer;

cancer is the "killer" disease; people who have cancer are "cancer victims." Ostensibly the illness is the culprit. But it is also the cancer patient who is made culpable. Widely believed psychological theories of disease assign to the luckless ill the ultimate responsibility both for falling ill and for getting well. And conventions of treating cancer as no mere disease but a demonic enemy make cancer not just a lethal disease but a shameful one.

—Susan Sontag ("Illness as Metaphor")

4. Frank evaluation of its [caffeine's] hazards is not easy. There is a vast literature on the effects of caffeine on the body, and for every study reaching one conclusion, seemingly there is another that contradicts it. Although most major health risks have been ruled out, research continues at a steady clip.

—Corby Kummer (*The Atlantic Monthly*)

Controlling Rhythm

Because end focus is such a common rhythm pattern, we can think of it as part of the contract between writer and reader. The reader expects the main sentence focus, the new information, to be in the predicate, unless given a signal to the contrary. But of course not all sentences are alike; not every sentence has end focus. In speech, especially, the focus is often shifted elsewhere. The speaker can easily stress the new information, no matter where in the sentence it appears. Consider, for example, these alternative ways of saying the motorcycle sentence, the variety of messages that are possible for the speaker:

BARBARA wrecked her motorcycle yesterday morning. [Not someone else.]
Barbara wrecked HER motorcycle yesterday morning. [Her own; not someone else's.]
Barbara wrecked her motorcycle yesterday MORNING. [Not in the afternoon.]

And we can add extra stress to *motorcycle:*

Barbara wrecked her MOTORCYCLE yesterday morning. [Not her car.]

Or we can give the whole sentence added emphasis:

Barbara DID wreck her motorcycle yesterday morning. [Believe me, I'm not making this up.]

The speaker is in control of the message that the listener is meant to hear. The spoken language is powerful, much more powerful than writing, far more capable of expressing feelings and nuances of meaning.

The *It*-Cleft

It's true that the speaker has a much easier job than does the writer in getting the message across and preventing misinterpretation. But the writer is certainly not powerless—far from it. As we saw earlier, the careful writer can take control simply by understanding the reader's expectations about the sentence and by making sure that the new information coincides with the prominent stress. You'll recall the second version of the motorcycle passage where the sensitive reader would almost certainly delay the stress until the word *yesterday*, the unit of new information. But in the following revision, the writer has left nothing to chance:

> Dennis told me that Barbara had an accident on the way to work this morning. But he apparently got his facts wrong. It was yesterday that she wrecked her motorcycle.

In this version it's impossible for the reader to misinterpret the emphasis on *yesterday* with the "it" construction, known as a **cleft sentence.** (The term *cleft* comes from the verb *cleave*, which means to divide or split.) The ***it*-cleft** enables the writer to shift the emphasis to any slot in the sentence, forcing the reader to focus on the structure following "it was" (or "it is," "it has been," etc.):

> It was Barbara who wrecked her motorcycle.
> It was her own motorcycle that Barbara wrecked.

Student writers are burdened with a great many myths about writing. You've probably been told at one time or another to avoid *I* or *you* or the passive voice—and, very possibly, the *it*-cleft as well. Many teachers and handbooks consider "it is" a weak sentence opener. In fact, however, the opposite is often true. The opening "it" construction enables the writer to point to the idea that should have the focus and to do so in a very decisive way.

One of the most famous opening *it*-cleft sentences begins Dickens' *A Tale of Two Cities:*

> It was the best of times, it was the worst of times. . . .

That sentence, in fact, goes on with eight more "it was" structures before the period. But we don't have to look at the past to find such openers.

The following passages are from a 1994 *Time* cover story on killer microbes by Michael D. Lemonick (the passages are not contiguous):

> It is tempting to think of the tiny pathogens that produce such diseases as malaria, dysentery, TB, cholera, staph and strep as malevolent little beasts, out to destroy higher forms of life. In fact, all they're trying to do is survive and reproduce, just as we are. Human suffering and death are merely unfortunate by-products.

> It is by killing individual cells in the body's all important immune system that the AIDS virus wreaks its terrible havoc. The virus itself isn't deadly, but it leaves the body defenseless against all sorts of diseases that are.

Stanley Weintraub begins the preface to his biography of Queen Victoria with an *it*-cleft:

> It has often been said that someone really worth writing about deserves reappraisal every twenty years.

And five paragraphs later:

> It is now a century and a half since a girl christened Alexandrina Victoria, eighteen years old and not quite five feet tall, became Queen of her country. . . .

Susan Sontag used an *it*-cleft in the passage about cancer we saw earlier:

> But it is also the cancer patient who is made culpable.

Such sentences are anything but weak. The *it* construction enables the writer to control the reader's valleys and peaks of stress, to determine precisely what the rhythm of the sentence will be.

Many of the myths about writing you've heard through the years, the various *dos* and *don'ts*, probably got started because inexperienced writers tend to overuse and misuse these structures. This is undoubtedly true with the *it*-cleft as well: The opening "it is" or "it was" is often misused. But when it is well used, it is efficient—and almost foolproof—in allowing the writer to direct the reader's focus.

The *What*-Cleft

Another kind of cleft sentence uses a *what*-clause in subject position; as with the *it*-cleft, here also a form of *be* separates the original sentence into two parts:

> Barbara wrecked her motorcycle.
> <u>What Barbara wrecked was her motorcycle</u>.

The ***what*-cleft** can also shift the original verb phrase into subject position; that shift will put the original subject in line for end focus:

> A branch lying across the road caused the accident.
> <u>What caused the accident was a branch lying across the road</u>.
> Thick fog reduced the visibility to zero.
> <u>What reduced the visibility to zero was the thick fog</u>.

Both of these examples could also be revised with the *it*-cleft:

> It was a branch lying across the road that caused the accident.
> It was thick fog that reduced the visibility.

The *There*-Transformation

Another method of changing word order to shift the stress is known as the ***there*-transformation:**

> A stranger is standing on the porch.
> There's a stranger standing on the porch.

> No concert tickets were available this morning.
> There were no concert tickets available this morning.

Again, this reordering puts the main stress on the subject by shifting its position. Remember that the normal subject position, the opening slot, is usually an unstressed valley in terms of the intonation pattern. This addition of *there*, known as an **expletive,** delays the subject, thereby putting it in line for stress.

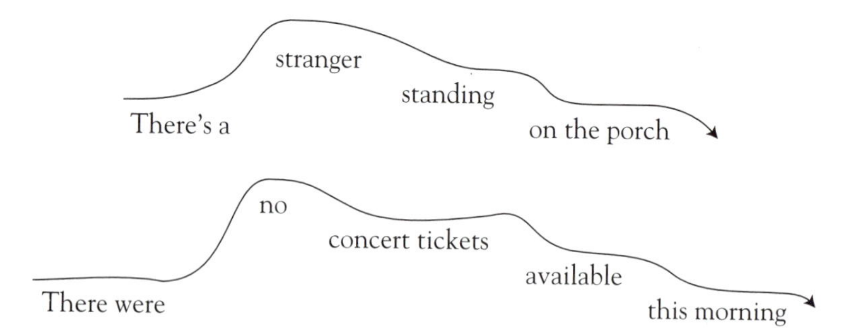

The last paragraph in the previous Exercise includes two *there*-transformations in the second sentence:

> There is a vast literature on the effects of caffeine on the body, and for every study reaching one conclusion, seemingly there is another that contradicts it.

Here the author undoubtedly wants the reader to put main stress on *vast literature* and on *another*. You also read a *there*-transformation in the Sontag paragraph:

> There is the "fight" or "crusade" against cancer. . . .

Do these writers consciously call up such rhythm-controlling devices from their grammar tool kits as they write? Do they deliberately say, "Time to use my trusty *it*-cleft or should I delay this subject with a *there*-transformation?"

No, they probably don't. They may not even have labels like "transformation" and "cleft" to describe those structures. But as experienced writers and readers, they're tuned into sentence rhythm as they compose—especially as they revise. Published paragraphs such as those in Exercise 5 did not spring fully developed from the heads of their authors. Those final drafts may have gone through many revisions. It's in the revision stage that writers experiment with such devices as the *it-* and *what-*clefts and the *there-*transformation and make decisions about their effectiveness. And you can be sure that in reading their own prose, whether silently or aloud, they are paying attention to sentence rhythm.

EXERCISE 7

Rewrite the following sentences, shifting the focus by using sentence transformations: the *it-*cleft, the *what-*cleft, and *there*. For example, you could use a cleft structure in the first sentence to focus either on Jody or on the flavor; in the second sentence, you could focus on the date or the place or the ship or the iceberg.

1. Jody loves chocolate ice cream.
2. The *Titanic* hit an iceberg and sank in the North Atlantic in 1912.
3. Our defense won the Stanford game in the final three minutes with a crucial interception.
4. Florida's agriculture and tourism industries will feel the sting when the African "killer" bee arrives in the 1990s as scientists expect. (*Orlando Sentinel*)
5. Tuesday's earthquake started with a small slip of the earth eleven miles beneath the ground. (Glennda Chui, *San Jose Mercury News*)
6. Hundreds of angry women were protesting the senator's position on day care at yesterday's political rally in the student union.
7. A month of unseasonably warm weather almost ruined the ski season last winter.
8. The Mississippi River and its tributaries overflowed their banks in the summer of 1993 and caused over $15 billion in damage to homes and farms in ten states.

Rhythm and the Comma

The sentence transformations with *it* and *what* and *there* are not the only ways we have to control the rhythm of sentences. Other ways, in fact, are much more common and, in most cases, more subtle. The phrase "in fact" in the preceding sentence illustrates one such method—a set phrase that interrupts the rhythm pattern. The inserted phrase not only adds a new intonation contour; it also adds emphasis to the subject. We can illustrate the difference with a picture of the contours:

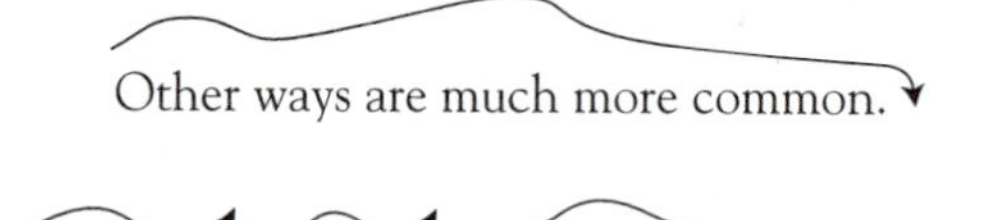

Other ways, in fact, are much more common.

The visual signal of the comma causes the reader to give added length and stress to the preceding word. And, as the contour lines illustrate, the sentence has gone from having one intonation contour to having three. The main focus is still on the new information at the end, but the sentence rhythm has changed, with part of the reader's attention shifted to the subject. Notice in the second version how much more length and stress you give to the subject headword, *ways*, when it is followed by a comma.

This role for the comma, to shift the peak of stress, is probably one you hadn't thought about before. You've probably considered the comma in the more traditional way, as a signaler of the pause in speech. But, as you learned in Chapter 1 regarding the sentence slots, not every pause translates to a comma in writing. And when we do include a comma, the pause goes beyond simple hesitation. It includes the rising intonation illustrated by the arrows, along with stress and added length given to the preceding word. Even the common *and* gets that extra attention in the second sentence of the previous paragraph. The inserted *as*-clause lengthens the opening *and;* because of the comma, that one word has its own intonation contour:

And, as the contour lines illustrate, the sentence . . .

Among the most versatile tools for manipulating sentence rhythm are the **conjunctive adverbs,** words and phrases that create cohesion between sentences with an adverbial emphasis—like the phrase *in fact* discussed earlier. Their versatility lies in their movability. That earlier sentence could have been written like this:

Other ways are much more common, in fact.

In this version, the word *common* gets all the attention.

Here are some other examples of sentences with movable phrases. You've read all of these previously in Chapters 1 and 2:

1. Writing, *of course*, requires much more conscious knowledge than does speech.
2. The study of rhetorical grammar, *then*, is essentially a matter of consciousness raising. . . .
3. These [connective words] are important, *of course;* they make the meaning clear.
4. In many questions, *for example*, the subject is buried in the predicate half of the sentence.

5. You might choose this pattern if, *for example*, you want to put the main emphasis. . . .
6. You'll discover, *however*, that sometimes you want to leave it [the word *that*] in to signal that a clause is coming.

Notice especially how many different places in these sentences a conjunctive adverb occurs: in (1) and (2) between subject and predicate; in (3) at sentence end; in (4) after the opening adverbial phrase and before the subject; in (5) between the subordinator and the clause it introduces; in (6) between the verb and the direct object. An important point to understand is that there are other places in all six of these sentences where that word or phrase could have been placed. Writers position these structures to help their readers read them: How do I want the reader to read this sentence? What is important here for the reader to stress? Will the reader understand how this sentence fits in with what follows?

Other familiar words and phrases in the same category include *in addition*, *meanwhile*, *in the meantime*, *instead*, *on the other hand*, *as a result*, *at any rate*, and *in conclusion*. You'll find a longer list on page 178. The movability and thus the versatility of these and other adverbial structures are discussed further in Chapter 7.

EXERCISE 8

1. Following is an early draft of the opening paragraph of a student essay. In making decisions about revising it, pay particular attention to sentence rhythm and focus and to the known–new contract. You can compare your revision to the student's final draft, reproduced in Answers to the Exercises in the back of the book.

It is a land where the sun doesn't shine for the entire winter. Warmth is a relative term; a heat wave happens when temperatures reach the fifties. Snowstorms and icy fog are typical of summer. Mosquitoes are the most abundant form of wildlife. They form dense, black swarms. Thousands of feet of permanently frozen ground lie inches below the spongy surface. Flying overhead, one sees nothing but a great expanse of what appears to be an Arctic wasteland. No trees and no signs of habitation are anywhere to be seen—just the tundra, a never-ending, dingy brown carpet. Why would anyone be concerned with this place, other than the 200 or so native inhabitants? Why? Because the frozen ground oozes black oil, making the coastal plain of the Arctic National Wildlife Refuge perhaps the most valuable piece of real estate in North America. Money and security are the interests behind those who wish to develop the land. They include oil companies, many Alaskans, and the Bush administration.

2. Reread the six passages that you revised for Exercise 5 in Chapter 2. Given what you have been reading in this chapter on rhythm—including end

focus, the cleft and *there* transformations, and commas—perhaps a re-revision would make them even more effective.

For Group Discussion

1. Several of the sentences in the following passage, from *The Birds* by Roger Tory Peterson, illustrate another method of putting the subject in line for main stress. Read the passage aloud and mark the peaks of stress. Using your understanding of the sentence slots, identify the subject and predicate of each clause. What technique has the author used to control the rhythm? (The sentences are numbered so that the discussion of them will be easier.)

[1] A bird's feathers have to do many things. [2] Not only must they provide lift surfaces for wings and tail, but they must protect the bird against the weather and insulate it against loss of heat. [3] Feathers come in almost infinite variety, but they fall into four main categories. [4] Most numerous are the contour feathers which coat the body, giving it a streamlined shape. [5] A house sparrow wears about 3,500 of these in winter, and they are so efficient at sealing in heat that it can maintain a normal temperature of 106.7°F. without difficulty in below-freezing cold. [6] Lying beneath them are the soft down feathers, also used for insulation. [7] Scattered among both types are the hair-like filoplumes which sometimes protrude from the coat and may serve as a kind of decoration, or possibly as sensory organs.

2. Read a draft of your own essay (or that of a classmate) with sentence rhythm in mind. (Don't hesitate to read it aloud and listen for your own peaks and valleys.) Think especially about end focus in connection with the known–new contract, as well as the difference in rhythm that commas make.

Power Words

We have just seen how conjunctive adverbs set off by commas can override the principle of end focus, the expected rhythm pattern. We've also seen how the sentence shifts with *it* and *there* change the emphasis. But some words are powerful enough to interrupt the usual rhythm pattern on their own—even without commas or sentence shifts.

Read the following pairs of sentences aloud and listen for the words that get main stress:

In the first gallery we admired a display of Tiffany glass.
In the first gallery we admired a magnificent display of Tiffany glass.

The senator spoke about the problems of the homeless.
The senator spoke eloquently about the problems of the homeless.

Both its meaning and its length may contribute to a word's inherent attention-getting power, as in the case of the adjective *magnificent* and the adverb *eloquently*. Words that convey strong emotions and words that have a superlative or absolute quality will be hard to compete with for attention in most sentences.

Adjectives and adverbs are especially powerful when they are qualified or intensified by another modifier (*absolutely ridiculous*, *thoroughly disgusting*, *especially powerful*) and when they are in the superlative degree, ending in *-est* or marked by *most* (*most aggressively*, *most incredible*). Noun phrases too have the power to take control of the sentence, especially when they include one of those powerful modifiers (*complete chaos*, *dangerous undertaking*, *overwhelming courage*, *bewildering array*).

Certainly a caveat is called for here. To label these words as power words is not necessarily to recommend that you use them. The point to remember is that when you do use them they will command attention. Like movie stars who inevitably create a stir wherever they go, these words will change the atmosphere of the sentences they inhabit. Here is what happened to the sentence about the senator's speech:

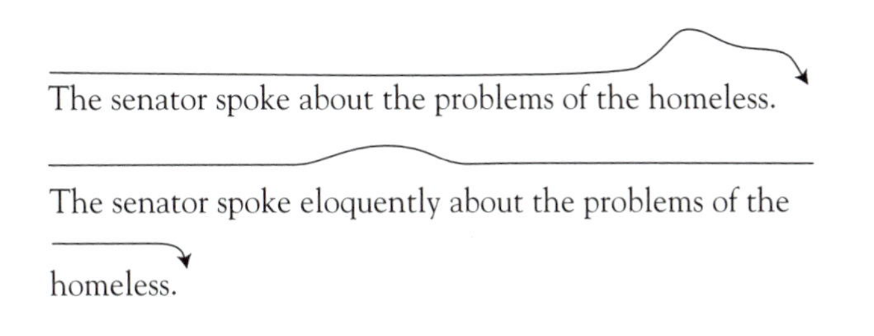

The word *eloquently* has shifted the limelight from the topic of the speech to the senator's style of speaking; and, in doing so, it has set up a different expectation in the reader. We would not be surprised if the subject of the next sentence turned out to be *he* or *she* (the senator) rather than *they* (the homeless).

It's important to recognize that in each example the word added—*magnificent*, *eloquently*—has changed a statement of fact into an arguable proposition. The reader has every right to expect supporting evidence for these opinions. What was there about the speech that was eloquent? In what way is the display magnificent? In other words, those power words that changed the rhythm have also changed the reader's expectations.

Correlative Conjunctions

Although conjunctions like *and*, *or*, and *but* are among our most common words (and you certainly have no problem in using them), there is a subclass of conjunctions that writers often overlook: the correlative conjunctions. They are *either/or*, *neither/nor*, *both/and*, *not only/but also*, and *not only/but . . . as well*.

They, too, are among the power words, those words that change the focus and rhythm pattern of the sentence and change the expectation of readers. When you read the following sentence, you probably give the loudest stress to *environment* and *scale:*

> Individuals and nations must learn to think about the environment on a worldwide scale.

Now add one word. Instead of the simple conjunction *and,* use the correlative *both/and* and listen to your rhythm pattern:

> *Both* individuals *and* nations must learn to think about the environment on a worldwide scale.

Your main stress has probably shifted to the subject, especially to *and nations.*

Now try it with *not only/but also* (or . . . *as well*):

> Not only individuals but also nations must learn to think about the environment on a worldwide scale.
>
> Not only individuals but nations as well must learn to think about the environment on a worldwide scale.

The subject has acquired even more emphasis.

You will look again at these powerful tools in Chapter 9 in the discussion of "The Long and the Short of Sentences."

For Group Discussion

Look for places in your own writing (or in that of your classmates) where you have used compound structures with *and* and *or.* Consider the possibility of turning the *and* into *both/and* or *not only/but also* and the *or* into *either/or.* Remember, however, that the correlative puts extra emphasis on that structure, especially on its second element. You'll want to make that change only if you intend for the reader to give it added attention. You may have to make other changes as well, to fulfill the reader's expectations.

RHETORICAL REMINDERS

Sentence Rhythm

Does the main stress in my sentences coincide with the new information?

Have I considered my reader's expectations by putting the new information in line for end focus, unless otherwise marked?

Controlling Rhythm

Have I used *there* and cleft sentences effectively—but not too frequently?

Have I placed interrupting words and phrases and clauses where they will be the most effective?

Power Words

Have I considered the impact of power words on the rhythm pattern?

Have I considered the contribution that correlative conjunctions could or do make to the rhythm and the reader's expectations?

PUNCTUATION REMINDER

Remember that a comma changes the rhythm of the sentence, adding length and stress to the preceding word.

Chapter 4

A Way with Words

Your intuitive understanding of sentences in your native language is more than matched by your remarkable way with words. The sentences that you automatically generate whenever the need arises are, of course, strings of individual words, which you select from an inventory, or **lexicon,** of many thousands of entries—an internal dictionary of sorts. The extent of your lexicon is impossible to measure with any accuracy, but chances are if you have grown up with English you understand well over half of the 150,000 words in a standard desk dictionary. How many of them are part of your active vocabulary is another matter; it's possible you use only 5,000 to 10,000 for most of the speaking and writing you do. On the other hand, that number could be closer to 20,000 or 30,000—even higher, perhaps, depending on your background, including the language you hear spoken around you, your level of interest in reading, your curiosity. But no matter what the extent of your active vocabulary, like all literate people, you recognize and understand many more words than you actually use, words that constitute your passive vocabulary.

Although it's useful to compare our internal lexicon to the dictionary, the analogy is not a very accurate one. Individual entries in our lexicon and their definitions are quite different from those in a standard dictionary. Our definitions are bound up with experience and memory, so they include all of the associations that the word holds for us, negative and positive. For example, think about your own personal definition of *mother* and *kindergarten* and *picnic* and *train* and *football;* it's obvious that no dictionary can describe the pictures that those words conjure up for you.

Although the size of a person's lexicon will vary from one individual to another and from one language to another, this remarkable way with words is universal: It holds true for native speakers of every language. If English is not your first language, your experience will determine the number of words in your vocabulary and the definitions you have for them. And in the discussion that follows, you will probably recognize, from your study of English, some of the restrictions on the ways in which words are arranged—restrictive rules that your classmates who are native speakers have never thought about before.

Lexical Rules

Even more impressive than the number of words and their associations in our memory are the grammatical rules and restrictions that determine how we put our words together into sentences. The following pairs of sentences illustrate how those rules and restrictions work—or fail to work:

> Kevin had some trouble last night with his homework.
> Paul had a trouble last night with his homeworks.
>
> Dr. Carroll owns a BMW.
> His wife is owning a pickup.
>
> Sue is being funny.
> Rob is being tall.
>
> Pam walked to school.
> Kate walked to home.
>
> Jim walked to town.
> Joe walked to city.
>
> The little children were afraid of the Halloween ghosts.
> The afraid children hid from the trick-or-treaters.
>
> I've given you the main reason for my decision.
> That reason for my decision is main.

You probably recognized that in each case the second sentence is ungrammatical—that is, it is not a sentence that a native speaker would say. A comparison of the two sentences in each pair should illuminate the kinds of lexical rules that operate in English.

The first pair illustrates the restriction that prevents us from saying "homeworks," a distinction we make between the **countable** and **noncountable nouns** in our lexicon: *Homework* is noncountable; it's a kind of **mass noun;** others in the class are *sugar* and *water* and *oil* and *cotton*. Another noncountable class is that of **abstract nouns,** such as *happiness* and *peace*. The first pair of sentences also demonstrates the restriction built into the **indefinite article,** *a* (or *an*), one of our **determiners,** or noun signalers. Noncountable nouns, such as *homework* and *happiness*, cannot be signaled by *a*, nor do they have a plural form: Native speakers simply do not say "homeworks" or "a happiness."

The verb *own*, as illustrated in the second pair of sentences, is called a **stative** verb; it describes an unchanging condition, or state. Because no change—no progress—is implied, the "progressive" form of the verb (the *-ing* form preceded by a form of *be* as an auxiliary) is simply not used.

The next pair illustrates the semantic qualities of adjectives: *Tall* is stative, so it cannot be used with the progressive "is being," which suggests a dynamic, or changeable, quality. The adjective *funny* includes both possible meanings: "Sue is funny" suggests a permanent characteristic of Sue's personality; "Sue is being funny" suggests a condition of the present moment.

For Group Discussion

If you were to hear someone say the following sentences, you could be quite sure you were hearing a nonnative speaker.

*We're going shopping for a new furniture.[1]
*Our furnitures are getting shabby.
*My family's healths are important to me.
*Kaleena is seeming sad today.
*I am not knowing Spanish very well.
*The pizza is being stale.
*The kids are not liking it.

Revise the sentences to make them grammatical. When you compare the two versions, you should be able to figure out which of your internal grammar rules has been broken.

The four sentences with *walked* in the list of pairs illustrate how arbitrary, or unsystematic, some of our rules are. There is something in our lexicon that restricts us from using the preposition *to* with *home*, although we do, of course, say "to town." The second pair with *walked* demonstrates the arbitrariness of determiners in some common situations. *City* takes the determiner; *town* does not. And although we do say, "I have *a* cold," we don't say, "I have *a* flu." Some of the rules for using determiners are different for British speakers. The British go "to hospital" and "to university," and they "look out of window." Americans go "to college" and "to school" but "to *the* university" and "to *the* hospital"; and we "look out of *the* window."

The last two pairs of sentences in the list illustrate a restriction on the position that the adjectives *afraid* and *main* can fill. Most adjectives can fill both the slot before the noun (the *nice* children) and the subjective complement slot after a linking verb or *be* (the children are *nice*); *afraid* and *main* are among a handful that cannot. These restrictions, too, are arbitrary.

[1]The asterisk signals, in this chapter and all subsequent chapters, that a sentence is ungrammatical or in some way unacceptable to a native speaker.

The grammar rules illustrated here are obviously not the kind that you studied in your grammar classes; chances are, you were not even aware that you follow rules like these when you speak and write. And certainly you don't want to worry about such rules—or even try to remember them. You couldn't remember them all even if you wanted to; in fact, no one has ever described them all. With these few we have just scratched the surface. We are looking at these rules simply to illustrate the kinds of information that our internal lexicon includes and to help you recognize and appreciate that your way with words is truly remarkable.

It is obvious that for a native speaker the restrictions illustrated by these pairs of sentences have somehow become internalized. Linguists sometimes describe such features as a built-in hierarchy, much like the taxonomy that scientists use in classifying plants and animals. Each level—phylum, class, order, family, genus, and species—includes features that differentiate it from the other levels. The farther down the hierarchy, the more specific the details that distinguish the classes. The following scheme illustrates certain features of nouns:

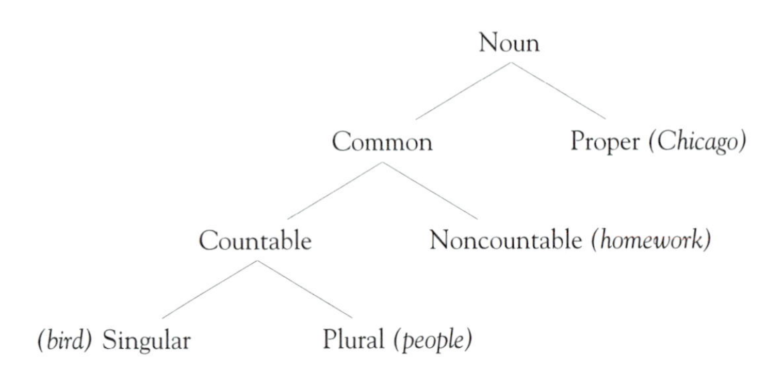

The restrictions built into the word will determine its place in the hierarchy; each word carries with it only those features in the higher intersections (or nodes) that it is connected with: *Homework* is a noncountable, common noun; *bird* is a singular, countable, common noun. Determiners, too, have such built-in features: The indefinite article, *a* (or *an*), includes "singular" and "countable," so we are restricted from using it with *homework*; it will signal only those nouns that fit in the lowest, left-hand branch, like *bird*. The **definite article,** *the*, is much more versatile as a determiner: It can signal nearly all nouns, even noncountables:

Have you finished the homework?
The happiness I felt at that moment is beyond description.

Many words in our lexicon can appear in both branches of a node, depending on their context. For example, some nouns can be both countable and noncountable:

I had a strange experience yesterday.
I've had experience working with animals.

I baked *a* pie today.
I'll have pie with ice cream, please.

Ron had two beers today already.
He drinks beer often.

The countable/noncountable feature applies also to certain signalers of nouns, such as *less/fewer, amount of/number of*, and *much/many*. The commercial that advertises a certain brand of soft drink as having "less calories" than another brand has failed to make the countable/noncountable distinction: *Calories* is a countable noun; the fact that it's plural tells us that. We generally reserve *less* for noncountables; the description of that soft drink should be "*fewer* calories." We would also talk about the "number of calories," not the "amount of calories," just as we would say "many calories," not "much calories." Such noncountables as *water* and *cotton* and *love* and *homework* pattern with "amount of" and "much"; *calories* does not.

For Group Discussion

A careful writer would avoid writing sentences like these two:

*There have been less bicycle accidents in the county this year.
*I have also noticed an increase in the amount of bicycles on the roads.

But there's no problem with these:

There are fewer students enrolled in the advanced ceramics class this year.
There is an increase in the number of students enrolled in the beginning course.

Think about where in the noun hierarchy you would find *accidents, bicycles, and students*, and *attention*. How would a careful writer revise those first two sentences? If you were helping a nonnative speaker revise those sentences, how would you explain the changes?

Would that careful writer avoid any of these?

There were less than a dozen bicycle accidents in the county this year.
We had fewer accidents than last year.
We have less dollars than we need.
We have less money than we need.
We have less than ten dollars to last until payday.

You probably gave that nonnative speaker some advice about the use of *less/fewer* and *amount of/number of*. Should you revise your explanation? In what way?

Semantic Features

All nouns have semantic features as well, features relating to their meaning. These features can also be pictured as a hierarchy. Countable nouns, for example, are either animate or inanimate:

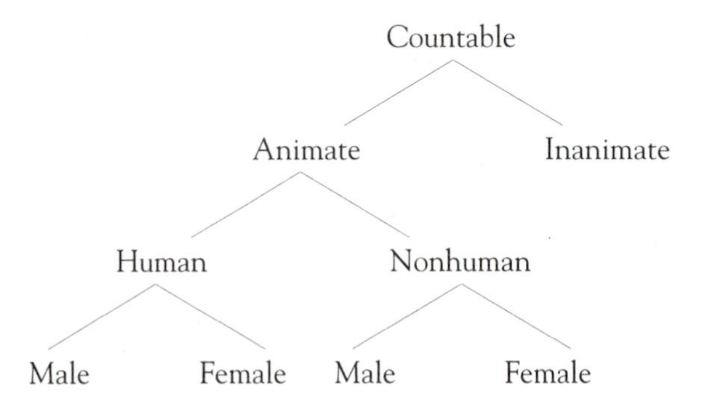

The branches at the bottom of the tree can be further branched into other features, including singular/plural and adult/child. The word *girl*, for example, includes the features "singular, child, female, human, animate, countable."

These built-in semantic features also account for both the meaning and the use of certain other words we select. For example, the animate/inanimate distinction often affects the selection of the verb. A verb such as *notice* or *think* requires a subject with the feature "animate"; it would not have an inanimate noun such as *rock* or *house* as its subject. Further, a verb such as *quibble* or *explain* requires still another feature, a "human" as well as "animate" subject; only human animals quibble and explain. The male/female distinction, built into many nouns (*woman*, *man*, *waiter*, *waitress*, *stallion*, *mare*), affects the choice of pronouns; and it may also affect other selections, such as certain adjectives: "A *ruddy* complexion" usually applies to men, "a *lovely* figure" generally to women. A similar built-in feature applies to such adjectives as *tall* (as we saw earlier), one that identifies it as "permanent" and thus restricts its use with *is being*.

Figurative Language

This scheme, showing the meaning of words in a hierarchy, should also illuminate the concept of **figurative language,** which involves a transfer of meaning. We use language figuratively when we deliberately bypass the hierarchies of meaning. For example, the writer who allows the wind to complain or the houses to stand at attention has moved the words *wind* and *houses* from the inanimate branch of the hierarchy to the animate or human branch. We call this transfer **personification.** Another kind of transfer is **metaphor.** The writer who calls the White House "a cabin in the bureaucratic woods" is imposing all of the characteristics of *cabin* on *White House*, as well as transferring the features of woods to bureaucracies; the writer who describes a ship as "cutting through the sea" has altered the features of both *ship* and *sea*.

For Group Discussion

1. Words are powerful. As a writer you can use to advantage the power that words hold to call up images in the mind of the reader. But to use words effectively, you have to understand as far as possible the meanings that are built into the reader's lexicon. Consider the following sets of related words: What features do the members have in common? What features separate them? In what context would one be more effective than another?

house/home	lad/boy/kid
hearth/fireplace	slumber/sleep/snooze
pleasure/fun/a good time	foolhardy/daring/rash/bold
companion/friend/buddy	change/alter
colleague/co-worker	dine/eat
picky/careful	careful/stingy/thrifty/tight
cocky/confident	clever/skillful/cunning
slim/skinny/lean/gaunt	great/wonderful/delightful/super

2. Many of the clichés that we are warned against are **similes,** comparisons that transfer the qualities of one thing (or person or animal) to another. Such similes become clichés when the reader knows exactly what's coming—that is, when there is no new information involved. The comparison will be much more effective when it evokes a fresh image, when it helps the reader see someone or something in a new way. No doubt you and all of your classmates could fill the following blanks with the same word; so instead of using the expected word, use an unexpected one to create a fresh image. For example, you might say, "Quiet as a sealskin coat."

sharp as ________________	mean as ________________
hot as ________________	light as ________________
cold as ________________	pretty as ________________
scared as a ________________	swear like a ________________
strong as ________________	weak as ________________
fast as ________________	ugly as ________________
worth its weight in ________________	tough as ________________
avoid like the ________________	sell like ________________

Parts of Speech

The traditional grammar course commonly opens with the classification of words into "parts of speech." You perhaps remember your own language arts classes from junior high, where you began your study of grammar by defining *noun* and *verb* and *adjective* and *adverb* and such. As you learned in the discussion of the lexicon, our internalized grammar includes rules and restrictions that determine how we use our words. In a sense, those rules constitute definitions of a sort for our word classes; so in this study of the parts of speech we will look at those internalized definitions.

We begin by classifying the words of our lexicon into two broad groups: **form classes** and **structure classes.** To understand the difference between the two groups, imagine an inexperienced speaker of English saying a sentence such as,

Stranger standing porch.

Even though it doesn't sound exactly like English, the sentence certainly communicates. Now imagine the same sentence spoken by an experienced speaker:

A stranger is standing on the porch.

or, perhaps,

That stranger is standing near the porch.

The added words make the message more explicit, of course, but the nouns and verb the first speaker used are adequate to get the gist of the message across. Those are the *form-class words;* the missing ones are the *structure-class words*, those that provide the grammatical connections.

In general, the form-class words—nouns, verbs, adjectives, and adverbs—provide the primary lexical content; the structure classes—determiners, auxiliaries, qualifiers, prepositions, conjunctions—explain the grammatical or structural relationships. Using a metaphor, we can think of form-class words as the bricks of the language and structure words as the mortar that holds them together.

Probably the most striking difference between the form classes and the structure classes is characterized by their numbers. Of the nearly half million words in our language, the structure words number only in the hundreds. The form classes, however, are large, open classes; new nouns and verbs and adjectives and adverbs regularly enter the language as new technology and new ideas require them. They are sometimes abandoned, too, as the dictionary's "obsolete" and "archaic" labels testify. But with few exceptions, the structure classes remain constant—and limited. We have managed with the very same small store of prepositions and conjunctions for generations, with few changes. It's true that we don't hear *whilst* and *betwixt* anymore, nor do we see them in modern prose and poetry, but most of our structure words are identical to those that Shakespeare and his contemporaries used.

In one way the contrast between the form and structure words is actually quite misleading. Even though the structure words number only a few hundred, they are by far the most frequently used words in the language. An amazing statistic was reported by G. H. McKnight in 1923: "[A] mere forty-three words account for half of the words actually uttered in English; and a mere nine account for fully a quarter of all spoken words."[2] The nine are *and*, *be*, *have*, *it*, *of*, *the*, *to*, *will*, and *you*.

[2]McKnight's research is reported by Cullen Murphy in "The Big Nine" (*The Atlantic Monthly*, March 1988).

Assuming that *be* and *have* are included because of their role as auxiliaries, there are no form-class words in the list. Except for the pronouns *it* and *you*, they are all structure-class words.

A third class, the **pronouns,** straddles the line between the form and structure classes. Many pronouns are like the form classes, insofar as they have variations in form; and of course they function as nouns, as substitutes for nouns and noun phrases. But they also belong with the structure classes: The possessive and demonstrative pronouns constitute important subclasses of the determiners (*my* house, *that* boat). Also, like the structure classes, pronouns are a small, closed class, admitting no new members. (We will take up pronouns in Chapter 5.)

As you read the descriptions of word classes in this and other chapters, don't make the mistake of thinking that here are pages of details to memorize. That's not the purpose of these descriptions, not at all. The purpose is, rather, to help you recognize in a conscious way some of those features of your lexicon that can help you to become a more thoughtful writer.

The Form Classes

Nouns, verbs, adjectives, and adverbs are called the "form" classes because each class has specific forms, a set of inflectional endings, or **inflections,** that distinguish them from all other classes. The feature of form is very useful in defining the class. For example, instead of defining *noun* in its traditional way, as "the name of a person, place, or thing," you can define it according to its form: "A noun is a word that can be made plural and/or possessive." And instead of defining *verb* as a word that shows action, which isn't very accurate, you can use the criterion of form, which applies to every verb, without exception: "A verb is a word that has an *-s* and an *-ing* form." These are the definitions built into your internal grammar system. Even though you may not be aware of these features, your internal linguistic computer makes use of them when you generate sentences.

Nouns

Nouns have an inflection for plural (*-s* or *-es*) and for **possessive case:**

SINGULAR	*PLURAL POSSESSIVE*	*SINGULAR POSSESSIVE*	*PLURAL*
cat	cats	cat's	cats'
treasure	treasures	treasure's	treasures'
fortress	fortresses	fortress's	fortresses'

Not every noun fits into the entire set, as we saw earlier in the case of noncountables such as *homework,* which has no plural. And some nouns have irregular plurals, an inflection other than *-s* or *-es: children, men, feet, mice, crises.* But certainly the vast majority of our nouns are inflected in this regular way, with *-s* (or *-es*) for those that have a plural form, with *s* for singular possessive and *-s'* or (*-es'*) for plural possessive.

It's easy to make mistakes in writing the plural and possessive of some nouns; read aloud the three inflected forms in the set of nouns—*cats, cat's, cats'*—and you'll understand why: They sound identical; in speech we make no distinction. The apostrophe is strictly an orthographic signal, a signal in the written language.

As you may know, the apostrophe is easy to misuse. It's not unusual to see it used mistakenly in plurals, especially if the plural looks a bit strange:

> *Fishing license's sold here.

This sign was spotted in the window of a sporting goods store; clearly, someone goofed. And a poster announcing the schedule of a musical group that reads,

> *Now playing Tuesday's at The Lounge,

is also wrong. We use the apostrophe with the *s* in the possessive case, not in the plural: *Joe's Bar & Grill, Tuesday's meeting.* The only exception to that rule occurs in the case of letters or numbers that would be unreadable without the apostrophe:

> There are three t's in my name.

And sometimes it occurs with decades:

> The 1960's were troubled times for many people.

In this latter case, however, it is even more common to see the decade referred to as "the 1960s"—without the apostrophe.

Probably the best rule of thumb to remember is that when you add an *s* sound, you add the letter *s*—in both plural and possessive: *cat, cat's, cats, cats'*. Words that end with an *s* (or an *s*-like sound), such as *fortress* or *church* or *dish*, require a whole syllable for the plural, an *-es: fortress/fortresses, church/churches, dish/dishes*. But we write the singular possessive just as we do with words like *cat:* We simply add *'s: fortress's, church's, dish's*. For the plural possessive, we simply add the apostrophe to the plural, as we do with *cats': fortresses', churches', dishes'*.

With nouns that already have one or more *s* sounds, we don't always add another when we make it possessive. For example, the word *Texas* has two *s* sounds in the last syllable (the letter *x* is actually a combination of two sounds: those of *k* and *s*); in speech when we make *Texas* possessive, we don't normally add another *s*, so in writing we add only the apostrophe to form the possessive case: *Texas' laws*. Another good example of this rule is the Biblical term "for righteousness' sake": We don't add another *s* sound to the word *righteousness* when we make it possessive.

Most names that end in a single *s* sound will have a second *s* sound for the plural and possessive, just as the word *fortress* does: *Ross's cat; I know two Rosses; Mr. Jones's cat; The Joneses' house; Dukakis's presidential campaign.*

Plural-only Forms. Some nouns, even when singular in meaning, are plural in form. One such group refers to things that are in two parts—that are bifurcated, or branching: *scissors*, *shears*, *clippers*, *pliers*, *pants*, *trousers*, *slacks*, *shorts*, *glasses*, *spectacles*. As subjects of sentences, these nouns present no problems with subject–verb **agreement:** They take the same verb form as other plural subjects do. Interestingly, even though a pair of shorts is a single garment and a pair of pliers is a single tool, we generally use the plural pronoun in reference to them:

> I bought a new pair of shorts today; they're navy blue.
> I've lost my pliers; have you seen them?

A different situation arises with certain plural-in-form nouns that are sometimes singular in meaning. Nouns such as *physics*, *mathematics*, and *linguistics*, when referring to an academic discipline or course, are treated as singular:

> Physics is my favorite subject.
> Linguistics is the scientific study of language.

But such nouns can also be used with plural meanings:

> The mathematics involved in the experiment are very theoretical.
> The statistics on poverty in this country are quite depressing.

Again, you can use your intuitive knowledge of pronouns to test these nouns:

> It [mathematics] *is* my favorite subject.
> They [the statistics on poverty] are quite depressing.

Collective Nouns. Collective nouns such as *family*, *choir*, *team*, *majority*, *minority*—any noun that names a group of individual members—can be treated as either singular or plural, depending on context and meaning:

> The family have all gone their separate ways. (they)

(It would sound strange to say "The family *has* gone *its* separate way.")

> The whole family is celebrating Christmas at home this year. (it)
> The majority of our city council members *are* Republicans. (they)
> The majority always rules. (it)

Certain noncountable nouns and indefinite pronouns take their number from the modifier that follows the headword:

> The remainder of the building materials are being donated to Habitat for Humanity.
> The rest of the books are being donated to the library.

The headwords *remainder* and *rest* are noncountable nouns in this context; their plurality clearly derives from the modifier, which determines the form of the verb. A singular noun in the modifier would change the verb:

> The remainder of the wood is being donated to Habitat for Humanity.
> The rest of the manuscript is being donated to the library.

Some of our indefinite pronouns, among them *some, all,* and *enough,* work in the same way:

> Some of the maps were missing.
> All of the cookies were eaten.

Again, notice what happens to the verb in such sentences when the noun in the *of* prepositional phrase is singular:

> Some of the water is polluted.
> All of the cake was eaten.

The pronoun to use in reference to these noun phrases will depend on the meaning, and it will usually be obvious:

> They [some of the maps] were missing.
> It [some of the water] is polluted.

One special problem occurs with the word *none,* which has its origin in the phrase *not one.* Because of that original meaning, many writers insist that *none* always be singular, as *not one* clearly is. However, a more accurate way to assess its meaning is to recognize *none* as the negative, or opposite, of *all* and to treat it in the same way, with its number determined by the number of the modifier:

> All of the *guests want* to leave.
> None of the *guests want* to leave.
>
> All of the *cookies were* left.
> All of the *cake was* left.
>
> None of the *cookies were* left.
> None of the *cake was* left.

These examples clearly suggest that in the case of noun phrases with collective nouns, certain noncountable nouns, and indefinite pronouns as headwords, the concept of number refers to the whole noun phrase, not just to the noun headword.

Proper Nouns. In contrast to **common nouns,** which refer to general things, places, attributes, and so on, **proper nouns** are those with a specific referent: *Empire*

State Building, Grand Canyon, William Shakespeare, London, The CBS Evening News, Aunt Mildred, November, Thanksgiving. Proper nouns name people, geographic regions and locations, buildings, events, holidays, months, and days of the week; they usually begin with capital letters. Most proper nouns are singular; exceptions occur with the names of mountain ranges (*the Rocky Mountains, the Rockies, the Andes*) and island groups (*the Falklands*), which are plural.

EXERCISE 9

Problems of subject–verb agreement sometimes occur when modifiers follow the headword of the subject noun phrase:

> *The instructions on the loan application form was very confusing.
> *This collection of poems by several of my favorite romantic poets were published in 1910.

In these incorrect examples, the writer has forgotten that the headword determines the number of the noun phrase. To figure out the correct form of the verb, you can use the pronoun-substitution test:

> The instructions [they] were very confusing.
> This collection [it] was published in 1910.

Now test the following sentences to see if they are grammatical:

1. The statement on the income tax form about deductions for children and other dependents were simply not readable.
2. The type of career that many graduates are hoping to pursue pay high salaries and provide long vacations.
3. Apparently the use of robots in Japanese factories have been responsible for a great deal of worker dissatisfaction.
4. The problems associated with government deregulation have been responsible for the economic plight of several major airlines in recent years.
5. The government's deregulation policy regarding fares have also resulted in bargains for the consumer.
6. The inability to compete with those low airline fares are also responsible for the financial problems of the bus companies.
7. The impact of computers on our lives is comparable to the impact of the industrial revolution.
8. This new book of rules with its 100 ways to play solitaire really amaze me.
9. Carmen's collection of computer games and board games were really impressive.
10. The amount of money and time I spend on computer games is more than I can afford.

Verbs

Although traditional grammar books often describe **verbs** in ways that make them seem complicated, they are really quite simple and systematic, especially when compared with verbs in other languages. With one exception, English verbs have only five forms—the base, or present tense, and four inflected forms:

PRESENT TENSE	*-S FORM*	*-ED FORM*	*-ING FORM*	*-EN FORM*
eat	eats	ate	eating	eaten
walk	walks	walked	walking	walked

The only verb that has more than these five forms is *be*, which has eight forms: *be, am, is, are, was, were, been, being.*

[Note: The past participle (*-en*) and the past tense (*-ed*) forms of **regular verbs** are identical: Both end in *-ed* (or, in some cases, *-d*, or *-t*). So to distinguish them, we give the past participle the label *-en*, the actual form it has in a number of **irregular verbs,** such as *eat* (*eaten*) and *break* (*broken*).]

In English we can get along with only these few forms of our verbs because we express differences in tense and mood mainly with the use of the auxiliary verbs *have* and *be* and with modals (*can, could, will, would, shall, should, may, might, must,* and *ought to*). French, on the other hand, expresses such differences with inflections: Where we have five forms, French has nearly eighty.

We form the *-ed* (the **past tense**) and the *-en* (the **past participle**) of almost all verbs—all but a hundred or so—by adding the inflectional suffix *-ed*. Some of our most frequently used verbs, however, including *eat*, are irregular; the irregularities affect only their *-ed* and *-en* forms, however; the *-s* and *-ing* forms are always the same. But even for the irregular verbs, it's very easy to figure out the members of the set just by using the verb in a sentence. When you generate a sentence with the word *yesterday*, your internal grammar rules will go to work, and you'll automatically insert the past tense (*-ed*) form:

Yesterday I <u>put</u> my coat in the closet.
Yesterday I <u>sang</u> a song.
Yesterday I <u>ate</u> some delicious scallops.
Yesterday I <u>walked</u> to town.

With the auxiliary *have*, you automatically use the past participle (*-en*):

I have <u>put</u> the coats on the bed.
I have <u>sung</u> many duets with Rosa.
I have <u>eaten</u> junk food all day.
I have <u>walked</u> home every day this week.

The **present participle,** the *-ing* form, is always used with a form of *be* as an auxiliary:

Sue was singing silly songs.
Bill is helping Dad.
Pat Paulsen has been campaigning for twenty-five years.

The *-s* form is used with singular nouns and third-person singular pronouns (*he*, *she*, *it*) to designate the present tense:

Rob usually sings off-key.
Bill helps his dad every Saturday.
Pat Paulsen campaigns for president every four years.

And, as strange as it may seem, the two present tense forms—both the base form and the *-s* form—can also denote the future when a time adverbial is included:

The bus leaves at noon tomorrow.

You can think of the verb as the pivotal slot in the sentence pattern, not only from the standpoint of position but also from the standpoint of its contribution to meaning and effectiveness. In Chapter 6 we will look further at the contribution of verbs, emphasizing the importance of their selection, including the sequence of tenses and the use of the passive voice.

Adjectives

A third open class of words is that of **adjectives,** which can sometimes be recognized by their comparative and superlative inflections, a semantic feature known as **degree:**

POSITIVE	*COMPARATIVE*	*SUPERLATIVE*
big	bigger	biggest
silly	sillier	silliest
intelligent	more intelligent	most intelligent

Note that *more* and *most* are variations of the inflections *-er* and *-est*.

A number of adjectives will not fit this set. For example, we do not say "the mainest reason" or "a more principal reason." The adjectives that do not take the inflections of degree will also not fit into the "adjective test frame":

The ______ NOUN is very ______.

The adjective test frame is useful in identifying adjectives: A word that will fit into both slots is an adjective—and most adjectives will work:

The frisky kitten is very frisky.
The comical clown is very comical.
The tough assignment is very tough.

The formula illustrates the two main slots that adjectives fill; as we saw earlier, however, not all adjectives fit both slots:

> *The principal reason is very principal.
> *The afraid children are very afraid.
> *The medical advice was very medical.

The test frame, then, can positively identify adjectives: Only an adjective will fit both slots. But it cannot rule them out—that is, just because a word doesn't fit, that doesn't mean it's *not* an adjective.

In Chapter 8 we'll look at adjectives as well as other structures in their role as adjectivals, or noun modifiers.

Adverbs

Our most recognizable **adverbs**—and the most common—are those that are formed by adding *-ly* to the adjective: *slowly, deliberately, exclusively, perfectly.* These are called adverbs of **manner.** Some common adverbs have the same form as the adjective: *fast, far, near, hard, long, high, late.* These are sometimes called **flat adverbs.**

Like adjectives, the *-ly* adverbs and the flat adverbs have comparative and superlative forms:

POSITIVE	*COMPARATIVE*	*SUPERLATIVE*
slowly	more slowly	most slowly
fast	faster	fastest

The comparative form of *-ly* adverbs, usually formed by adding *more* rather than *er,* is fairly common. However, the superlative degree of the *-ly* adverbs—*most suddenly, most slowly, most favorably*—is rare enough in both speech and writing to have impact when used; these forms invariably call attention to themselves and in most cases will carry the main stress:

> The committee was most favorably disposed to accept the plan.
> The crime was planned most ingeniously.

A great many adverbs have no endings that distinguish them as adverbs, nor are they used with *more* or *most.* Instead we recognize them by the information they provide, by their position in the sentence, and often by their movability:

Time:	now, today, nowadays, yesterday, then, already, soon
Duration:	always, still
Frequency:	often, seldom, never, sometimes, always

Place:	here, there, everywhere, somewhere, elsewhere, upstairs
Direction:	away
Concession:	yet, still

There are also a number of words that can serve as either prepositions or adverbs: *above, around, behind, below, down, in, inside, out, outside, up.*

Derivational Affixes

Besides the inflectional endings that identify the form classes, we also have an extensive inventory of **derivational affixes,** suffixes and prefixes that provide great versatility to our lexicon by allowing us to shift words from one class to another and/or to alter their meanings.

NOUN	*VERB*	*ADJECTIVE*	*ADVERB*
exclusion	exclude	exclusive	exclusively
denial	deny	deniable	deniably
beauty	beautify	beautiful	beautifully
economy	economize	economical	economically
continuation	continue	continual	continually
peace	pacify	peaceful	peacefully

Some of our suffixes change the meaning rather than the class of the word: *boy/boyhood; citizen/citizenry; king/kingdom; terror/terrorism.* Prefixes, too, generally change the meaning of the word rather than the class: *un*deniable, *pro*-American, *inter*action, *intra*murals, *il*legal, *dis*enchanted. Some prefixes enable us to derive verbs from other classes: *en*chant, *en*courage, *en*able, *de*rail, *de*throne, *be*witch, *be*devil, *dis*able, *dis*member.

This remarkable ability to expand our lexicon with uncountable new forms provides yet more evidence (if we needed more) for the idea of the inherent language expertise that native speakers possess. With this system of word expansion it's easy to understand why no one has yet come up with a definitive number of words in English. And although we follow certain rules in shifting words from one class to another, there is no real system: We can take a noun like *system,* turn it into an adjective (*systematic*), then a verb (*systematize*), then a noun again (*systematization*). There's also the adverb *systematically* in that set; and the same base, *system,* produces *systemic* and *systemically.* But we can't distinguish between those adjectives that pattern with *-ize* to form verbs (*systematize, legalize, realize, publicize*) and those that pattern with *-ify* (*simplify, amplify, electrify*).

EXERCISE 10

Fill in the blanks with variations of the words shown on the chart, changing or adding derivational morphemes to change the word class. In some cases, you may think of more than one possibility.

	NOUN	VERB	ADJECTIVE	ADVERB
1.	grief			
2.		vary		
3.				ably
4.		defend		
5.				quickly
6.			pleasant	
7.	type			
8.		prohibit		
9.				critically
10.			valid	
11.		appreciate		
12.	danger			
13.		accept		
14.			pure	
15.		steal		

EXERCISE 11

We have seen how easy it is to shift words from one class to another by a simple change in form. One such shift is that of verb to noun, which we call **nominalization.** The most common noun-forming suffix we add to verbs is *-ion* or one of its variations, *-tion*, *-ation*, *-sion*, (*action*, *abolition*, *legalization*); others are *-ment* (*accomplishment*); *-ance* (*acceptance*); *-al* (*arrival*); and *-ure* (*departure*). The ease with which we nominalize verbs, however, can become a trap for the unwary writer; their overuse tends to produce an impersonal and abstract style.

(1) Identify the nominalizations in the following passages—that is, nouns that have been made from verbs; then (2) revise the sentences by turning the nouns back into verbs, whenever possible.

1. A bill under consideration by the Senate would create changes in the way the IRS deals with taxpayers.
2. The bill requires notification of taxpayers in writing before the IRS could begin the seizure of their property.
3. The bill is aimed at preventing the IRS from the collection of taxes in ways that create hardships.
4. The IRS Commissioner has expressed opposition to the adoption of the bill. He says that the correction of abuses can be handled by the agency under existing laws.
5. Congressional opponents of the bill have made the claim that its implementation would cost more than $200 million a year.
6. An occurrence that brought nationwide attention to the problems that

taxpayers encounter was the seizure of a savings account in the amount of $70.76 belonging to a nine-year-old girl.

EXERCISE 12

The following paragraph, altered from its published version, is now overloaded with nominalizations. Sometimes you can fix an overly abstract sentence by asking yourself, "Who is doing what?" In other words, check to see that the "agent," the actual "doer" of the verb occupies the subject slot. Revise the paragraph with this "agent-as-subject" principle in mind. Then compare your revision with the published version, which you will find in the Answers to the Exercises.

Here's a hint to get you started: The first sentence, with "suburbanization" as the subject, has *not* been altered. So start your revision with the second sentence.

> Since 1945, suburbanization has been the most significant fact of American social and political life. The people responsible for the compiling of the 1970 census caught its magnitude with the observation that for the first time more people in metropolitan areas resided outside the boundaries of cities than within them. The 1980 figures represent a confirmation of this trend and a measurement of its acceleration. Moreover, the explosion of the population of the suburban areas has been accompanied by a marked decline in the population of cities. The result has been a steady growth of suburban power in American politics. The changing numbers have made its dominance inevitable, but the fact that the participation of suburbanites in registration and voting produced a much larger percentage than did the participation of city dwellers has resulted in an acceleration of the shift.

For Group Discussion

Read a draft of your essay (or that of a classmate), paying special attention to the choice of words. Are there any nominalized verbs that might be more effective in their role as verbs? Think about the "agent-as-subject" principle: "Who is doing what?" If the subject slot contains an abstraction instead of the agent, the actual doer, the sentence might be a candidate for revision. Listen for the peaks of stress with "power words" as well. Be sure that the stress is where it ought to be.

RHETORICAL REMINDERS

Have I selected words with clear and precise meanings?

Have I considered the countable/noncountable features of nouns in using such modifiers as *less/fewer, amount of/number of*, and *much/many?* Have I been careful to recognize the singular/plural aspect of the subject noun phrase, especially when tricky words like collective nouns and plural-only forms are involved?

PUNCTUATION REMINDER

The apostrophe added to a noun turns it into the possessive case:
cat/cat's (singular); cats/cats' (plural).

Chapter 5

Understanding Pronouns

One word that accurately describes the place of pronouns in English is the adjective *ubiquitous*—a word that may be new to your lexicon. It means "everywhere present, constantly encountered, widespread"—and that's what pronouns are. You will rarely encounter a passage of two or more sentences that doesn't contain several pronouns. In fact, the sentence you just finished reading contains three. (And this first paragraph contains ten.)

We looked briefly at pronouns in earlier chapters when we substituted them for noun phrases in order to demonstrate whether the subject of the sentence was singular or plural and to figure out where the subject ended and the predicate began:

U.S. mileage standards [*they*] are a scandal.
Management as a practice [*it*] is very old.
Linda's sister [*she*] graduated from nursing school.

Those substitutions—*they*, *it*, and *she*—are among the personal pronouns, the kind you probably recognize most readily. But there are many other classes of pronouns as well—reflexive, demonstrative, relative, indefinite, and others. In this chapter we will look at all of the pronouns, concentrating especially on those members of various classes that sometimes cause problems for writers.

Again, don't make the mistake of thinking that this is a list for you to memorize. It's not that at all. The purpose of describing our inventory of pronouns is to raise your consciousness about this important category of the lexicon and to point out those areas that require some thought on the part of writers.

Personal Pronouns

The easiest way to understand the system of **personal pronouns** is in terms of **person** and **number.** The forms in parentheses (possessive, objective) are variations in **case,** the choice of which is determined by the pronoun's function in the sentence.

PERSON	NUMBER	
	Singular	**Plural**
1st	I (my, me)	we (our, us)
2nd	you (your, you)	you (your, you)
3rd	he (his, him) she (her, her) it (its, it)	they (their, them)

Number, of course, refers to the singular/plural distinction. *Person* is related to point of view, the relationship of the writer to the reader or listener. The reference of the first person includes the writer or speaker; second person refers exclusively to the person addressed; third person refers to "third parties," someone or something other than the speaker or the person addressed.

Point of View

You're probably familiar with the concept of person in connection with composition, when you make a decision regarding the point of view to adopt: Shall I use *I?* Shall I use *you?* Or shall I stick to third person? Many kinds of essays are written in first person—more than you might think. Personal narratives, of course, are nearly always first person, but so are many others. In fact, it would probably be accurate to say that most essay writers use first person somewhere in their text.[1] The exceptions are business and scientific reports and historical essays, which are often strictly third person. Newspapers and newsmagazines also stick to third person when reporting the news. But writers of editorials and syndicated columns and feature stories regularly use both first and second person. And it's certainly a common point of view in textbooks, such as this one, where sentences with *we* and *our* and *you* and *your* appear on every page.

If it's true that first person is a common point of view, then why do teachers so often rule it unacceptable in the essays they assign? (That's another of the myths in the student writers' baggage: "Don't use I.") Very likely you've had an English teacher in high school or college who required you to use third person. One reason for that proscription against first person is undoubtedly the bad writing that so often results, with *I* turning up as the subject of almost every sentence—as if the writer, the "I," were the topic being discussed. A good compromise for some writing assignments

[1]Among the thirty-three essays in *A World of Ideas: Essential Readings for College Students* (Lee A. Jacobus, ed., St. Martin's Press, 1986), only two are strictly third person. The other thirty-one, all by famous, well-established writers of the past and present, include pronouns in the first person.

may be to use the first person in the introduction and conclusion, where the writer sets the tone and takes a stance, then third person for the body of the essay.

The most common use of first person in professional writing is the plural—*we* and *us* and *our* rather than *I* and *me* and *my*. The result is a kind of collective first person (sometimes referred to as the "royal we" or the "editorial we"). You'll find that collective first person in the preamble to the Constitution: "We the people . . . for ourselves and our posterity. . . ." The *we* in this book is also that collective *we*. For example, the second paragraph in this chapter begins, "We looked briefly at pronouns in earlier chapters when we substituted. . . ." And following is another example, a first-person passage from *A Brief History of Time* by Stephen W. Hawking:

> Now at first sight, all this evidence that the universe looks the same whichever direction we look in might seem to suggest there is something special about our place in the universe. In particular, it might seem that if we observe all other galaxies to be moving away from us, then we must be at the center of the universe.

Here the first-person plural is especially effective, where the writer wants the reader to be included in his description of the universe.

Before leaving the subject of point of view, we should mention the use of *you*, the second-person pronoun. You'll notice that many of the sentences in the foregoing paragraphs, as well as the sentence you're reading now, include *you* as the subject. That *you*, of course, stands for you, the reader of *Rhetorical Grammar*. But *you* does not always address the reader; it is often used in a more general sense, with a meaning more like that of the third person. Notice the use of *you* in this passage from *Broca's Brain* by Carl Sagan, describing an excursion into the back rooms of the Museum of Man in Paris:

> Most of the rooms were evidently used for storage of anthropological items, collected from decades to more than a century ago. <u>You</u> had the sense of a museum of the second order, in which were stored not so much materials that might be of interest as materials that had once been of interest. <u>You</u> could feel the presence of nineteenth-century museum directors engaged, in their frock coats, in goniometrie and craniologie, busily collecting and measuring everything, in the pious hope that mere quantification would lead to understanding.

Here *you* takes the place of *one* or a *person;* it is not "you, the reader."

Some teachers, however, still prefer *one* to this general *you:*

> When *one* sees the Golden Gate Bridge for the first time, the sight is simply breathtaking.

The problem that <u>one</u> creates is obvious to the ear: The sentence sounds formal and British, like something Prince Charles would say. In American English, we use *you* rather than *one* to convey that third-person indefinite sense:

When you see the Golden Gate Bridge for the first time, the sight is simply breathtaking.

The sentence with *you* is technically second person, but the meaning is closer to the indefinite third-person *one*.

In another passage from *A Brief History of Time*, Hawking uses mainly the second person, but in one sentence he switches to the first with *we* and *our:*

> Any physical theory is always provisional, in the sense that it is only a hypothesis: you can never prove it. No matter how many times the results of experiments agree with some theory, you can never be sure that the next time the result will not contradict the theory. On the other hand, you can disprove a theory by finding even a single observation that disagrees with the predictions of the theory. As philosopher of science Karl Popper has emphasized, a good theory is characterized by the fact that it makes a number of predictions that could in principle be disproved or falsified by observation. Each time new experiments are observed to agree with the predictions the theory survives, and our confidence in it is increased; but if ever a new observation is found to disagree, we have to abandon or modify the theory. At least that is what is supposed to happen, but you can always question the competence of the person who carried out the observation.

We should note that it is not at all unusual to "mix" the point of view, as Hawking does here. A first- or second-person passage will always include pronouns in the third person. And many essays that are essentially third person have an occasional *we* or *our* or *you*. There is no rule that says good writing should not have that versatility of view.

EXERCISE 13

1. The following passage is an adulterated version of the opening of an essay by Annie Dillard, from her Pulitzer Prize-winning narrative *Pilgrim at Tinker Creek*. (Dillard is also the author of the weasel passage in Chapter 1.) You'll notice that these two first-person paragraphs include twelve clauses with *I* as subjects: Four of these *I*'s are not in the original. Your job is to put the passage back into its prize-winning form.

Yesterday, I set out to catch the new season, and instead I found an old snakeskin. I was in the sunny February woods by the quarry; I found the snakeskin lying in a heap of leaves right next to an aquarium someone had thrown away. I don't know why that someone hauled the aquarium deep into the woods to get rid of it; it had only one broken glass side. The snake found it handy, I imagine; snakes like to rub against something rigid to help them out of their skins, and the broken aquarium looked like the nearest likely object. Together the snakeskin and the aquarium made an interesting scene on the forest floor. I thought it looked like an exhibit at a trial—circumstantial evidence—of a wild scene, as though a snake had burst through the broken side of the aquarium, burst through his ugly old skin, and disappeared, perhaps straight up in the air, in a rush of freedom and beauty.

I could see that the snakeskin had unkeeled scales, so I knew it belonged to a non-poisonous snake. It was roughly five feet long by the yardstick, but I'm not sure because it was very wrinkled and dry, and every time I tried to stretch it flat it broke. I ended up with seven or eight pieces of it all over the kitchen table in a fine film of forest dust.

(You can read the original in the Answers section in the back of the book.)

2. Revise the Hawking passages to eliminate the use of first and second person. How would you characterize the difference in tone and style of the two versions? What is the effect on the reader?

For Group Discussion

Here's another *I*-filled passage, this one from Judy Syfer's essay "Why I Want a Wife," which first appeared in *Ms.* magazine in December of 1971. The thirteen *I*'s in this paragraph are all in the original; no changes have been made.

> I want a wife who will take care of my physical needs. I want a wife who will keep my house clean. A wife who will pick up after my children, a wife who will pick up after me. I want a wife who will keep my clothes clean, ironed, mended, replaced when need be, and who will see to it that my personal things are kept in their proper place so that I can find what I need the minute I need it. I want a wife who cooks the meals, a wife who is a *good* cook. I want a wife who will plan the menus, do the necessary grocery shopping, prepare the meals, serve them pleasantly, and then do the cleaning up while I do my studying. I want a wife who will care for me when I am sick and sympathize with my pain and loss of time from school. I want a wife to go along when our family takes a vacation so that someone can continue to care for me and my children when I need a rest and a change of scene.

How do you react to that proliferation of *I*'s? Are they appropriate?

The Missing Pronoun

The scheme of personal pronouns on page 68 may look complete—and, unfortunately, it does include all we have. But, in fact, it has a gap, one that is responsible for a great deal of the sexism in our language. The gap occurs in the third-person singular slot, the slot that already includes three pronouns representing masculine (*he*), feminine (*she*), and neuter (*it*). You'd think that those three would be up to the task of covering all the contingencies, but they're not. For third-person singular we have no choice that is sex-neutral. When we need a pronoun to refer to an unidentified person, such as "the writer" or "a student" or just "someone," our long-standing tradition has been to use the masculine:

> The writer of this news story should have kept <u>his</u> personal opinion out of it.
> Someone left <u>his</u> book on the table.

But that usage is no longer automatically accepted. Times and attitudes change, and we have come to recognize the power of language in shaping those attitudes. So an important step in reshaping society's view of women has been to eliminate the automatic use of *he* and *his* and *him* when the gender of someone referred to could just as easily be female.

In a paragraph we looked at in Chapter 3 in connection with sentence rhythm, the writer has made an effort to avoid sexism with the generic *salesperson,* a title that has all but replaced the masculine *salesman.* But notice the pronoun in the last sentence:

> Never invest in something you don't understand or in the dream of an artful salesperson. Be a buyer, not a sellee. Figure out what you want (be it life insurance, mutual funds or a vacuum cleaner) and then shop for a good buy. Don't let someone else tell you what you need—at least not if <u>he</u> happens to be selling it.
>
> —Andrew Tobias

In speech we commonly use *they* for both singular and plural:

> Don't let someone else tell you what you need—at least not if <u>they</u> happen to be selling it.

Eventually, perhaps, the plural pronoun will take over for the singular; in the second person (*you/your/you*), we make no distinction between singular and plural, so it's not unreasonable to do the same in the third person. But such changes come slowly. What should we do in the meanwhile?

One common, but not necessarily effective, way to solve the problem of the pronoun gap is with *he or she:*

> . . . at least not if <u>he or she</u> happens to be selling it.

An occasional *he or she* will work in most situations like this one, but more than one in a paragraph will change the rhythm of the prose, slow the reader down, and call attention to itself when such attention is simply uncalled for.

The awkwardness of *he or she* in a passage becomes even more obvious when the possessive and objective case pronouns are also required. Avoiding sexist language by using *his or her* and *him or her* as well as *he or she* will quickly render the solution worse than the problem. Here, for example, is a passage from a 1981 issue of *Newsweek:*

> To the average American, the energy problem is mainly his monthly fuel bill and the cost of filling up his gas tank. He may also remember that in 1979,

and way back in 1974, he had to wait in long lines at gasoline stations. For all of this, he blames the "Arabs" or the oil companies or the government, or perhaps all three. Much of the information that he gets from the media, as well as his own past experience, tells him that energy prices will continue to go up sharply and that gas lines are going to come back whenever a conflict flares up in the Middle East.

—Fred Singer, "Hope for the Energy Shortage"

Now imagine a version in which the problem of sexism has been solved with *he or she:*

> To the average American, the energy problem is mainly his or her monthly fuel bill and the cost of filling up his or her gas tank. He or she may also remember that in 1979, and way back in 1974, he or she had to wait in long lines at gasoline stations. For all of this, he or she blames the "Arabs" or the oil companies or the government, or perhaps all three. Much of the information that he or she gets from the media, as well as from his or her own past experience, tells him or her that energy prices will continue. . . . *Enough!*

That's only one short paragraph. Imagine reading a whole essay. Clearly, there are better solutions to the problem.

Because we do have a sex-neutral pronoun in the plural, often that singular noun can be changed to plural. In the *Newsweek* article, for example, the writer could have started out by discussing "average Americans":

> To average Americans, the energy problem is mainly their monthly fuel bill and the cost of filling up their gas tank.

That revision, of course, has changed the relationship of the writer to the reader: The writer is no longer addressing the reader as an individual—a change the writer may not want. Often, however, the plural is an easy and obvious solution. For example, in the following passages from books about language, the change to plural does not affect the overall meaning or intent:

> Of all the developments in the history of ~~man~~ *the human race*, surely the most remarkable was language, for with it ~~he was~~ *our ancestors were* able to pass on ~~his~~ *their* cultural heritage to succeeding generations who then did not have to rediscover how to make a fire, where to hunt, or how to build another wheel.

— Charles B. Martin and Curt M. Rulon

> It has been said that whenever ~~a person~~ *people* speak~~s~~, ~~he~~ *they* ~~is~~ *are*
>
> either mimicking or analogizing.
>
> — Charles Hockett

We should emphasize that these three examples of sexist language were written at least a decade ago, when the masculine pronoun was the norm. Chances are, none of them would have been written in this way today. All of us who are involved with words, who are sensitive to the power of language, have gone through a consciousness raising in the matter of sexist language.

Let's assume that Fred Singer, the *Newsweek* writer, insists on maintaining the singular "average American." What other means would he have for eliminating the sexism of the masculine pronouns? In some cases, he could use different determiners. For example, he needn't write "*his* monthly fuel bill" and "*his* gas tank"; *the* will do the job. And in the last sentence, "*his* own past experience" could become "past experience" or, simply, "experience" without losing any information; "tells *him*" could become "says" or "suggests." He could probably get by with a single *he or she*, to replace the *he* of the second sentence; the other sentences with *he* can be revised with different subjects. Here's one possibility:

> To the average American, the energy problem is mainly the monthly fuel bill and the cost of filling up the gas tank. He or she may also remember in 1979, and way back in 1974, waiting in long lines at the gasoline stations. Who gets the blame for all of this? The "Arabs" or the oil companies or the government, or perhaps all three. The media, as well as the consumer's past experience, suggest that energy prices will continue to go up sharply and that gas lines are going to come back whenever a conflict flares up in the Middle East.

In the last sentence we've substituted "the consumer" for "the average American."

Here, then, are some of the ways in which you can make up for the pronoun gap when you write and/or revise your own sentences:

1. USE THE PLURAL:
   Every writer should be aware of the power of language when <u>he</u> chooses <u>his</u> pronouns.
   Revision: Writers should be aware of the power of language when <u>they</u> choose <u>their</u> pronouns.
2. USE *HE OR SHE* if you can use it only once:
   Revision: Every writer should be aware of the power of language when <u>he or she</u> chooses pronouns.
3. AVOID *his* as a determiner, either by substituting another one or, in some cases, deleting the determiner:
   The writer of the news story should have kept <u>his</u> opinion out of it.
   Revision: The writer of the news story should have kept (<u>all</u>) opinion out of it.

4. TURN THE CLAUSE INTO A VERB PHRASE, THUS ELIMINATING THE PROBLEM SUBJECT:
   Revision: Every writer should be aware of the power of language when choosing pronouns.

This fourth method of revision is often a good possibility because the offending pronoun nearly always shows up in the second clause of a passage, often as part of the same sentence. In our example, we have turned the complete subordinate clause into an elliptical clause—that is, a clause with something missing. In this case what's missing is the subject. (The elliptical clause, which has some hidden pitfalls, is discussed further in Chapter 7.)

5. REWRITE THE ADVERBIAL CLAUSE AS A RELATIVE (WHO) CLAUSE:
   When a person buys a house, he should shop carefully for the lowest interest rate.
   Revision: A person who buys a house should shop carefully for the lowest interest rate.

The relative clause with its neutral *who* eliminates the necessity of a personal pronoun to rename *a person*.

6. CHANGE THE POINT OF VIEW:
   2nd person: As a writer you should be aware of the power of language when you choose (your) pronouns.
   1st person: As writers, we should be aware of the power of language when we choose (our) pronouns.

EXERCISE 14

1. Rewrite the *Newsweek* passage using the second person. (Note: You might begin with "If you are an average American . . .")
2. The following passage was written in 1944, at a time when the masculine pronoun was accepted as the generic singular. Revise it to reflect today's concerns about sexism in language.

> Of all born creatures, man is the only one that cannot live by bread alone. He lives as much by symbols as by sense report, in a realm compounded of tangible things and virtual images, of actual events and ominous portents, always between fact and fiction. For he sees not only actualities but meanings. He has, indeed, all the impulses and interests of animal nature; he eats, sleeps, mates, seeks comfort and safety, flees pain, falls sick and dies, just as cats and bears and fishes and butterflies do. But he has something more in his repertoire, too—he has laws and religions, theories and dogmas, because he lives not only through sense but through symbols. That is the special asset of his mind, which makes him the master of earth and all its progeny.
>
> —Susanne K. Langer, "The Prince of Creation," *Fortune* (January 1944)

3. It's not surprising to see the masculine pronoun used generically in a passage written in 1944; now, however—fifty years later—it is surprising. Yet the following passage, published in *USA Today* (June 8, 1994), was part of a graduation speech given by Andy Rooney, correspondent for *60 Minutes*, in 1994 at Gettysburg College, a coeducational college:

> An education is good for its own sake—not necessarily because you use it to make money. An education is a lifelong comfort to anyone who has one, and there's no reason an educated person shouldn't make a living with his hands. The notion that someone who works with his hands isn't also working with his head is wrong. It's possible to work with your head without moving a muscle, but it's not possible to work with your muscles without using your head, too.

Revise the passage to include women among those educated people who can make a living with their hands.

We and Us as Determiners

The possessive case of pronouns is the form we generally use as determiners, the signalers of nouns: *my* house, *our* friends, *their* new car. In some circumstances, however, with the first person plural pronoun (*we*, *us*, *our*), the subjective and objective cases act as determiners. They aren't very common in this function, so writers are sometimes unsure of the form:

We students got together and demonstrated against the proposed tuition increase.
The boss required us waiters to share our tips with the busboys and dishwashers.

The form of the pronoun is determined by the function of the noun being signaled: When it's a subject, as with *students*,the form is *we*; when it's an object, as with *waiters*, the form is *us*.

Personal Pronoun Errors

Case

Among the most common pronoun errors that writers make are the errors of **case.** As you'll recall, case refers to the change that pronouns undergo on the basis of their function in the sentence. Following are the various forms for the three cases, which we saw earlier in the chart on page 68, where they are arranged according to number and person:

Subjective:	I	we	you	he	she	it	they
Possessive:	my (mine)	our (ours)	your (yours)	his (his)	her (hers)	its (its)	their (theirs)
Objective:	me	us	you	him	her	it	them

The subject slot of the sentence, of course, takes the **subjective case.** The subjective case is also traditionally used in the subjective complement slot following *be* as the main verb. For example, when a phone caller says,

> "May I speak with Ann?"

Ann will reply,

> "This is she,"

unless she wants to be informal, in which case she might reply,

> "Speaking."

At any rate, she would not sound grammatical if she said,

> "This is her."

On the other hand, the formal "It is I" is often replaced with the less formal "It's me," and nobody gets upset. In many writing situations, however, the informal "It's me" would be inappropriate. The writer who thinks that "It is I" is too formal (and sometimes it does sound stuffy) can probably find a way around it without being nonstandard.

In Chapter 1 the transitive verbs were defined as those with direct objects. When a pronoun fills that object slot, we use the **objective case:**

> My roommate helped <u>me</u> with my biology assignment.

You'll recall that the Pattern 6 sentence has a second object slot: the indirect object. It, too, takes the objective case when it's filled by a pronoun:

> Marie gave <u>him</u> a gift.

The other object slot we've been seeing in our sentences is that of object of the preposition. It's another that takes the objective case:

> Marie gave a <u>gift to him</u>.
> I walked to town <u>with him</u>.
> I walked to town <u>with Joe and him</u>.
> Joe walked to town <u>with him and me</u>.
> Marie walked *between* <u>Joe and me</u>.

Pronouns in the **possessive case** function as determiners, or noun signalers. The alternative forms of the possessive case, shown on the chart in parentheses, are used when the headword of the noun phrase, the noun, is deleted:

This is *my* bicycle. This bicycle is mine.
This is her bicycle. This is hers.

We should note that *nouns* in the possessive case function in the same way:

This is Pete's bicycle. This is Pete's.

Most of the case errors that writers make occur with the subjective and objective cases. And most of them probably occur as the result of hypercorrection:

*There's no rivalry between my brother and I.
*The supervisor told Jenny and I that we might get a raise next week.

In both cases, the noun/pronoun compound is functioning as an object, so the correct pronoun choice is *me*, not *I*. This is a common error, however, possibly because people remember being corrected by their parents or teachers when they said such sentences as

Me and Bill are going for a bike ride. ("No, dear. Bill and *I*.")
Bill and me are going to be late. ("No, dear. Bill and *I*.")

As a consequence of those early lessons, some people simply find it hard to say "my brother and me" or "Jenny and me," no matter what function the pronoun has in the sentence. The correct version of those sentences is,

There's no rivalry between my brother and me.
The supervisor told Jenny and me that we might get a raise next week.

The Unwanted Apostrophe

Perhaps the most common writing error of all—and not just among students—occurs with the pronoun *it:*

*The cat caught it's tail in the door.

Here's the rule that's been broken with the word *it's:*

Personal pronouns have no apostrophes in the possessive case.

If you check the chart showing the case of the personal pronouns on page 76, you'll see that there are no apostrophes. Notice that the rule also applies to the alternative forms of the possessive—*hers* and *his* and *yours* and *theirs*—those that are used when the headword of the noun phrase is deleted. They have no apostrophe either. (For these pronouns, the rule is more logical because *their* and *his* and *her* and *your* are already in the possessive case.)

This is their bicycle. / This is theirs.
This is her bicycle. / This is hers.
Where is *your bicycle?* / Where is yours?

When we say that *it's* can mean only "it is" or "it has," we are actually stating an exception to the general apostrophe rule. In every other use of the *apostrophe* + *s*—that is, when we add *'s* to nouns and indefinite pronouns—there are three possible meanings. In the first two examples below, the apostrophe signals a **contraction,** where part of a word—in fact, a whole syllable—has been deleted; the third example illustrates the possessive case:

1. John's coming. / Someone's coming. = *is coming*
2. John's been here. / Someone's been here. = *has been*
3. John's hat is on the table. / Someone's hat is on the table. = possessive case

It's certainly understandable for writers to treat *it* in the same way, to assume that the possessive case of *it* is formed by using the apostrophe with the *s*, as in the case with nouns and indefinite pronouns—in other words, that the word *it's* has the same three possible meanings that *John's* does. But it doesn't.

The error probably occurs so easily because *it* is the only personal pronoun that gets that added *s*, as nouns do. The other personal pronouns actually have new forms for the possessive case, as the chart on page 76 shows: *I* becomes *my* in the possessive; *he* becomes *his; she* becomes *her; you* becomes *your; we* becomes *our;* and *they* becomes *their. It* is unique in form.

Here's what you have to remember—and check for: When you add *s* to *it*, you're actually writing "it is" or "it has"; the possessive case has no apostrophe. Because *it* is such a common word, and because the unwanted apostrophe is such an easy error to slip in, you should probably make a point of double-checking all instances of *its* and *it's* during your final proofreading.

In the next chapter, "Choosing Verbs," we will look at the rhetorical effect of contractions like "Someone's coming" and "John's been here." They add an informality to your writing; they have an effect on your personal voice.

The Ambiguous Antecedent

Another error that turns up with personal pronouns is the ambiguous **antecedent**—the pronoun that has more than one possible referent:

> When Bob accidentally backed the car into the toolshed, it was wrecked beyond repair.

Here we can't be sure if the pronoun *it* refers to the car or to the toolshed.

> Just before they were scheduled to leave, Shelley told Devon that she couldn't go after all.

Here we may suspect that *she* refers to Shelley—but we can't be sure. And the careful writer wouldn't make us guess.

> When the first-night audience was invited backstage to meet the cast, they had a wonderful time.

Here we assume that it's the audience that had a wonderful time; but the reader has every right to assume that a pronoun will refer to the last-mentioned possibility—in this case, *the cast*.

> Uncle Dick and Aunt Teresa took the kids to their favorite restaurant for lunch.

Whose favorite restaurant?

The ambiguous antecedent often gets resolved by the context; within a sentence or two the reader will very likely understand the writer's intention. But not always. And, of course, the reader shouldn't have to wait.

The Vague Antecedent

Our use of pronouns is dictated by our internal rules. In Chapter 1, in connection with the sentence slots, you saw how automatically you use pronouns when you substituted them for noun phrases:

> U.S. mileage standards are a scandal.
>
> They are a scandal.

Here's a similar one:

> My sister's boyfriend works for a meat-packing company.
>
> He works for a meat-packing company.

As you can clearly see, the pronoun stands in for the entire noun phrase, not just for the headword—and certainly not for a modifier of the headword. Now look at the following sentences with that principle in mind:

> The neighbor's front porch is covered with trash, but *he* refuses to clean it up.
> The neighbor's dog gets into my garbage every week, but *he* refuses to do anything about it.
> My sister's boyfriend works for a meat-packing plant. *She's* a vegetarian.
> It's hard to keep track of the Administration's stand on immigration. *They* say something different every week.

Last summer I didn't get to a single baseball game, even though *it*'s my favorite sport.

Notice what has happened. The subject of the second clause in each case is a pronoun. But its antecedent is not a complete noun phrase; it's only a noun modifier. The problem is not with communication: The reader will understand these sentences. And in a conversation we might not even notice anything amiss. But there is a problem of fuzziness that could easily cause a blip in the reader's comprehension. As writers we have the obligation to consider the reader's expectations, to get rid of the fuzziness caused by vague antecedents.

The problem in the following sentence is different from the problem with *it* in the previous example. Here the pronoun has what is called "**broad reference.**" The antecedent for *it* is the idea of the whole preceding clause:

I just found out that my roommate is planning to withdraw from school. It really shocked me.

Again, the reader encounters a pronoun that has no clear antecedent. Like the previous examples, the sentence is grammatical but fuzzy.

You can help the reader it by replacing the pronoun with a noun phrase:

Her decision really shocked me.

You'll see this same sentence discussed in the section on demonstrative pronouns. And you'll read about the problem of vague antecedents again in the discussion of the relative pronouns in Chapter 8 under the heading "The Broad-Reference Clause."

Reflexive Pronouns

Reflexive pronouns are those formed by adding *-self* or *-selves* to a form of the personal pronoun: *myself*, *ourselves*, *yourself*, *yourselves*, *himself*, *herself*, *itself*, *themselves*. The standard rule for using the reflexive is straightforward. We use it as an object in a sentence when its antecedent is the subject:

John cut himself.
I glanced at myself in the mirror.
Jack cooked an omelet for Barbara and himself.
I cooked breakfast for Kelly and myself.

The tendency toward hypercorrection occurs with the reflexives as well as with the personal pronouns. It's quite common to hear the reflexive where the standard rule calls for *me*, the straight objective case:

*Tony cooked dinner for Carmen and *myself.*
*The boss promised Pam and myself a year-end bonus.

Note that the antecedent of *myself* does not appear in either sentence. Another fairly common nonstandard usage occurs when speakers use *myself* in place of *I* as part of a compound subject:

*Ted and myself decided to go out and celebrate.

These nonstandard ways of using the reflexive are probably related to emphasis as well as to hypercorrection. Somehow the two-syllable *myself* sounds more emphatic than either *me* or *I*.

The nonstandard use of the reflexive occurs only with the first-person pronoun, *myself*, not with *himself* or *herself*. In the case of third person, the personal pronoun and the reflexive produce different meanings:

John cooked dinner for Jenny and himself (John).
John cooked dinner for Jenny and him (someone else).

Intensive Reflexive Pronouns

When we use the reflexive to add emphasis to a noun, we call it the **intensive reflexive pronoun.** It can appear in a number of positions:

I myself prefer classical music.
I prefer classical music myself.
Myself, I prefer classical music.

Each of these versions produces a different rhythm pattern. In the first version, the main stress falls on *myself*, whereas in the second it probably falls on *classical*. In the third, added stress will be given to *I*.

Reciprocal Pronouns

Each other and *one another* are known as the **reciprocal pronouns.** They serve either as determiners (in the possessive case) or as objects, referring to previously named nouns: *Each other* refers to two nouns; *one another* refers to three or more, a distinction that careful writers generally observe.

David and Ann help each other.
They even do each other's laundry.
All the students in my peer group help one another with their rough drafts.

Demonstrative Pronouns

The **demonstrative pronouns** are used as determiners. They include the features of "number" and "proximity."

PROXIMITY	*NUMBER*	
	Singular	***Plural***
Near	this	these
Distant	that	those

That documentary we saw last night really made me think, but this one is a waste of time.
Those trees on the ridge were almost destroyed by the gypsy moths, but these seem perfectly healthy.

Like other determiner classes, the demonstrative pronoun can be a substitute for a noun phrase (or other nominal structure) as well as a signal for one:

These old shoes and hats will be perfect for the costumes.
↓
These will be perfect for the costumes.

To be effective, however, the demonstrative must replace or stand for a clearly stated antecedent. In the following example, *that* has no clear antecedent; there is no noun phrase in the first sentence that the demonstrative *that* stands for:

My roommate just told me she's planning to withdraw from school. *That* came as a surprise.

Here the subject, *that*, refers to the whole idea in the first sentence, not to a specific noun phrase, as pronouns usually do. Such sentences are not uncommon in speech, nor are they ungrammatical. But when a *this* or a *that* (or *it*) has this kind of **broad reference,** you can usually improve the sentence by providing a noun headword for the demonstrative pronoun—in other words, by turning the pronoun into a determiner, by using a complete noun phrase in place of the pronoun:

That decision came as a surprise.
or
That news came as a surprise.

When you don't provide that headword, you are making the reader do your work. If you have trouble pinning down the precise noun, you might be tempted to leave it out. But if you, the writer, have trouble, think of the problem the reader will have in trying to interpret your fuzzy pronoun.

EXERCISE 15

Edit the following passages, paying special attention to the pronoun problems.

1. The National Academy of Sciences has reported that 90 percent of all the fungicides, 60 percent of all herbicides, and 30 percent of all pesticides used in the United States are capable of causing cancer. This will result in an estimated 1.4 million cancer cases and will slightly increase each American's chance of contracting the disease in their lifetime.
2. The goal of animal-rights activists is not just to prevent animal cruelty, as they advocated in earlier times, but also to promote the idea that they have intrinsic value, that they have a right to live. As a result of their efforts, the Public Health Service has revised their policy regarding the treatment of laboratory animals.
3. When my sister Beth asked me to go to Salem with her to visit our grand-mother, I had no idea that she was sick. We were almost there before she told me she had had stomach cramps since early morning. Our grandmother took one look at her and called the doctor, then drove her to the hospital, which turned out to be a good decision. It turned out to be appendicitis.

Indefinite Pronouns

The **indefinite pronouns** include a number of words that we use as determiners:

Quantifiers:	enough, few, fewer, less, little, many, much, several, more, most
Universals:	all, both, every, each
Partitives:	any, either, neither, none, some

One is also commonly used as a pronoun (as are the other cardinal numbers—two, three, etc.) along with its negative, *none*. As a pronoun, *one* often replaces only the headword, rather than the entire noun phrase:

The blue shoes that I bought yesterday will be perfect for the trip.
The blue ones that I bought yesterday will be perfect for the trip.

The personal pronoun, on the other hand, would replace the entire noun phrase:

They will be perfect for the trip.

The universal *every* and the partitives *any*, *no*, and *some* can be expanded with *-body*, *-thing*, and *-one:*

	body		body		body		body
some	thing	every	thing	any	thing	no	thing
	one		one		one		one (two words)

These pronouns can take modifiers in the form of clauses:

> Anyone *who wants extra credit in psych class* can volunteer for tonight's experiment.

They can also be modified by verb phrases:

> Everyone *reporting late for practice* will take fifteen laps.

And by prepositional phrases:

> Nothing *on the front page* interests me anymore.

And, unlike most nouns, they can be modified by adjectives that follow the headword:

> I don't care for anything *sweet*.
> I think that something *strange* is going on here.

Notice the strong stress that you put on the postnoun adjective.

The Everyone/Their Issue

The question of number—that is, whether a word is singular or plural—often comes up in reference to the indefinite pronouns *everyone* and *everybody*. In form they are singular, so as subjects they take the -*s* form of the verb or auxiliary in the present tense:

> Everyone is leaving the room at once.

An illustration of the scene described by this sentence, however, would show more than one person—more than two or three, probably—leaving the room, even though the form of *everyone* is singular. In spite of this anomaly, the issue of subject–verb agreement is not a problem.

But often such a sentence calls for the possessive pronoun. And when it does, the traditional choice has been the singular masculine:

> Everyone picked up his books and left the room.

But that makes no sense—even if the *everyone* refers to men only. And it certainly makes no sense if the group of people includes women. The only reasonable solution is the plural, in spite of the singular form of *everyone:*

Everyone picked up their books and left the room.

Unfortunately, even though the solution may be reasonable, your teacher is likely to mark *their* an error of pronoun/antecedent agreement.

It is interesting to discover that the problem arises only with the possessive pronoun. No one disputes the correctness of the subjective case, they:

The teacher asked everyone to leave, and *they* did.

Certainly *he* would make no sense at all. The objective case, too, requires the plural:

Everyone in the class cheered when the teacher told them the test had been canceled.

There is simply no logic in insisting on the singular for the possessive case when both logic and good grammar call for the plural in every other situation.

It's true that in form *everyone* is singular; this is also true of collective nouns, such as *crowd* or *group*. But these nouns call for plural pronouns when the members of the collection are seen as individuals:

The crowd began to raise their voices.
Everyone in the group began to raise their voices.

No matter how logical it may be to use the plural pronoun in reference to these indefinite pronouns, to do so contradicts the advice in most handbooks, most of which take the traditional view that *everyone* and *everybody* are singular and cannot be replaced by *they*. If you feel uneasy about using the plural because your reader—your composition teacher, perhaps, or your boss—may take the traditional view, you can always avoid the problem by substituting a different subject:

All of the people began to raise their voices.
All of the students picked up their books and left the room.

English is such a versatile language that we nearly always have alternatives.

EXERCISE 16

Edit the following passages, paying particular attention to the nonstandard use of pronouns and to those with unclear referents.

1. I recall with great pleasure the good times that us children had at our annual family reunions when I was young. Our cousins and ourselves,

along with some younger aunts and uncles, played volleyball and softball until dark. They were a lot of fun.

2. Aunt Yvonne and Uncle Bob always brought enough homemade ice cream for them and everyone else as well. There was great rivalry, I remember, between my brother and I over who could eat the most. Nearly everyone made a pig of himself.
3. It seemed to my cousin Terry and I that the grownups were different people at those family reunions. That may be true of family reunions everywhere.
4. Nowadays my father seems to forget about them good days and concentrates on the sad ones instead. He often tells my brother and myself about his boyhood during the Great Depression. He remembers the long years of unemployment for he and his whole family with very little pleasure. That doesn't really surprise me, because they were hard times.

For Group Discussion

You saw the following paragraph at the opening of Chapter 1. Given its length, you're probably not surprised to learn it includes twelve pronouns, from four different subclasses: personal, relative, demonstrative, and indefinite. The pronoun *it* accounts for six of the twelve, the first two in reference to *pyramid*, the other four to *management*.

> Management as a practice is very old. The most successful executive in all history was surely that Egyptian who, 4,500 years or more ago, first conceived the pyramid, without any precedent, designed it, and built it, and did so in an astonishingly short time. That first pyramid still stands. But as a discipline, management is barely fifty years old. It was first dimly perceived around the time of the First World War. It did not emerge until the Second World War, and then did so primarily in the United States. Since then it has been the fastest-growing new function, and the study of it the fastest-growing new discipline. No function in history has emerged as quickly as has management in the past fifty or sixty years, and surely none has had such worldwide sweep in such a short period.
>
> —Peter F. Drucker

Examine the sentences that include the four instances of *it* in reference to *management*. Consider ways of revising them that would cut down that number. One thing to think about is the place and frequency of the antecedent word, *management*.

In addition to the twelve pronouns, the paragraph also includes two instances of the word *so* in its role as a "proform." What does it stand in for?

RHETORICAL REMINDERS

Point of View

Have I chosen an effective—and natural—point of view?

In my first person passages, have I kept the number of *I*'s to a minimum?

Sexism

Have I avoided sexism in my choice of pronouns?

Have I avoided the awkward *he/she* and *his/her?*

Case

Have I used the objective case (*me*, *him*, *her*) for object slots in the sentence?

Have I avoided "between______and I?"

Have I kept apostrophes out of possessive pronouns (*its*, *hers*, *theirs*)?

Antecedents

Have I avoided ambiguous antecedents? Does my reader understand the referent of every *he*, *his*, *him*, *she*, *they*, and so on?

Reflexives

Have I used the reflexive pronoun (*-self*, *-selves*) only in object positions and only when the referent precedes it in the sentence?

Broad Reference

Have I avoided the fuzzy use of the broad-reference *this* and *that?*

Chapter 6

Choosing Verbs

If you were asked to describe what makes poetry different from prose, what features would you mention? Its imagery? Its rhythm? The emotional response it evokes? The control of language, perhaps? Certainly one difference is the obvious control, the careful selection of words. Poets budget their words carefully. Of course, good prose writers select their words carefully, too; they adhere to a word budget. And an important difference between good and bad prose is just that—the budgeting, the careful selection of words.

Here, for example, are the words of two prose writers, both of whom know how to budget. The first is the nature writer Hal Borland, who for many years wrote editorials on the outdoors for the *New York Times*. If it weren't for the prose form of this paragraph, which opens a short essay called "The Miracle of the Bud," you could easily mistake it for poetry.

> The earth teems now with the unseen miracle of new roots groping downward and young shoots reaching for the light and sun; but all around us, in plain sight, is the equal miracle of the buds. Out of the buds, so countless and so commonplace, come this world's green leaves, its wealth of bloom, the surging growth of twig and branch and stem. The miraculous surrounds us now.
>
> —*Sundial of the Seasons*

The second is from *The Lives of a Cell: Notes of a Biology Watcher* by the scientist Lewis Thomas:

> Watching television, you'd think we lived at bay, in total jeopardy, surrounded on all sides by human-seeking germs, shielded against infection and

> death only by a chemical technology that enables us to keep killing them off. We are instructed to spray disinfectants everywhere, into the air of our bedrooms and kitchens and with special energy into bathrooms, since it is our very own germs that seem the worst kind. We explode clouds of aerosol, mixed for good luck with deodorants, into our noses, mouths, underarms, privileged crannies—even into the intimate insides of our telephones. We apply potent antibiotics to minor scratches and seal them with plastic. Plastic is the new protector; we wrap the already plastic tumblers of hotels in more plastic, and seal the toilet seats like state secrets after irradiating them with ultraviolet light. We live in a world where the microbes are always trying to get at us, to tear us cell from cell, and we only stay alive and whole through diligence and fear.

One common feature that these passages share is their vivid, active verbs. In the Borland passage, for example, the verbs give life to the description of buds: *teems, groping, reaching, come, surging, surrounds*. Not all of these are predicating, or main, verbs; some function here as modifiers, but their verbness remains intact, contributing to the dynamic quality of the description. And in just the first sentence of the Thomas paragraph we find *watching, think, lived, surrounded, seeking, shielded, enables*, and *killing*.

When you get to the study of adverbials (Chapter 7) and of noun phrases (Chapter 8), you'll discover that sentences provide many places, not just the main predicate, for including verbal ideas. "New roots groping downward" and "young shoots reaching for the light and sun" are noun phrases with verbs—participles—as modifiers. Verbs can also substitute for noun phrases, as gerunds; and subordinate clauses (adverbials) and relative clauses (adjectivals) always have predicating verbs. With so many possible slots for verbs, then, it's important for the writer to choose them carefully, to give them every opportunity to do effectively what they do best: provide the action, the movement, the life, the focal point of the sentence. The sentence pivots on its verbs.

In this chapter we will focus on verbs from two perspectives: effective diction and effective grammar.

Verbs and Diction

Diction refers to word choice. Diction will be effective only when the words are appropriate for the audience and purpose, when they convey your message accurately and comfortably. The idea of comfort may seem out of place in connection with diction, but, in fact, words can sometimes cause the reader to feel uncomfortable. You've probably experienced such feelings yourself as a listener—hearing a speaker whose words for one reason or another strike you as inappropriate and make you feel uncomfortable. Writing can provoke those same feelings in a reader.

As a reader, you will usually spot an inappropriate word simply because it calls attention to itself—negative, uncomfortable attention. As a writer, you must learn to spot your own inappropriate words. Probably the most common such attention-getter is the word, often a verb, that is too formal for its purpose and audience.

Sometimes, of course, the opposite problem occurs: a word too informal for its purpose. But student writers are more likely to have the mistaken notion that writing calls for a sophisticated vocabulary. And so they look for words that demonstrate that sophistication. One consequence of that inappropriate word choice is the loss of their personal voice.

Your Personal Voice

As a writer, one of the most important questions you can ask yourself is one that concerns your "personal voice": "Does the language I'm using sound natural, like something I'd really say?" You've probably had the experience, when reading a letter from someone you know well, of hearing that person's voice. That's the same experience you should have in reading your own prose: You should hear your own personal voice coming through. But if what you've written doesn't sound like you, like anything you'd ever say, then you should reconsider your choice of words or style of phrasing.

This is not to suggest that writing is exactly like speech; it's not, of course. In our everyday conversation with family and friends, we use informal words and phrases that we rarely see in writing, and we commonly use sentence fragments. Further, in writing we use certain modifiers, such as nonrestrictive clauses and phrases, and transition words and phrases, such as the *further* at the beginning of this sentence, that we rarely use in speaking. But even when we include those structures, we should be able to recognize our words as our own.

Using a personal voice certainly does not require using the first person, nor does it mean being informal or conversational. Rather, "personal" in this sense means "natural," language that a real person would use. We have all had the experience of reading legal language and various official pronouncements that sound anything but natural; in fact, we've come to expect that nonpersonal voice in certain kinds of documents. But we don't expect such "legalese" or "bureaucratese" in the essays and articles and reports we read; likewise, we shouldn't use it in the essays and articles and reports that we write.

To hear the difference between the impersonal style and the "personal voice," compare the first sentence of the previous paragraph with a revised version. Read both of them aloud:

> *Original:* Using a personal voice certainly does not require using the first person, nor does it mean being informal or conversational.
>
> *Revision:* Utilizing a personal voice is not contingent upon the adoption of the first person point of view in one's writing, nor is it necessarily to be regarded as synonymous with a writing style that could be termed informal or conversational.

No one's personal voice sounds like that: People don't talk that way, and good writers don't write that way. But inexperienced writers sometimes do. Here, for example, is the opening of a law school applicant's short essay in response to the question "Why do you want to study law?"

It has long been a tenet of my value system that as a capable individual I have a social and moral duty to contribute to the improvement of the society in which I live. It seems that the way to make a valuable contribution is by choosing the means that will best allow me to utilize my abilities and facilitate my interests.

In spite of the first person point of view—the use of *I*—there's nothing "personal" in those lines. If the author had been asked in a face-to-face interview why she wanted to go to law school, she certainly would not have begun her answer with "It has long been a tenet of my value system." Never in her life has she begun a sentence that way. Instead, she would have said "I believe" or "I've always thought." But like many inexperienced writers she associated formal writing with lofty phrases and uncommon words.

A "personal voice" does not, of course, preclude the use of big words or uncommon words. Nor does the expression "big words" refer to the number of syllables. It means pretentious or fancy words, words that call attention to themselves. The word *tenet* as used in the law school statement, is one such pretentious word; it's out of place. Even the Declaration of Independence, with its formal, ceremonial language, uses the simple word *truths:*

We hold these truths to be self-evident.

Chances are that Thomas Jefferson didn't consider, even in his first draft,

We hold these tenets of our value system to be self-evident.

There are times, of course, when an uncommon word is called for, a word with the precise meaning you want. All of us have in our passive vocabulary words that we rarely, if ever, use in speaking; and using them when they're called for does not mean giving up our personal voice. The mere fact that a word is infrequent does not make it pretentious. In the opening sentence of the previous paragraph, for example, the verb is *preclude*. It's not a common word, but there's certainly nothing fancy or pretentious about it: It's simply the most precise word for the job.

Another problem with pretentious language is the flabbiness that it produces, such as "utilize my abilities and facilitate my interests." Verbs like *utilize* and *facilitate* may sound impressive, but what do they really mean? *Utilize* simply means *use:* "to use my abilities." And it would probably surprise the law school applicant to learn that *facilitate* does not mean "to carry out," as she apparently assumed; it means "to make easier." So "facilitate my interests" is not only pretentious; it is meaningless.

Another kind of pretentious diction, which we saw in Chapter 4, can occur when we rob verbs of their verbness by turning them into nouns, a process called nominalization:

to make a discovery *instead of* to discover
to conduct an investigation *instead of* to investigate

to make an accusation *instead of* to accuse
to make a recommendation *instead of* to recommend

"Pretentious" may be too strong a word to use for nominalization; the nouns made from verbs in the previous list are certainly common words. And sometimes, of course, the nominal version of the word is called for. But too often the result is the same kind of flabbiness that comes with using fancy words. (We'll look at other aspects of nominalization later in this chapter when we consider the concept of agency—that is, the idea of the actor, or agent, as subject.)

Remember that "rhetorical effect" refers to the effect that the writer's words have on the reader. Are the words convincing? The answer is determined in large part by the reader's perception of the writer's authority. The writer's voice, of course, influences that perception. To achieve an effective voice, then, you should aim for an appropriate tone, avoiding those pretentious words and lofty phrases that obscure meaning and call attention to themselves.

The Rhetoric of Contractions

Contractions are useful tools. They not only affect the writer's personal voice, they can also make an important contribution to the rhythm of sentences. We will look at them here in this chapter on verbs because, with few exceptions, the auxiliary verb is involved: It is itself contracted, or it is attached to the contracted *not*.

Although contractions are much more common in conversation than in writing, the two principal kinds occur frequently in all but the most formal writing situations:

Negative:	*can't, don't, won't, couldn't, doesn't, isn't,* etc.
Auxiliary verb:	*I'd, she'll, they're, we've, he's,* etc.

The contracted forms of *be* can also occur when they function as the main verb:

You're happy.
I'm sad.

The contracted *is* is especially common with *it* and *there:*

It's a nice day today.
There's a storm due tomorrow.

If you think about—and listen for—sentence rhythm, you'll understand the contribution that contractions make in eliminating or greatly diminishing a syllable. As you read the following passages, consider how different the sentences would be without the contractions they include:

> Cats, I surmise, seem unsocial to us only because we aren't good at recognizing the signals of other species. We interpret cat signals as telling us, for

instance, that the cat doesn't care about us and doesn't miss us when we're gone. If people were giving off similar signals, our interpretation would probably be right. But they're not people, and we're wrong.

—Elizabeth Marshall Thomas, "Strong and Sensitive Cats"
(*The Atlantic Monthly*, July 1994)

All left-handers know that they are different, different in ways that can make everyday life seem like a trip to a foreign country without a phrasebook. Lefties have roughly the first year or two of their lives to prepare for the obstacle course they'll encounter; until they're a couple of years old, infants frequently use both hands interchangeably. It's when children begin to master fine motor skills that a dominant hand emerges.

—Nancy Shute, "Life for Lefties: From Annoying to Downright Risky"
(*Smithsonian*, December 1994)

If you use ready-made phrases, you not only don't have to hunt about for words; you also don't have to bother with the rhythms of your sentences, since these phrases are generally so arranged as to be more or less euphonious.

—George Orwell, "Politics and the English Language,"
Shooting an Elephant and Other Essays

You may have noticed that none of the examples, either in the lists or in the quoted passages, involve nouns—only pronouns. Contractions with nouns—"My dog'll eat anything"; "The Senate's accomplished a lot lately"—are fairly common in conversation and in written quotations and dialogue, but they are rare in most writing situations. However, contractions with pronouns are anything but rare—in spite of the warnings against using them you may have heard or read. That kind of advice does not reflect actual usage. Even fairly formal written prose commonly includes the contracted *not*, as the Orwell passage illustrates. And in negative questions, the contracted form is essentially required:

Hasn't the winter weather been wonderful?
Shouldn't the tax laws be revised?

In the uncontracted form, the *not* predominates, changing the intended emphasis, if not the meaning:

Has the winter weather not been wonderful?
Should the tax laws not be revised?

An interesting feature in negative statements is that often the writer has more than one contraction to choose from.

She is not here.
She's not here. / She isn't here.

Both contracted forms are less formal than the original, of course, but there's also a difference between the two: In the version with the diminished *not (isn't)*, the reader will probably put more emphasis on *here*—and may then expect a different follow-up sentence:

> She isn't here. She's in class.
> She's not here. I don't know where she is.

If you want to insure that the reader puts strong stress on the negative, you can use the uncontracted *not*—with or without the contracted *is*. Another difference between these two contracted versions is the number of syllables. The sentence with *isn't* has four syllables; the one with *not* has only three—a rhythm difference that in a given situation may be important.

In some cases where there's a choice of contractions, you may also notice a difference in formality, with the uncontracted *not* on the more formal side:

> I won't be there. / I'll not be there.
> I haven't finished. / I've not finished.
> I wouldn't go there if I were you. / I'd not go there if I were you.

Even though the second version in each case includes a contraction, it has a rather formal tone.

It's important to recognize the connection between the level of formality and the use of contractions: In general, the more formal the writing, the fewer contractions you'll find, or want to use, especially contracted auxiliaries. However, in most of the writing you do for school or on the job, the occasional contraction will certainly be appropriate. It's important to recognize the contribution that contractions can make to your personal voice.

Choosing Precise Verbs

A well-chosen verb not only heightens the drama of a sentence and makes its meaning clear; it sends a message to the reader that the writer has crafted the sentence carefully, that the idea matters. Sometimes the culprit that keeps a sentence from sending that message is the two- or three-word verb, known as an **idiom:** *turn down, bring about, bring on, put up with, stand for, think up, take off, take up, do away with, get on with, give up*. There's nothing wrong with these common verbs—and they certainly are common, part of our everyday speech. But the single-word near-synonym may be more precise—and it's always tighter:

> The legislature turned down the governor's compromise proposal/the legislature *rejected* . . .
> The lawyers for the defendant turned down the prosecutor's offer of a plea bargain/the lawyers for the defendant *refused* . . .
> The police are looking into the rumors about corruption/the police are *investigating* . . .
> The police are looking into the evidence/the police are *analyzing* . . .

The police are looking carefully at the evidence/the police are *scrutinizing* . . .
The police are looking below *the surface*/the police are *probing* . . .

Certainly another difference between an idiom or a phrase and its one-word counterpart is the level of formality: *To scrutinize* and *to probe* sound more formal than *to look into* or *to look carefully*. In informal contexts, the idiom may be the best choice—for example, in a personal essay or narrative, or for a general audience, such as you might address in a letter to the editor of a newspaper. But for research papers or technical reports—and certainly for résumés and letters to prospective employers—the single-word version might be more effective. So one step in your revision process is to look carefully at (to *scrutinize*) the verbs that you have chosen—and recognize that you have a choice.

You may also have introduced some flabbiness simply by selecting a common garden-variety verb: *have, make, go, do, say, get, take*. (In many cases they are verbs that take part in idioms.) Because these verbs have so many nuances of meaning, you can often find a more precise one. For example, where you have selected the verb *make*, you could probably express yourself more exactly with *constitute, render, produce, form, complete, compel,* or *create*, all of which are indexed under *make* in Roget's *Thesaurus*, along with *make believe, make good* (demonstrate), *make out* (discover, know, interpret), and *make up* (complete).

It's important to note, too, that these alternatives to *make* are not uncommon or esoteric words; they're certainly a part of your active vocabulary. Unfortunately, however, the precise verb doesn't always come to mind when you need it—especially when you're composing the first draft. Rather than stop right there in mid-sentence or mid-paragraph to find it, just circle the word you've used—or highlight it with boldface type if you're using a word processor. Then, during the revision stage you can take time to think about it again. At that point, in fact, you may want to consult your dictionary or thesaurus just to remind yourself of some of these more specific verbs.

(A word of warning: Every word in the thesaurus is not for you. If it's not your word, if you're not sure of it, if it doesn't sound natural in your voice, then don't use it. Sometimes the dictionary will be a better reminder: It will usually have each synonym in context, along with the distinctive meanings of each.)

The Overuse of Be

Another major culprit contributing to flabbiness is the overuse of the linking *be* (*am, is, are, was, were, have been, is being, might be*, and so on) as the main verb. You'll recall from Chapter 1 that the *be* patterns commonly serve not only as topic sentences but as supporting sentences throughout the paragraph. You may be surprised, in checking a paragraph or two of your own prose, at how often you've used a form of *be* as the link between the known and the new information. An abundance of such examples—say, more than two or three in a paragraph—constitutes a clear "revise" message.

The following revised examples, sentences from this chapter, illustrate the substitution of more active, meaningful verbs:

Original: Poets are careful to budget their words
Revision: Poets *budget* their words *carefully*.

Original: The precise verb isn't always available when you need it.
Revision: The precise verb *doesn't* always *come to mind* when you need it.

Original: As a writer, you must be aware of your own inappropriate words
Revision: As a writer, you must *learn to spot* your own inappropriate words.

Original: In fact, we are not surprised to see that nonpersonal voice in certain kinds of documents.
Revision: In fact, *we've come to expect* that nonpersonal voice in certain kinds of documents.

Original: Further, in writing there are certain modifiers, such as nonrestrictive clauses and phrases . . . , that we rarely use in speaking.
Revision: Further, in writing *we use* certain modifers. . . .

In this last example the culprit is an unnecessary *there are*. In Chapter 3, you'll recall, we looked at this *there*-transformation as well as the cleft transformation *it is*, both of which take *be*—and neither of which should be overused.

In Chapter 10, in the discussion of appositives, you'll learn about another revision technique for eliminating the linking *be*. Meanwhile, don't worry if you can't find an alternative. The sentence with a linking *be* is often the most straightforward, natural structure for making your point—as this author concluded in reconsidering this sentence. For further examples of *be* sentences that could be revised, you can turn to almost any paragraph in this book.

EXERCISE 17

Revise the following passages by finding more precise alternatives to the italicized verbs. In some cases you will have to make changes other than just the verb substitution.

1. The small band of rebels *fought off* the army patrol for several hours, then *gave up* just before dawn. News reports about the event did not *give any specific details about* how many troops were involved.
2. The majority leader *has* a great deal of influence in the White House. He can easily *find a way around* the established procedures and go directly to the president, no matter what his party affiliation.

3. Several economists are saying that they *look forward to* an upturn in the stock market during the second half of the year. Others, however, maintain that interest rates must *stop their fluctuating* if the bull market is to prevail.
4. The night-shift workers took their complaints to the shop steward when the managers tried to *force* them into *giving up* their ten-cent wage differential.
5. The chairman of the Senate investigating committee *spoke against* the practice of accepting fees for outside speeches. He said that the new rules will *put a stop to* all such questionable fund raising. To some observers, such practices *are the same thing as* bribery. Several senators have promised to *come up with* a new compromise plan.
6. Dorm life changed drastically when colleges *did away with* their traditional "in loco parentis" role. In the old days, of course, there were always students who *paid no attention to* the rules. At some schools, where the administration would not *put up with* violations, students were routinely *kicked out*.

For Group Discussion

A sign that greets the visitors at the entrance to the San Diego Wild Animal Park reads as follows:

> Please do not annoy, torment, pester, plague, molest, worry, badger, harry, harass, heckle, persecute, irk, bullyrag, vex, disquiet, grate, beset, bother, tease, nettle, tantalize, or ruffle the animals.

What you expect to read, of course, is "Do not feed the animals." And, even though the sign doesn't say not to, no one feeds the animals either!

Put your heads together and come up with a comparable sign for some of the other written edicts we encounter. Consult your thesaurus only as a last resort.

No loitering

No shirt, no shoes, no service

No parking

No smoking

Please do not block the entrance

Verbs and Grammar

There are two main grammatical features of verbs that will be especially useful for you to understand in a conscious way. One is the selection of **tense,** especially for those sentences where you have more than one clause and, thus, a decision to make about the **sequence of tenses.** The second is the concept of **agency,** which involves an understanding of the relationship of the subject and verb, whether or not the subject is the agent, or actor. Included under the heading of agency is the feature of **voice**—whether the verb is active or passive.

Tense

For experienced speakers, the selection of tense is rarely a problem, even in writing, especially for sentences with only one clause.

SIMPLE PRESENT: BASE AND -S FORM

- *"Habitual" or "timeless" present:*
  Kevin has a chemistry exam every Thursday.
  We have earthquakes in California quite often.
- *Present point in time:*
  I understand your position.

PRESENT PROGRESSIVE: -ING FORM WITH A FORM OF BE

- *Present action of limited duration:*
  Sherry is taking computer science this semester.

  Note: Both this form and the simple present can indicate future time with the addition of an appropriate adverbial:
  The bus leaves at seven.
  We are having pizza tonight.

SIMPLE PAST: -ED FORM

- *Specific point in the past:*
  The Loma Prieta earthquake struck at 5:04 P.M. on October 17, 1989.
- *Period of time in the past:*
  In 1993 we lived in Idaho.

PAST PROGRESSIVE: -ING FORM WITH THE PAST OF BE (WAS OR WERE):

- *Past action of limited duration* (often to show one particular action during a larger span of time):
  Larry was sleeping during the history lecture.
  I was trying to study last night during the party, but it was no use.

PRESENT PERFECT: -EN FORM (PAST PARTICIPLE) WITH A FORM OF HAVE:

- *Completed action extending from a point in the past to either the present or the near present or occurring at an unspecified past time:*
  The leaves have turned yellow already.
  I have finished my work.
  I have memorized several of Frost's poems.

PAST PERFECT: THE PAST PARTICIPLE WITH THE PAST OF HAVE (HAD):

- *Past action completed before another action in the past:*

The telecast of the World Series had just started when the earthquake struck.
I had answered only half the questions when the proctor called out, "Time's up."
By the time the police arrived, the crowd had begun to attack the picket line.

The past perfect is one of the tenses most likely to be a problem—most likely to be used ineffectively. In the foregoing examples, the writer is referring to more than one point or period of time in the past. Actually three different times are included in these sentences, given the writer's point of view in the present:

PAST PERFECT	*PAST*	*PRESENT*
prior to "then"	*"then"*	*"now" (at this writing)*
had started	struck	
had answered	called out	
had begun	arrived	

Here are some other sentences expressing the past that include more than one clause:

We lived in Colorado when I was a boy.
My family had lived there for six years before we moved to Texas.

Note that in the first sentence the two clauses describe the same period of time; the simple past—*lived* and *was*—is appropriate because the verbs refer to simultaneous happenings. In the second sentence, however, the time expressed by *had lived* precedes the event described in the *before* clause. It's not unusual to see or to hear sentences such as the last one with the simple past in both clauses.

My family lived there for six years before we moved to Texas.

But careful writers would use *had lived* to maintain the time distinction.

Another situation that calls for a careful selection of tenses occurs with what is called the "hypothetical past":

If we had invited George, he would have *come*.

Inexperienced writers sometimes make the mistake of including the modal auxiliary *would* in both clauses:

*If we would have invited George, he would have *come*.

Here the "conditional" meaning is expressed by *if*, so *would* is simply redundant.

The *if* clause can also denote what is called the **subjunctive mood,** to express a condition contrary to fact or contrary to the belief or expectation of the speaker:

If George <u>were</u> here, we would probably be playing charades.

In the subjunctive we avoid the *-s* form of the verb: "If George *were*," not *was*. We should note, too, that the subjunctive applies in the *if* clause only when the sentence expresses a wish or a condition contrary to fact or expectation:

If I <u>were</u> rich, I'd be driving a BMW.
If George <u>were</u> here, I just know he'd have us playing charades.

It does not apply in *if* clauses that express contingencies or possibilities:

If the mail *is* late again today, I'm going to complain.
If the store *was* closed, why were you gone so long?
If George *was* here earlier, why didn't he leave a message?

EXERCISE 18

Select a paragraph or page from an essay you have written or one you are currently working on. List the main verbs in all the clauses.

1. What percentage are a form of *be* or *have?* (Remember that both *have* and *be* can serve as auxiliaries; count them only in their role as main verb.)
2. Consider whether your verbs are as precise as they could be. Use your dictionary or thesaurus to find synonyms that might be more precise.
3. Note the two- or three-word idioms you have used. Try to find single-word substitutes and compare the effect.

Agency

The concept of agency might be easier to understand if we used the police officer's word *perpetrator* instead of *agent*. The **agent** in the sentence is the perpetrator—generally human (or animate)—of the action specified by the verb, the responsible party. In the **active voice,** the agent functions as the subject:

The <u>acting commissioner</u> canceled the World Series.

This is the basic transitive sentence: Agent—Action—Objective (or Goal). In Chapter 1 our sample transitive sentence is

<u>My roommate</u> baked this apple pie.

Here the agent is *my roommate*. Like all transitive sentences in the active voice, we learn "who is doing what."

So why is the concept of agency important for writers to understand? It's important because too often the inexperienced writer obscures the agent in various ways, sometimes by using the passive voice when an active sentence would be stronger; sometimes by turning verbs into nouns—the process called nominalization (see Exercises 11 and 12 in Chapter 4); sometimes by using a verb phrase or clause as subject when the direct Agent—Action—Goal sentence would be more effective (you'll see examples of these structures in Chapter 8). Writers who understand these sources of lame and flabby sentences will have the tools both for recognizing them and for revising them.

The Passive Voice

When a sentence is in the **passive voice,** it is the goal, not the agent, that fills the subject position:

> The World Series was canceled by the acting commissioner.

Notice how we have transformed the original sentence, in which "the World Series" is the direct object and "the acting commissioner" is the subject. And the passive version of our other transitive sentence is

> This apple pie was baked by my roommate.

You'll notice that in the passive voice of both sentences the verb includes *be* as an auxiliary followed by the *-en* form, the past participle; the agent, when it does appear, will be the object in a *by* prepositional phrase.

It's possible that everything you've heard about the passive voice up to now has been negative; English teachers often declare it out of bounds. Such edicts come about—those "pass" comments appear in the margins—because students so often use passives when they shouldn't; and it's true that ineffective passives do stand out. But there's a great deal of misunderstanding about the passive. It's both simplistic and inaccurate to flatly rule it out; all good prose includes both active and passive voice.

EXERCISE 19

It's important to recognize the passive voice when you see it—so that you'll know when you've used it and thus will use it deliberately and effectively. In the first section of this exercise, you'll transform active sentences into the passive voice; in the second part you'll do the opposite—the passive into the active. And in the third part, the voice of the sentence is not identified: You'll have to figure it out.

A. Transform the following active sentences into the passive voice; remember that the direct object of the active functions as the subject in the passive.

1. My roommate wrote the lead article in today's *Collegian*.
2. Bach composed some of our most intricate fugues.
3. My brother-in-law builds the most expensive houses in town.
4. He built that expensive apartment complex on Water Street.
5. The county commissioners try out a new tax-collection system every four years.

B. Transform the following passive sentences into the active voice; remember that the subject of the passive is the direct object in the active. (Note: If the agent is missing, you will have to supply one to act as the subject for the active.)

1. The football team was led onto the field by the cheerleading squad.
2. This year's cheerleading squad was chosen by a committee last spring.
3. Bill's apartment was burglarized last weekend.
4. A snowstorm is predicted for this weekend.
5. The election of the student body officers will be held on Tuesday.

C. First decide if the following sentences are active or passive; then transform them.

1. John Kennedy was elected president in 1960.
2. Bill's grandmother nicknamed him Buzz when he was a baby.
3. You should read the next six chapters before Monday.
4. The cities in the Northeast have been affected by migration in recent years.
5. Thousands of northern workers have found good jobs in the Sunbelt.
6. In the 1980s, the taxpayers were cheated out of huge sums by the managers of Savings and Loan institutions.
7. The street lights on campus are finally being repaired.
8. Our company is trying out a new vacation schedule this year.
9. They will close the plant for two weeks in July.
10. Several new provisions were added to the Federal Tax Code in 1994.

Using the Passive Voice. The main strength of the passive voice is that it enables the writer to shift the focus of the sentence. In Chapter 3 we examined other devices for shifting the focus and altering rhythm—among them the *there*-transformation, which moves the subject into the position of main stress, and cleft sentences with *it* and *what*, which enable the writer to focus on almost any segment of the sentence. The passive transformation has the same effect of shifting parts of the sentence from their "home base."

The passive voice may also be called for when the agent is unknown or has no bearing on the discussion:

> In 1905 the streets of Patterson, California, were laid out in the shape of a wheel.

> So far as we know, from Einstein's Special Theory of Relativity, the universe is constructed in such a way (at least around here) that no material object and no information can be transmitted faster than the velocity of light.
>
> —Carl Sagan, *Broca's Brain*

> The Vikings have had a bad press. Their activities are equated with rape and pillage and their reputation for brutality is second only to that of the Huns and the Goths. Curiously, they also have been invested with a strange glamour which contradicts in many ways their fearsome image.
>
> —James Graham-Campbell and Dafydd Kidd, *The Vikings*

The author's purpose in the last passage is not to explain who equates the Vikings with rape and pillage or who invests them with glamour. The use of the passive puts these statements in the category of accepted beliefs.

In some cases the passive voice is simply more straightforward:

> Joe was wounded in Vietnam.

And sometimes, in order to add modifiers to the agent, we put it where we can do so more conveniently, at the end of the sentence:

> Early this morning my poodle was hit by a delivery truck traveling at high speed through the intersection of James Avenue and Water Street.

Note that if the agent were in subject position, the result would be a fairly wide separation of the subject headword and the verb:

> Early this morning a delivery truck traveling at high speed through the intersection of James Avenue and Water Street hit my poodle.

The choice, of course, will also depend on where the main focus should be.

The passive voice is especially common—and deliberate—in technical and scientific writing, in legal documents, and in lab reports, where the researcher is the agent, but to say so would be inappropriate:

> *Active:* I increased the heat to 450° and allowed it to remain at that temperature for twenty minutes.
>
> *Passive:* The heat was increased to 450° and allowed to remain at that temperature for twenty minutes.

Sometimes writers shift the focus for the purpose of transition. You'll recall that in most sentences the new information, which is where the main focus will occur, is at or near the end, in object position, while the known information is in the subject slot. However, if the direct object is the known information, it can be shifted to the subject slot by means of the passive transformation. That opening information will provide transition from the previous sentence.

Here, for example, is a paragraph from a *Time* article by Michael D. Lemonick about the destruction of the Brazilian rain forests. Note that in the second sentence, which is passive, the subject provides that transition:

> If Americans are truly interested in saving the rain forests, they should move beyond rhetoric and suggest policies that are practical—and acceptable—to the understandably wary Brazilians. Such policies cannot be presented as take-them-or-leave-them propositions. If the U.S. expects better performance from Brazil, Brazil has a right to make demands in return. In fact, the U.S. and Brazil need to engage in face-to-face negotiations as part of a formal dialogue on the environment between the industrial nations and the developing countries. The two sides frequently negotiate on debt refinancing and other issues. Why not put the environment at the top of the agenda?

In the first sentence, *policies* is new information; in the second, it is known.

In the following paragraph from Jane Brody's *Good Food Book*, note the underlined passive. The subject (*children's taste for salt*) is the old information in the clause; the "by" phrase—the agent—is new, the point of focus.

> Human beings are born with the ability to taste salt, but our taste for a high-salt diet is an acquired one. Newborns do not particularly like salty foods. But when given them, after a while they acquire a taste for salt, and by early to middle childhood they prefer salted foods to those that are unsalted. A long-term study under the direction of Dr. David L. Yeung, a nutritional scientist at the University of Toronto, showed that children's taste for salt at the age of 4 <u>is determined</u> by how much salt their parents feed them in infancy. A preference for salt does not develop in cultures where salt is not added to foods. In such societies, even the adults do not like salt.

And in the following passage, the first paragraph of E. B. White's Introduction to the second edition of Strunk and White's *Elements of Style*, you'll see another example of how the passive voice provides transition by allowing the old information to open the sentence:

> At the close of the first World War, when I was a student at Cornell, I took a course called English 8. My professor was William Strunk, Jr. A textbook required for the course was a slim volume called The Elements of Style, 1919. <u>The book was known on the campus in those days as "the little book,"</u> with the stress on the word "little." <u>It had been privately printed by the author.</u>

The subjects of those two final passive sentences, *the book* and *it*, are in both cases the known information, referring to "the slim volume" in the paragraph's third sentence.

EXERCISE 20

1. The verb *is determined* is not the only passive verb in the previous paragraph from Jane Brody's *Good Food Book*. Identify the others; why has Brody used passive instead of active? Would any of them be more effective in the active voice? Why or why not?
2. Surely the most famous words in our country's history are those written by Thomas Jefferson in the Declaration of Independence. Here is the opening of the Declaration's second paragraph:

> We hold these truths to be self-evident, that all men are created equal, that they are endowed by their Creator with certain unalienable Rights, that among these are Life, Liberty and the pursuit of Happiness. That to secure these rights, Governments are instituted among Men, deriving their just powers from the consent of the governed. That whenever any Form of Government becomes destructive of these ends, it is the Right of the People to alter or to abolish it, and to institute a new government, laying its foundation on such principles and organizing its powers in such form, as to them shall seem most likely to effect their Safety and Happiness. Prudence, indeed, will dictate that Governments long established should not be changed for light and transient causes; and accordingly all experience hath shown, that mankind are more disposed to suffer, while evils are sufferable, than to right themselves by abolishing the forms to which they are accustomed.

   Underline the passive sentences. Rewrite all or some of them in the active voice and compare the two versions.

3. The following paragraph is the beginning of a short description of Jefferson by Lee A. Jacobus:

> Thomas Jefferson, an exceptionally accomplished and well-educated man, is probably best known for writing the Declaration of Independence, a work composed under the eyes of Benjamin Franklin, John Adams, and the Continental Congress, which spent two and a half days going over every word. The substance of the document was developed in committee, but Jefferson, because of the grace of his style, was chosen to do the actual writing. The result is one of the most memorable statements in American history.

   Again note the use of the passive voice. Write an active version and compare the two.

Misusing the Passive Voice. Certainly the passive voice has a place in every kind of writing; it is a legitimate tool—but like any tool it must be right for the job. Too often the purpose of the passive voice is simply to obscure the agent. For example, one of the most common responses that governmental investigative committees hear from individuals accused of mismanagement is

"Yes, Senator, mistakes were made."

And the passive is common in the "official" style used by bureaucrats:

> It was reported today that the federal funds to be allocated for the power plant would not be forthcoming as early as had been anticipated. Some contracts on the preliminary work have been canceled and others renegotiated.

Such "officialese" or "bureaucratese" takes on a nonhuman quality because the agent role has completely disappeared from the sentences. In the foregoing example we do not know who is reporting, allocating, anticipating, canceling, or renegotiating.

This kind of agentless passive is especially common in official news conferences, where press secretaries and other government officials explain what is happening without revealing who is responsible for making it happen:

> Recommendations are being made to the Mexican government concerning their economic problems.
> A tax hike has been proposed, but several other solutions to the federal deficit are also being considered.
> The president has been advised that certain highly placed officials are being investigated.

The faceless passive does an efficient job of obscuring responsibility, but it is neither efficient nor graceful for the writing that most of us do in school and on the job.

Sometimes the inexperienced writer resorts to the passive voice simply to avoid using the first-person point of view. Here is a gardener's active account of spring planting written in the first person (*we*):

> In late April, when the ground dried out enough to be worked, we planted the peas and onions and potatoes and prepared the soil for the rest of the vegetables. Then in mid-May we set out the tomato and pepper plants, hoping we had seen the last of frost.

Certainly the first person as used here would seem to be the logical choice for such a passage; nevertheless, some writers take great pains to avoid it—and, unfortunately, some writing texts, for no logical reason, warn against using the first person (see the discussion of point of view on pages 68–70). The result, as applied to the foregoing paragraph, is a gardener's passive account of spring planting—without the gardener:

> In late April, when the ground dried out enough to be worked, the peas and onions and potatoes were planted and the soil was prepared for the rest of the vegetables. Then in mid-May the tomato and pepper plants were set out in hopes that the frost was over.

This revision is certainly not as stilted as the earlier examples of agentless prose, but it does lack the live, human quality that the active version has.

Here's another example of the passive, typical of the student writer who has managed to avoid using *I*, perhaps because the paper has too many of them already or because the teacher has ruled out the first-person point of view:

> The incessant sound of foghorns could be heard along the waterfront.

But remember that English is a versatile language; first person is not the only alternative to the passive. You don't have to write, "I [or we] heard the sound of foghorns. . . ." Here's a version of the sentence using *sound* as the verb:

> The foghorns sounded along the waterfront.

And here's one that describes the movement of the sound:

> The incessant sound of foghorns floated across the water.

Many times, of course, the writer simply doesn't realize that the passive voice may be the culprit producing the vagueness or wordiness of that first draft. For example, a student writer ended his family Christmas story with an impersonal, inappropriate passive:

> That visit from Santa was an occurrence that would never be forgotten by the family.

Clearly, he needed to ask himself, "Who was doing what?"

> The family would never forget that visit from Santa.

And if for purposes of transition or rhythm he had wanted to retain *visit* as the subject, he could easily have done so in an active way:

> That visit from Santa became part of our family legend.

The student's original sentence ("That visit . . . was an occurrence") actually has two red flags besides the passive that should have signaled the need for revision: *be* as the main verb and the nominalized *occurrence*—the verb *occur* turned into a noun. All are possible weak spots, the kinds of signals you should be alert for in the revision stage.

EXERCISE 21

1. The writer of the following passage has managed to avoid using the first-person point of view but in doing so has obliterated any resemblance to a personal voice. Revise the passage, avoiding both the passive and the first person. Remember to think about the agent as subject.

The woods in the morning seemed both peaceful and lively. Birds could be heard in the pines and oaks, staking out their territory. Squirrels could be seen scampering across the leaves that covered the forest floor, while in the branches above, the new leaves of the birches and maples were outlined by the sun's rays. The leaves, too, could be heard, rustling to the rhythm of the wind.

2. Identify the passive verbs in the following passage from *Stalking the Wild Asparagus* by Euell Gibbons. Why do you think he chose the passive instead of the active voice? Can you improve the passage by revising some or all of the sentences?

Wild food is used at our house in a unique method of entertaining. Our "wild parties," which are dinners where the chief component of every dish is some foraged food, have achieved a local fame. Many different meals can be prepared almost wholly from wild food without serving anything that will be refused by the most finicky guest. Such dinners are remembered and talked about long after the most delicious of conventional dinners have been forgotten.

The Abstract Subject

As you have learned in the foregoing discussion of the passive voice, the agent—the perpetrator—is not always the subject of the sentence; in some passive sentences it doesn't appear at all. However, the more concrete and active the sentence, the more likely the agent will function as the subject—or at least make an appearance. The more abstract and passive the sentence, the more likely the agent will be missing.

One common cause of abstraction is the sentence with a preponderance of nominalized verbs—verbs that have been turned into nouns. The word *occurrence* in the previous discussion is one such example; we saw other nominalizations in Chapter 4 in connection with the discussion of derivational affixes, the word endings that change the class of the word. Remember that a verb is an action word: A verb *shows* the action; but a noun simply *names* the action:

The president's <u>opposition</u> to abortion has caused many prochoice organizations to work against his reelection.

There is a growing <u>recognition</u> that forests are more valuable when left standing.

Our language, of course, is filled with nominalized verbs—most of which are useful, legitimate ways of expressing ideas. In the second sentence of this paragraph, for example. you saw *discussion* and *connection*, both of which began as verbs (*discuss*, *connect*) and are now ordinary, everyday nouns.

But because nominalized verbs are so common and so easy to produce, they can become a trap for the unwary writer, introducing abstraction where concrete ideas belong. It's during the revision stage of writing that you'll want to be on the lookout. Ask yourself, is the agent there and, if so, is it functioning as the subject? In other words, does the sentence explain *who is doing what?* If the answer is no, your sentence may be a prime candidate for revision.

Another source of abstraction and flabbiness is the sentence with a verb phrase or a clause as subject, rather than the usual noun phrase. When you study these structures in Chapter 8, you'll see that they are grammatical, common substitutes for noun phrases. But because they are abstractions, they too may be pitfalls for the unwary writer. Again, the source of the problem may be that of the missing or misplaced agent:

> The buying of so many American companies and so much real estate by the Japanese is causing concern on Wall Street.
>
> With the opening of the East Bloc nations to democracy and capitalism, what is happening is that American companies are looking for ways of expanding their markets and their product lines to take advantage of the situation.
>
> Analyzing the situation in China has shown that opportunities for investment are growing.

Although we need context to tell us the best way of revising these sentences, we can see and hear a problem. The sentences seem to be about actions—but they can't show the action in a strong and concrete way because the agents of those actions are not there in subject position. This kind of agentless sentence should send up a red flag—a signal that here's a candidate for revision.

EXERCISE 22

Revise the following passages, paying special attention to ineffective passives, unnecessary nominalizations, and problems of agency. The first three items are the examples from the preceding discussion. Remember to ask yourself, "Who is doing what?"

1. The buying of so many American companies and so much real estate by the Japanese is causing concern on Wall Street.
2. With the opening of the East Bloc nations to democracy and capitalism, what is happening is that American companies are looking for ways of expanding their markets and their product lines to take advantage of the situation.
3. Analyzing the situation in China has shown that opportunities for investment are growing.
4. In the biography of Lyndon Johnson by Robert Caro, an account of the Senate election of 1948 is described in great detail.
5. When Julie filled out an application for a work-study job, she was surprised to learn that a detailed financial statement would have to be submitted by her parents.
6. Getting his new pizza shop to finally turn a profit has meant a lot of hard work and long hours for Tim.

7. The overuse of salt in the typical American diet has had the result of obscuring the natural taste of many foods. Nutritionists maintain that a reduction in people's dependence on salt would lead to an enhancement of taste and heightened enjoyment of food.
8. The measurement of the Earth's fragile ozone layer was one of the important missions undertaken by the crew of the space shuttle *Atlantis*. The shuttle was launched in October of 1994. The mission lasted ten days. Humans are put at greater risk of skin cancer, cataracts, and other ailments because of overexposure to ultraviolet radiation. Crops can also be spoiled and underwater food sources devastated as a result of too much direct sunlight. A vast ozone "hole" over Antarctica from September to December every year is particularly worrisome to scientists.

RHETORICAL REMINDERS

Verbs and Diction

Can I hear my personal voice in the words I've written?

Have I kept my use of the linking *be* to a minimum?

Could I improve the effectiveness of my diction by substituting precise single-word synonyms for my phrasal verbs?

Are any contractions I have used appropriate for my audience and purpose?

Verbs and Grammar

In sentences with more than one clause, do the tenses accurately describe the time relationship?

Have I put the agent in subject position whenever possible?

Have I used the passive voice effectively?

Chapter 7

Adding Adverbials

You may recall from Chapter 1 that a few basic sentence patterns like these

Noun Phrase	**Transitive Verb**	**Noun Phrase**
(Subject)		*(Direct Object)*
Noun Phrase	**Linking Verb**	**Adjective**
(Subject)		*(Subjective Complement)*

represent the underlying skeletal structures of all our sentences. Of course, not many of the sentences we actually speak and write are quite that simple: Most have flesh on those bare bones. We add that flesh in three principal ways: (1) by expanding the individual slots, (2) by putting patterns together into coordinate structures, and (3) by adding one or more optional slots—among them, our versatile adverbials.

Although the term *adverbial* may be unfamiliar, you know "adverb" as one of the parts of speech, one of the four form classes you read about in Chapter 4. Among the adverbs are some of our most common words designating time and place: *then, now, here, there, soon, never, always, sometimes, often*. The easiest ones to recognize are those that end in *-ly*: *slowly, carefully, quickly, peacefully, probably*. We have thousands of such *-ly* adverbs, simply because there are thousands of adjectives like *slow* and *careful* and *quick* and *peaceful* and *probable* that we can convert to "adverbs of manner," as these adverbs are called, simply by adding *-ly*.

But adverbs are not the only words that add information about time and place and reason and manner to our sentences; phrases and clauses can also function in an adverb-like way. **Adverbial** is the term that names that function. In the following sentences, the adverbial information is provided by prepositional phrases, subordinate clauses, a verb (infinitive) phrase, and a noun phrase, in addition to adverbs:

1. On Tuesday night we ordered pizza because no one wanted to cook.
   (prep. phrase) *(sub. clause)*
2. The fans cheered wildly when Fernando stepped up to the plate.
   (adverb) *(sub. clause)*
3. Suddenly Paul walked out the door, without a word to anyone.
   (adverb) *(prep. phrase)* *(prep. phrase)*
4. There's a film crew shooting a movie near the marina.
   (prep. phrase)
5. I got up early this morning to study for my Spanish test.
   (adverb)(noun phrase) *(infinitive phrase)*
6. On its last assignment in outer space, *Voyager 2* photographed the
   (prep. phrase)
   rings of Saturn.

It's not only the variety of form that makes adverbials so versatile and so important for writers; it's also their movability and, consequently, their potential for providing transition and for changing sentence rhythm. You'll recall from the discussion of rhythm in Chapter 3 that our sentences have a regular beat, a rhythm pattern that usually begins with a valley of low stress. The subject in that opening position, as it commonly is, will be in line for low stress—and rightfully so, because the subject is generally the known information. But if we want to add stress to the subject for any reason, we can insert an adverbial to fill the opening valley so that the subject will be in line for a peak. For example, listen carefully to the intonation contours of these sentences as you read them aloud; listen for the words that get stress:

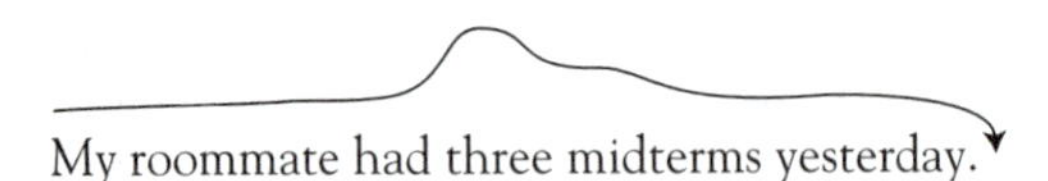

My roommate had three midterms yesterday.

Yesterday my roommate had three midterms.

In the second version, *yesterday* delays the subject, putting it in line for a peak of stress—not a high peak, to be sure, but at least a rhythm beat that it does not have in the opening position.

Another function of that opening adverbial is to provide cohesion, the tie that connects a sentence to what has gone before. In Chapter 2 we saw examples of the cohesion provided by known information, a pronoun or noun phrase that repeats information from the previous sentence. In Chapter 4 we looked at the cohesive effects produced by certain stressed words, words that the reader expects because of what has gone before. What opening adverbials do so well is to provide road signs that connect the sentences and orient the reader in time and place. Notice in the following paragraphs from *The Sea Around Us* how Rachel Carson opens her sentences with adverbials. (These are not contiguous paragraphs.)

> In modern times we have never seen the birth of an island as large as Ascension. But now and then there is a report of a small island appearing where none was before. Perhaps a month, a year, five years later, the island has disappeared into the sea again. These are the little, stillborn islands, doomed to only a brief emergence above the sea.
>
> Sometimes the disintegration takes abrupt and violent form. The greatest explosion of historic time was the literal evisceration of the island of Krakatoa. In 1680 there had been a premonitory eruption on this small island in Sunda Strait, between Java and Sumatra in the Netherlands Indies. Two hundred years later there had been a series of earthquakes. In the spring of 1883, smoke and steam began to ascend from fissures in the volcanic cone. The ground became noticeably warm, and warning rumblings and hissings came from the volcano. Then, on 27 August, Krakatoa literally exploded. In an appalling series of eruptions, that lasted two days, the whole northern half of the cone was carried away. The sudden inrush of ocean water added the fury of superheated steam to the cauldron. When the inferno of white-hot lava, molten rock, steam, and smoke had finally subsided, the island that had stood 1,400 feet above the sea had become a cavity a thousand feet below sea level. Only along one edge of the former crater did a remnant of the island remain.

Opening adverbials like these are especially common in narrative writing, the story or explanation of events through time. In fact, you'll notice that most of these adverbial openers provide information of time.

The Prepositional Phrase

No doubt our most common adverbial, other than the adverb itself, is the **prepositional phrase,** a two-part structure consisting of a **preposition** and its **object,** usually a noun phrase. In fact, of the twenty most frequently used words in English, eight are prepositions: *of, to, in, for, with, on, at,* and *by.*[1] Here are some examples of adverbial information that prepositional phrases can provide:

Direction: toward the pond, beyond the ridge, across the field
Place: near the marina, on the expressway, along the path, behind the dormitory, under the bridge

[1]This frequency count, based on a collection of 1,014,232 words, is published in Henry Kuçera and W. Nelson Francis, *Computational Analysis of Present-Day English* (Providence: Brown University Press, 1967).

Time: on Tuesday afternoon, at noon, in modern times, in the spring of 1883
Duration: until three o'clock, for several days, during spring break, throughout the summer months
Manner: in an appalling series of eruptions, without complaint, with dignity, by myself, in a frenzy
Cause: because of the storm, for a good reason

The Proliferating Prepositional Phrase

You'll recall from Chapter 4 the reference to the "big nine," those nine words that constitute 25 percent of our spoken language. Among them are the prepositions *of* and *to*. Because they are so common, those two prepositions are especially vulnerable to proliferation. Both occur in countless idioms and set phrases. For example, we regularly use *of* phrases with numbers and with such pronouns as *all, each, some,* and *most:*

one of the guests, all of the people, some of the students, most of the problems, the rest of the time, half of the food, each of the parts

Of is also used to indicate possessive case, as an alternative to *s:*

the capacity of the trunk, the base of the lamp, the opening night of the new show, the noise of the crowd

And we use it to show direction and position and time:

the front of the house, the top of the bookcase, the back of the page, the end of the play

The preposition *to*, in addition to its directional meaning (to the store, to town), is used with verbs as the "sign of the infinitive" (to run, to play). And both *of* and *to* phrases are commonly used as adjective complements:

Brad is afraid to fly (of flying).
I am sure of my facts.
He is certain to win (of winning).
He is sure of himself.

Prepositions also pattern with verbs to form phrasal verbs (we saw these in Chapter 6), many of which are endowed with new, idiomatic meanings:

look up, bring up, turn on, live down, bring about, bring on, put up with, stand for, hand in, pull through, help out, think up, take off, take up, do away with, get away with, pass out, give up

Because there are so many such situations that call for prepositions, it's not at all unusual to find yourself writing sentences with prepositional phrases strung together in chains. You can undoubtedly find many such sentences in the pages of this book. In fact, the sentence you just read ended with two: "*in* the pages *of* this book." It would be easy to imagine even more: "in the pages of this book about the grammar of English for writers." As you edit what you have written, it's important to tune in to the rhythm of the sentence; a long string of short phrases is a clue that suggests revision. Ask yourself if those prepositional phrases are proliferating awkwardly.

Awkwardness is not the only problem—nor is it the most serious. The sentence that ends with a long string of prepositional phrases often loses its focus. Our usual rhythm pattern, which follows the principle of end focus, calls for the new information to be the last or next-to-the-last structural unit. Notice, for example, what happened to that altered sentence in the previous paragraph. Here's the original; read it aloud and listen to the stress:

> You can undoubtedly find many such sentences in the pages of this book.

Chances are you put stress on *many* and on *this book*. Now read the altered version:

> You can undoubtedly find many such sentences in the pages of this book about the grammar of English for writers.

Because you expected the sentence to have end focus, you probably found yourself putting off the main stress until you got to *writers*. But that last unit (starting with *about*), consisting of three prepositional phrases, is known information. Not only should it get no stress, it shouldn't be there at all. That kind of unwanted repetition of known information is what we call **redundancy.**

Here's another illustration of this common source of redundancy—an edited version of the opening sentences from the previous paragraph:

> Awkwardness is not the only problem with those extra prepositional phrases in our sentences—nor is it the most serious of the writer's problems. The sentence that ends with a long string of prepositional phrases often loses its focus on the main point of the sentence that the writer intended it to have.

Those redundant modifiers add to the total number of words—and that's about all they add. Clearly, they have added no new information. And they have obliterated the original focus.

Sometimes the culprit producing those extra prepositional phrases is the process of nominalization, which we looked at in Chapter 4 in connection with the parts of speech and in Chapter 6.

> A bill under consideration by the Senate would create changes in the way the IRS deals with taxpayers.

Consideration is a noun that in its former life was a verb (*consider*). Turning it back into a verb not only makes the sentence more direct by putting the agent in the subject position; it also eliminates two prepositional phrases:

> *Revision:* The Senate is considering a bill that would change the way the IRS deals with taxpayers.

In the following example the direct version has again eliminated two *of* phrases:

> The bill requires notification of taxpayers in writing before the IRS could begin the seizure of their property.
>
> *Revision:* The bill requires the IRS to notify taxpayers in writing before seizing their property.

Again, the words in this sentence that should send up the red flag to suggest revision are *notification* and *seizure*, both of which are nouns made from verbs.

EXERCISE 23

The problem with proliferating prepositional phrases lies not only in their ungraceful rhythm but also in the resulting lack of focus—a more serious error. The following are altered versions of paragraphs you read in Chapter 3. Read them aloud, paying particular attention to the intonation, including the points of main stress. Remember that redundant information may be the culprit that keeps the sentence from having a clear focus. Think about new information as you revise them to give them a clearer focus. (You may compare your edited version with the originals on pages 34 and 35. They are items 1 and 2 of Exercise 6 and the paragraph following the exercise, headed "Controlling Rhythm.")

1. Never be an investor in something you don't understand or in the dream of an artful salesperson of some product. Be a buyer, not a sellee. Figure out for yourself what you want to buy (be it life insurance, mutual funds or a vacuum cleaner for the home) and then shop for a good buy before making up your mind. Don't let someone else tell you what the necessities for your life are—at least not if he happens to be the salesman who wants to sell it to you.
2. Plaque has almost become a household word in this country. It is certainly a household problem for most people. But even though everyone is affected by it every day few people really understand the seriousness of plaque in their daily lives or the importance of controlling it. Plaque is an almost invisible sticky film of bacteria that in the case of all of us continuously forms throughout the day and night. Plaque germs are constantly multiplying and building up on the teeth. Any dentist will tell you that controlling

plaque from forming is the single most important step to better oral health for people everywhere.

3. Because end focus is such a common rhythm pattern in our sentences, we can almost think of it as a contract between writer and reader. The reader has an expectation that the main sentence focus will be in the predicate of the sentence, unless given a signal to the contrary that it has some other focus. But of course all sentences are not alike in every respect; not every sentence has end focus as its rhythm pattern. In speech, especially, the focus is often shifted elsewhere to some other word or phrase. Consider, for example, these alternative ways of speaking the motorcycle sentence in a conversation with someone, the variety of messages that are possible for the speaker to express in saying this sentence.

The Subordinate Clause

Another common structure that adds adverbial information is the **subordinate clause:**

> The fans cheered when Fernando stepped up to the plate.
> We ordered *pizza because no one wanted to cook*.
> When the inferno of white-hot lava, molten rock, steam, and smoke had finally subsided, the island . . . had become a cavity. . . .

As you can see from the examples, without the opening word of the clause—the **subordinator** (also called **subordinating conjunction**)—those clauses would be complete sentences:

> Fernando stepped up to the plate.
> No one wanted to cook.
> The inferno of white-hot lava . . . had finally subsided.

The word *clause* is, in fact, nearly synonymous with *sentence*. You'll recall from Chapter 1 that the sentence patterns you learned are essentially clause patterns. All sentences are clauses, but not all clauses are sentences. Only when a clause can function independently is it a sentence. A clause that is embedded in another sentence—as a modifier, for example—is a **dependent clause.** The subordinator that opens the adverbial clause robs it of its independence.

The purpose of the subordinator is to indicate the relationship of the clause to the main sentence: The clause introduced by *when* adds time information; introduced by *because*, it tells why. We have many such subordinators, words and phrases that connect the clause for a specific purpose. Among the most common are *if, since, while, although, even though, after, before, as if, as long as, as soon as, provided that*, along with *when* and *because*.

Subordinate clauses are certainly common structures in our language. We use them automatically and often in conversation. But in writing they are not automatic; nor are they always used as effectively as they could be. Two problems that show up fairly often are related to the meaning of the sentence:

1. The wrong idea gets subordinated;
2. The meaning of the subordinator is imprecise.

Here, for example, are two related ideas that a writer might want to combine into a single sentence:

> We worked hard for our candidates.
> We suspected that our candidates didn't stand a chance.

Here are some possibilities for connecting them:

> While we worked hard for our candidates, we suspected they didn't stand a chance.
> Although we worked hard for our candidates, we suspected they didn't stand a chance.
> We worked hard for the candidates, even though we suspected they didn't stand a chance.

We need context, of course, to know precisely how the relationship between hard work and the chances of winning should be expressed; but given no other information, the last version expresses what would appear to be the logical relationship.

Perhaps an even more common problem than the imprecise subordinator is the compound sentence with no subordination—the sentence with two independent clauses, two equal focuses, that would be more accurate and effective with a single focus. Here, for example, is the beginning of a paragraph from a *New York Times* article about sleep by Erik Eckholm. The paragraph preceding this one gives examples of accidents on the job connected with work schedules:

> The biological clock is flexible enough to adjust to slight changes in a person's work schedule, but in many industries rotations in shift work are so drastic that they play havoc with body rhythm, leaving employees unable to sleep at home and impairing their productivity at work.

In form this is a compound sentence, two clauses connected by *but*, one of our coordinating conjunctions. But the substance and focus of the two clauses are not equal: The statement in the second clause is clearly the main idea, the new information. The idea in the first clause, although it has not previously appeared in the article, is information the reader is assumed to know, the known information. Making the first clause subordinate will help the reader focus on the new idea:

> Although the biological clock is flexible enough to adjust to slight changes in a person's work schedule, in many industries rotations in shift work are so drastic that they play havoc with body rhythms, leaving employees unable to sleep at home and impairing their productivity at work.

Although has now subordinated the first clause, signaling the reader that the main idea is coming later.

The *Because*-Clause Myth

Because a subordinate clause looks so much like a full sentence (remember, it consists of a sentence preceded by a subordinator), it is a prime candidate for fragmenthood—that is, a part of a sentence punctuated as a full sentence. One of the most common such fragments is, apparently, the *because*-clause:

> Everyone agreed that our midterm was unfair. Because Professor Middleton included questions about cases we hadn't discussed in class. It turns out she hadn't even assigned them.

It appears that some teachers have discovered a sure-fire way to prevent such fragments: Ban *because* as a sentence opener. As a result, many student writers don't understand that *because* can, indeed, open a sentence, just as all the other subordinators can—*since*, *when*, *after*, *if*, *although*, *as soon as*, and the rest. Like the other adverbials, subordinate clauses can occupy a variety of slots in the sentence.

The Movability of Subordinate Clauses

The movability of subordinate clauses is especially important from a rhetorical point of view. As a sentence opener, the clause often supplies the transition from the previous sentence or paragraph, usually with a cohesive link of known information, as in our revision of the paragraph about sleep. The main focus, the new information, will generally occupy the main clause. The old standard rule of putting subordinate ideas in subordinate clauses and main ideas in main clauses is probably more accurately stated as "known information in the opening subordinate clause, new information in the main clause." Another example appears in Rachel Carson's paragraph about Krakatoa: The opening *when*-clause links the previous description of the "inferno"—that is, the volcano eruption—to a description of its aftermath. The general information in the *when*-clause is known, details of volcanic eruptions the reader is expected to recognize. The new information, the reason for the sentence, follows in the main clause.

Although most subordinate clauses occupy either the opening or closing slots of the sentence, they can also occur in the middle, between the subject and predicate or between the verb and complement. In this position the clause will be set off by commas, one before and one after:

I learn later that night, when ties are loosened during a coffee break, that I am wrong. (James R. Chiles, *Smithsonian*)
My brother, when he was only four years old, actually drove the family car for about a block.

That interruption in the usual flow of the sentence slows the reader down. Notice also that it adds stress and length to the word just preceding the clause, and it changes the rhythm pattern. That's the same principle we saw at work in Chapter 3, when we manipulated the intonation contour of the sentence by shifting word order and changing the punctuation. Ordinarily the subject is in an unstressed valley; it is old information. But a parenthetical comment following it, a word or a phrase or a clause set off by commas, as in the second example, will put the subject in a position of stress; the reader will give it extra length and emphasis. Compare the stress given to *brother* in the previous example with the following revisions, where the subordinate clause either opens or closes the sentence:

When he was only four years old, my brother actually drove the family car for about a block.
My brother actually drove the family car for about a block when he was four years old.

And it's not only a difference in the stress on *brother* that makes the inserted *when*-clause noteworthy: That internal positioning of the subordinate clause is unusual; it sends a message to the reader that says, "Pay attention. I did this on purpose."

Punctuation of Subordinate Clauses

There is one standard punctuation rule that applies to the subordinate clause:

A subordinate clause that opens the sentence is always set off by a comma.

This rule applies no matter how short that clause may be:

If you go to the party, I'll go too.
Even though I'll be bored, I guess I'll go to the party.
When Eric calls, ask him to bring some pizza.

When the subordinate clause closes the sentence, the punctuation will vary, depending on the relationship of the information in the subordinate clause to that of the main clause. As a general rule, when the idea in the main clause is conditional upon or dependent upon the idea in the subordinate clause, there is no comma. For example, the idea of the main clause—the opening clause—in the following sentence will be realized only if the idea in the subordinate clause is carried out; thus, the main clause depends on the *if* clause:

I'll go to Sue's party if you promise to be there.

But in the next sentence the subordinate clause does not affect the fulfillment of the main clause:

I'm going to the party at Sue's on Saturday night, even though I know I'll be bored.

In general, clauses introduced by *even though* and *although* are preceded by commas; those introduced by *if* and *because* are not. The use of the final subordinate clause is probably one of the least standardized of our punctuation rules. This is one situation where you can use your voice to help you decide about punctuation; if you put extra stress on the last word in the main clause, or if you detect a slight change in the pitch of your voice at the end of the main clause, you probably need a comma.

EXERCISE 24

Combine each of the following groups of sentences into a single sentence by using subordination. In some cases you will want to reword the sentence. Remember that the subordinator you select will signal the relationship between the two ideas. You can probably come up with more than one possibility for each.

1. The famous Gateway Arch is in St. Louis.
   Kansas City claims the title "Gateway to the West."
2. Our spring semester doesn't end until the second week of June.
   Many students have a hard time finding summer jobs.
3. Thomas Jefferson acquired the Ozark Mountains for the United States in 1803.
   That was the year of the Louisiana Purchase.
   We bought the Louisiana Territory from Napoleon.
4. What is called the Snake River Country includes nine million acres.
   It includes small parts of Montana, Wyoming, Oregon, and Washington.
   Its nine million acres take in almost the entire state of Idaho.
5. The neighbors added a pit bull to their pet population, which now numbers three unfriendly four-legged creatures.
   We have decided to fence in our back yard.
6. The human circulatory system is a marvel of efficiency.
   It is still subject to a wide variety of degenerative diseases.
7. Carbohydrates—starches—are the body's prime source of energy.
   Fad diets that severely restrict the intake of starches are nearly always ineffective.
   Such diets can also be dangerous.

8. Our congressman knows that the majority of voters in this district are upset with their tax rates.
   They also don't like the way their tax dollars are being spent.
   He has made "No New Taxes" the main theme of his reelection campaign.
9. Auto companies offered enticing cash rebates to buyers of new cars last January.
   Car sales increased dramatically.
10. By 1890 the buffalo population of the West had been nearly wiped out.
    It now numbers about 60,000.
    About 400 ranchers in Colorado are raising buffalo for meat.

Elliptical Subordinate Clauses

One common variation of the subordinate clause is the **elliptical clause,** one in which something is deleted. Elliptical clauses introduced by the "time" connectors *while* and *when* are especially common:

> While waiting for the bus, we saw the police arrest a pickpocket at the edge of the crowd.
> When stripped of its trees, the land becomes inhospitable.

Here the deletions of the subject and part of the verb have produced tighter structures, and there is certainly no problem in interpreting the meaning. The understood subject in the elliptical clause is also the subject of the main clause:

> While we were waiting for the bus
> When the land is stripped of its trees

This feature of elliptical clauses—let's call it a "rule"—is an important one for the writer to recognize:

> The subject of the main clause is always the understood subject of the elliptical clause as well.

This rule simply reflects the interpretation that the reader expects. Unfortunately, it is not always followed. Note what has happened in the following sentence:

> *While waiting for the bus, the police arrested a pickpocket at the edge of the crowd.

This sentence reports—no doubt inadvertently—that it is the police who were waiting for the bus. We call that a "dangling" elliptical clause. The writer should not expect the reader to give the sentence any other interpretation.

Quite often the sentence with a dangling clause or phrase offers no problem of understanding; the writer's intention is clear. Nevertheless, the reader may hesitate or feel uneasy or be aware of a problem with the connection:

> *While at the shopping center yesterday, mobs of people were exchanging Christmas presents.

There's certainly no problem of interpretation here, but there is a kind of fuzziness. The use of *while* suggests that the speaker or writer was at the shopping center; it sets up a certain expectation in the reader of what the subject of the main clause will be. The sentence that follows clearly thwarts that expectation. One way to correct the problem is to write out the subordinate clause in full:

> While I was at the shopping center yesterday . . .

Another way, which would be equally effective, would be to delete the subordinator, thus turning that opening elliptical clause into a prepositional phrase, a straight adverbial of place:

> At the shopping center yesterday, mobs of people were exchanging Christmas presents.

This version eliminates the stated presence of the writer, changing the point of view somewhat but retaining the content.

The problem of dangling also occurs in prepositional phrases that have verbs or verb phrases as objects:

> *Since <u>leaving school</u>, good jobs have not been easy to find.
> *Before <u>going to class this morning</u>, the bookstore was crowded.

These phrases are almost identical to the elliptical subordinate clauses. The only difference is that they cannot be expanded to full clauses simply by adding a subject; they would also require a change in the form of the verb:

> Since I left school . . .
> Before I went to class . . .

Nevertheless, the underlying clausal meaning is clear, and the same rule applies: The subject of the main clause is also the subject of the verb in the prepositional phrase. Without that subject–verb relationship, the phrase is dangling.

In introductory position the dangling clause or verb phrase is fairly obvious, once you've been made aware of the problem. However, when the dangling phrase or clause closes the sentence, its "dangling" nature is not as noticeable:

*Jobs have not been easy to find since leaving school.
*The subway is better than the bus when late for work.

Here the reader gets to the end of the main clause with no unfulfilled expectations and can simply supply a subject for that ending adverbial from the context. Even though the dangling may not be as obvious, the problem of fuzziness remains. It's the kind of sentence that careful writers avoid.

The Elliptical Clause of Comparison. The elliptical clause of comparison is different from the other elliptical clauses in that only the elliptical version is grammatical:

I'm a week older than Terry [is old].
My sister isn't as tall as I [am tall].
or
I'm a week older than Terry *is* [old].
My sister isn't as tall as I *am* [tall].

Recognizing such comparisons as clauses will help you understand why it is nonstandard to use *me* in such sentences:

*My sister isn't as tall as me.
*My roommate doesn't work as hard as me.

In standard, formal usage the pronoun will be in the subjective case, not the objective, because it is the subject of the underlying elliptical clause:

My roommate doesn't work as hard as I work.

Sometimes writers and speakers make mistakes with *like* as well as with *as*. But *like* is different from *as:* It does not always introduce a clause; in fact, it's more likely to be a preposition and thus take the objective case:

My sister looks like me.
The picture in the paper looks like him.

In these two sentences there is no underlying clause. But in the following sentences, *like* introduces an elliptical clause:

She plays the violin like a professional.
He throws a fast ball just like Greg Maddux.

In these sentences there is an underlying clause:

She plays the violin like a professional plays the violin.
He throws a fast ball just like Greg Maddux throws a fast ball.

The ellipses in such comparisons can produce ambiguity when the main clause has more than one possible noun phrase for the subordinate clause to be compared with:

> Joe likes Tracy better than Pat.
> The University of Nevada–Las Vegas beat Fresno State worse than Arizona.

In these sentences we don't know if the comparison is between subjects or objects because we don't know what has been left out. We don't know whether

> Joe likes Tracy better than Pat [*likes Tracy*].
> or
> Joe likes Tracy better than [Joe likes] *Pat.*

And we don't know whether

> UNLV beat Fresno State worse than [UNLV beat] Arizona
> or
> UNLV beat Fresno State worse than Arizona [beat Fresno State].

These elliptical clauses of comparison are especially tricky. Always look them over carefully to make sure you haven't misled your reader.

For Group Discussion

1. Using your understanding of elliptical clauses, explain how it's possible for both of the following sentences to be grammatical:
   My little sister likes our cat better than me.
   My little sister likes our cat better than I.
2. The following sentences are both illogical and ungrammatical. Explain the source of the problem.
   *The summer temperatures in the Santa Clara Valley are much higher than San Francisco.
   *The Pirates' stolen base record is much better than the Twins.

EXERCISE 25

Rewrite the following sentences to eliminate the dangling elliptical clauses and prepositional phrases. In some cases you may want to complete the clause; in others you may want to include its information in a different form.

1. Before mixing in the dry ingredients, the flour should be sifted.

2. Lightning flashed constantly on the horizon while driving across the desert toward Cheyenne.
3. There was no doubt the suspect was guilty after finding his fingerprints at the scene of the crime.
4. While waiting for the guests to arrive, there were a lot of last-minute details to take care of.
5. If handed in late, your grade on the term project will be lowered 10 percent.
6. After filling the garage with lawn furniture, there was no room left for the car.
7. While collecting money for the Women's Resource Center, the generosity of strangers simply amazed me.
8. The employees in our company who smoke now have to go outside of the building during their breaks if they want a cigarette, since putting the smoking ban into effect a month ago.
9. When revising and editing your papers, it is important to read the sentences aloud and listen to the stress pattern.
10. Your sentences will be greatly improved by eliminating dangling phrases and clauses.

Infinitive (Verb) Phrases

Another adverbial form in the list of sample sentences at the opening of the chapter—in addition to the adverbs, prepositional phrases, and subordinate clauses—is the **infinitive** phrase:

> I got up early this morning <u>to study for my Spanish test</u>.

The infinitive is usually easy to recognize: the base form, or present tense, of the verb preceded by *to*, sometimes called "the sign of the infinitive." "Infinitive," in fact, is often the label, or name, we use when we discuss a verb. For example, we might refer to "the verb *to go*" or "the verb *to have*."

The problem of "dangling" that comes up with the elliptical subordinate clause also applies to the adverbial infinitive phrase. As with other verbs, the infinitive needs a subject; the reader assumes that its subject will be the subject of the main clause, as it was in the earlier example:

> I got up early to study for my Spanish test.

Here *I* is the subject of *study* as well as of *got up*. When the subject of the infinitive is not in its expected place, the infinitive dangles:

> *<u>To keep your grades up</u>, a regular study schedule is important.

*For decades the Superstition Mountains in Arizona have been explored in order to find the fabled Lost Dutchman Mine.

Certainly the problem with these sentences is not a problem of communication; the reader is not likely to misinterpret their meaning. But in both cases a kind of fuzziness exists that can be cleared up with the addition of a subject for the infinitive:

To keep your grades up, you ought to follow a regular study schedule.
For decades people [or adventurers or prospectors] have explored the Superstition Mountains in Arizona to find the fabled Lost Dutchman Mine.

The dangling infinitive, which is fairly obvious at the beginning of the sentence, is not quite so obvious at the end, but the sentence is equally fuzzy:

*A regular study schedule is important to keep your grades up.

Two rules will help you use infinitives effectively:

The subject of the adverbial infinitive is also the subject of the sentence or clause in which the infinitive appears.

An infinitive phrase that opens the sentence is always set off by a comma.

The punctuation rule does not apply to adverbial infinitives in closing position; in fact, the opposite is generally true: A comma will rarely be called for when the infinitive closes the sentence.

And, as with other adverbials, it's possible to insert the adverbial infinitive in an almost parenthetical way, in which case commas—or even dashes—would be called for:

According to nutritionists, dieting, to have lasting effects, should be undertaken as a lifelong program of sensible eating habits.

Movability and Closure

The movability of adverbials, which enables us to vary our sentences and to change their emphasis, includes a risk for the unwary writer—the risk of losing the reader. As readers, we expect verbs to follow subjects, complements of various kinds to follow verbs, and adverbial phrases and clauses to open or close the sentence. Deviation from that norm comes as a surprise. As writers, we like to include surprises from time to time, but when we do, we should do so for a reason—and within reason.

In the discussion of movable adverbial clauses, we saw two examples in which the placement of the clause changed the stress pattern of the sentence. Here is one of them:

My brother, <u>when he was only four years old</u>, actually drove the family car for about a block.

In spite of the interruption of normal word order, the sentence is short and direct enough for the reader to recognize where it is headed and to experience a sense of closure, or completion. The reader experiences a beginning, a middle, and an end. Given a more complex interrupter, however, the reader is likely to be confused:

My brother, when he was only four years old and so short that all we could see were two small hands holding on to the steering wheel and a tuft of blonde hair, actually drove the family car for about a block.

Here the detour of that interrupting clause takes us too far from the path; we don't have enough information to know where we're headed. And when we do finally get back to our original clause, we've forgotten where we started. We have had to keep too many ideas on hold. Before we can experience a sense of closure, we have to go back to reconsider the opening of the clause. This is the kind of a sentence that produces an "awk" in the margin—when the reader happens to be your English teacher.

EXERCISE 26

(1) Underline all of the adverbial structures in the following sentences. (2) Identify the form of each: adverb, noun (or noun phrase), prepositional phrase, verb phrase, or subordinate clause. (3) Identify the kind of information it provides: time, frequency, duration, place, reason, manner, condition.

1. To save money, I often eat lunch at my desk.
2. After breakfast let's take the bus to the shopping center.
3. After my dad retired from the navy, he started his own business.
4. We furiously cleaned house to get ready for the party.
5. As soon as the guests left, we collapsed in a heap on the couch.
6. The legislature held a special session last week to consider a new tax bill.
7. When October came, the tourists left.
8. Victoria was crowned queen of England when she was only eighteen years old.
9. African killer bees are slowly making their way northward.
10. At last report, they had reached the southern border of Texas.
11. We stayed home last night because of the snowstorm.
12. If there is no further business, the meeting stands adjourned.

For further practice with adverbials, change the form of the adverbial while retaining the information.

For Group Discussion

Select a passage from an essay you have written or one you are currently working on. Note the various adverbials that open and close your sentences. What forms have you used? Do your opening adverbials, if any, provide a bridge of known information or provide transition by orienting the reader in terms of time or location or reason? If none of your sentences have opening adverbials, consider whether any might be more effective if they did.

The Adverbials of Emphasis

As we have seen, the adverbials are versatile structures. They provide their information of time, place, manner, and the like in a variety of shapes; and they give the writer special flexibility because they can fill so many different slots—at the beginning, the middle, and the end of sentences. But there's another group of adverbials, mainly single-word adverbs, whose purpose is to emphasize a particular structure and thus control the pace and rhythm of the sentence.

Read the following sentences and note where you apply the main stress:

> I hardly slept last night.
> I slept hardly at all last night.
> My roommate also had trouble sleeping.
> Some people are always looking for trouble.
> Joe tells me that he rarely stays awake past midnight.
> The country has never before faced the kind of crisis it faces with AIDS.
> Scientists will surely find a cure for AIDS before long.
> Many people assumed that by now the mystery of AIDS would have been solved.

You probably put the emphasis on *hardly*, *all*, *also*, *always*, *rarely*, *never before*, *surely*, and *by now*.

Given these examples, you can think of other words that you use for emphasis: other negatives, such as *seldom*, *barely*, *scarcely*; other time and frequency words, such as *afterwards*, *finally*, *sometimes*; and others expressing duration, such as *already*, *no longer*, *still*.

It's possible, of course, to write sentences in which these words would not have main stress, where the principle of end focus, for example, would still be in effect. But certainly these are words that you, as a writer, need to recognize; they often wield the power in a sentence, controlling its intonation contour and making a difference in the message.

The Common *Only*

One of our most versatile—but also most frequently misused—adverbials of emphasis is the common *only*. Like other emphasizers, *only* can change the focus of the sentence by directing the reader's attention to a particular word:

> I'm taking only twelve credits this semester.
> The car only looks old; it's really quite new.
> Joe isn't only handsome; he's rich too.
> Paul cleans house only on Saturdays.

When you read these sentences you'll find yourself putting nearly equal emphasis on both *only* and the word that follows it.

But there's also a common problem with *only;* It's frequently misplaced—and most of the time we don't even notice!

> I'm only taking twelve credits this semester.
> Paul only cleans house on Saturdays.
> We're only going to be gone for two or three days.
> Jane refuses to watch the Super Bowl; she only likes baseball.

Even song writers get it wrong:

> I only have eyes for you.

A well-placed *only* can strengthen the sentence focus. It sends a message to the reader that the writer has crafted the sentence carefully.

The Qualifiers

In the description of parts of speech in Chapter 4, we divided the words of our language into two general classes: the form classes and the structure classes. **Qualifiers** belong with the structure classes. They qualify or intensify adverbs and adjectives, so their function is actually different from that of the adverbials. We will look at them here in connection with adverbials because their effect is much like that of the adverbials of emphasis.

Among the most common words that qualify adjectives and adverbs are *very*, *quite*, *rather*, *too*, *still*, *even*, *much*, and *fairly*. Some adverbs of manner, the *-ly* adverbs, are themselves used as qualifiers with certain adjectives: *dangerously* close, *particularly* harmful, *absolutely* true. Qualifiers give writers few problems unless they overuse them. (One of the most overused in both speech and writing is *really*.) Experienced writers take special care in choosing a word with a precise shade of meaning, so a qualifier or intensifier may not be necessary. For example, instead of describing a person as "really nice" or "very nice" or "very beautiful," the experienced writer might say "cooperative" or "charming" or "lovely" or "stunning." The inexperienced writer might describe someone as "walking very fast," where the experienced writer would say "hurried" or "dashed" or "bolted." In most cases the difference is not a matter of knowing "big" words or unusual words. The difference is a matter of precision, of choosing words carefully. Such precision, even in small details, can make a difference in the overall effect on the reader.

One further caveat concerns the use of qualifiers with certain adjectives that have "absolute" meanings. Careful writers try to avoid *very* with *perfect* or *unique* or *round*. Although we might say "absolutely perfect" to emphasize the perfection, to say "very perfect" would probably have a negative effect on the reader. And certainly as careful users of language we should respect the meaning of *unique:* "one of a kind." *Round* and *square* have meanings in our lexicon other than their geometric absolutes, so it is possible for the shape of an object to be "nearly round" or "almost square" But qualifiers such as *very* or *quite* are best reserved for other kinds of qualities.

EXERCISE 27

As you read the following sentences, pay particular attention to the italicized words; replace them with words that are more precise.

1. Ben was so *very careful* about his wardrobe, he had his ties pressed after every wearing.
2. The guest speaker's *really strong* denunciation of our foreign policy seemed *quite out of place* at the awards banquet.
3. The foreman gives his orders in a *very abrupt* way.
4. To me, the tropical garden is the most *intriguing* display in the conservatory. *Completely covered* with orchids and vines, the towering palm trees and *really unusual* large-leafed plants seem to belong in a fairy tale.
5. It is usually *an absolute waste of time* to argue with radicals of any persuasion; they are unlikely to be influenced by mere reason.
6. Our host's *overly enthusiastic* welcome embarrassed me: First he kissed me on both cheeks; then he bowed and kissed my hand.
7. The basketball players seemed *really tired* as they took the court for the second half.
8. Our history teacher was *extremely upset* when he discovered that almost half the class had cheated on the midterm exam.
9. The choir members were *really excited* about their summer trip to Europe.
10. The members of Congress were *really very surprised* at the extent of voter cynicism toward Washington.

Rhetorical Reminders

Placement of Adverbials

Have I considered transition and cohesion and the known/new contract in using adverbials?

Do my opening subordinate clauses contain the known information?

Proliferating Prepositions

Have I avoided strings of prepositional phrases that obscure the focus of the sentence and add no new information?

Understood Subjects

Is the understood subject in every elliptical clause also the subject of the main clause?

Is the subject of every adverbial infinitive also the subject of the main clause?

Emphasis

Have I paid attention to the power of adverbs to change the sentence stress?

Word choice

Have I selected modifiers with precise meanings so that such qualifiers as *very* and *really* may not be necessary?

PUNCTUATION REMINDERS

Set off a subordinate clause that opens the sentence with a comma.
Set off an infinitive phrase that opens the sentence with a comma.

Chapter 8

The Texture of Noun Phrases

Fiction writers know the importance of "texture"—those telling details that enable the reader to picture the people and places and events in the writer's imagination:

> The fairgrounds weren't crowded this early on opening day. Except for the carousel, most of the midway rides and game booths weren't set up yet. But the freshly painted dairy barns sparkled white in the sunshine, the stalls had been draped with colored bunting and decorated with cedar boughs and wildflowers in sap pails, and as the farmer moved quietly along the aisles with hay and grain and wheelbarrows carrying out manure, there was an anticipatory, festive air about the scene that reminded me of Christmas.
>
> —Howard Frank Mosher, *Northern Borders*

> She was back at her board, ironing, when she heard feet sucking in the mud of the back yard.
>
> —Richard Wright, *Bright and Morning Star*

> Now the days were shorter and colder, and the trees emptied oceans of leaves on the lawn but remained, somehow, as full as ever, so you'd finish raking and look upward to see a great wash of orange and yellow just waiting to cover the grass again the minute your back was turned.
>
> —Anne Tyler, *The Accidental Tourist*

Some of those details are provided by the adverbials, as we saw in Chapter 7—structures of various forms that add information of time and place and reason and manner. This chapter describes another source of texture—modifiers in the noun phrase: ***adjectivals.***

The Adjectival Slots

In Chapter 1 we described the sentence as a series of slots. It can be useful to think of the noun phrase in this way too: the headword noun as the central, pivotal slot, with the various structures that function as adjectivals in the slots before and after it:

determiner adjective noun NOUN prepositional phrase verb phrase clause

In most noun phrases the first slot is occupied by the determiner, the noun signaler—words like *the* and *a* and *my*; the other slots are ordered in a very systematic away, with single word modifiers—adjectives and nouns—before the headword, phrases and clauses following it.

a strange **experience**
(det.) (adjective)
those city **folks**
(det.) (noun)
my **friend** from Little Rock
(det.) (prepositional phrase)
a great **wash** of orange and yellow
(det.) (adj.) (prepositional phrase)
an **aquarium** filled with exotic fish
(det.) (verb [participial] phrase)
an anticipatory, festive **air** that reminded me of Christmas
(adj.) (adj.) (clause)

When we have multiple adjectivals in a noun phrase—and we often do—they appear in that order:

the lovely rose **gardens** in Portland
(det.) (adj.) (noun) (prep. phrase)
my **uncle** from Minnesota, who loves cold weather
(det.) (prep. phrase) (clause)
a strong, sensitive **album** recorded by Tracy Chapman
(det.) (adj.) (adj.) (verb phrase)

We can even fill all the slots at once:

an exciting new spy **novel** about international drug dealers
(det.) (adj.) (adj.) (noun) (prep. phrase)
written by John Thomchick, which has been praised by the reviewers
(verb phrase) (clause)

It's important to remember that we're looking at the noun phrase in all of its functions, not just in its role as subject. As you recall from Chapter 1, noun phrases also fill the direct object, indirect object, objective complement, and subjective complement slots in the sentence patterns; another common function for the noun phrase is in the prepositional phrase, the object of the preposition. You can see, then, that noun phrases provide a great many opportunities for the writer to add texture to sentences.

In the following sections we will look briefly at each of the forms that fill the adjectival slots: determiners, adjectives, nouns, prepositional phrases, verb phrases, and clauses.

Determiners

Most nouns require a **determiner,** the noun signaler that occupies the opening slot in the noun phrase. The determiner class includes articles, possessive nouns, possessive pronouns, demonstrative pronouns, and numbers, as well as a variety of other common words. In both speech and writing you select most determiners automatically. But sometimes in your writing you will want to give that selection deliberate thought.

As the first word in the noun phrase, and thus frequently the first word of the sentence and even of the paragraph, the determiner can provide a bridge between ideas. The selection of that bridge can make subtle but important differences in emphasis, providing transition for the reader—and it can certainly change the rhythm of the sentence:

> <u>The</u> decision that Ben made was the right one.
> <u>That</u> decision of Ben's was the right one.
> <u>Ben's</u> decision was the right one.
> <u>Every such</u> decision Ben made . . .
> <u>His</u> decision . . .
> <u>Such a</u> decision might have been questionable . . .
> <u>A</u> decision like that . . .

In selecting determiners, then, writers have the opportunity to make subtle distinctions and to help their readers move easily from one idea to the next in a meaningful way.

For Group Discussion

In Chapter 4 we looked briefly at the semantic features of nouns that regulate our selection of determiners. For example, the indefinite article, *a*, signals only countable nouns, while the definite *the* can signal both countables and noncountables. Another difference between them is connected to new and known information. Only at a noun's first mention do we use the indefinite *a* (or *some*); subsequent references take *the* or another definitive determiner (*this, that, these, those, his,* etc.).

All of the determiners are missing from the following passages. Add them to all the nouns that need them. You'll discover, when you compare your versions with those of your classmates, that for some nouns there are choices—not only a choice of determiner but in some cases a choice of whether or not to use a determiner.

A. Dorothy was little girl who lived on farm in Kansas. Tornado struck farm and carried her over rainbow to land of Munchkins. Soon afterwards she met scarecrow who wanted brain, tin man who wanted heart, and lion who wanted courage. On way to Emerald City four friends met wicked witch who cast spell on them in field of flowers. Witch wanted magic shoes that Dorothy was wearing. When they reached city, as you recall, they met wizard. Story has happy ending.

B. Planet has wrong name. Ancestors named it Earth, after land they found all around them. So far as they thought about planet as whole, they believed for centuries that surface consisted almost entirely of rocks and soil, except for smallish bodies of water like Mediterranean Sea and Black Sea. They knew about Atlantic, of course, but they regarded it as relatively narrow river running around rim of world. If ancients had known what earth was really like they undoubtedly would have named it Ocean after tremendous areas of water that cover 70.8 percent of surface.

—adapted from *The Sea* (Time-Life Books)

There were several nouns in those passages that you left bare, without determiners. Why? How do their semantic features differ from the nouns that needed them? In how many cases did you have a choice of adding a determiner or not?

Does your use of *a* and *some* coincide with the earlier description of indefinite determiners for new information and definite determiners for known information?

Adjectives and Nouns

Adjectives and nouns fill the slots between the determiner and the headword. When the noun phrase includes both, they appear in that order:

DETERMINER	*ADJECTIVE*	*NOUN*	*HEADWORD*
a	dismal	weather	forecast
the	new	pizza	shop
an	important		decision
my		career	decision
your	important	career	decision

The adjective slot frequently includes more than one adjective modifying the headword:

a covert military operation

an unusual financial arrangement

You'll notice that there are no commas in the preceding noun phrases, even though there are several modifiers in a row. But sometimes commas are called for. A good rule of thumb is to use a comma if it's possible to insert *and* between the modifiers. We would not say "a covert and military operation" or "an unusual and financial arrangement." However, we would say "an exciting and innovative concept," so in writing that phrase without *and*, we would use a comma:

an exciting, innovative concept
an anticipatory, festive air

In general, our punctuation system calls for a comma between two adjectives when they are of the same class—for instance, when they are both subjective qualities like "festive" and "exciting" and "innovative." However, in the adjective phrases we saw without commas—*covert military operation* and *unusual financial arrangement*—the two adjectives in each pair are different kinds of qualities. The easiest way to decide on punctuation is to remember *and:*

Use a comma between prenoun modifiers if it's possible to use *and*.

Sometimes prenoun modifiers are themselves modified or qualified:

a highly unusual situation

a really important decision

When the first modifier is an *-ly* adverb, as in these two examples, we do not connect it with a hyphen. With other adverbs, however, and with nouns and adjectives as modifiers, we do use a hyphen for these prenoun compound modifiers:

the English-speaking world
a four-door minivan

Here the hyphen makes clear that *English* modifies *speaking* rather than *world* and that *four* modifies *door*, not *minivan*.

Here are some other examples of hyphens with prenoun modifiers:

a problem-solving approach
a poor inner-city neighborhood

a fuel-injected engine

a bases-loaded home run

a small-town high school teacher

a well-developed paragraph

a fast-moving train

Another occasion for hyphens in preheadword position occurs when we use a complete phrase in the adjective slot:

an off-the-wall idea

the end-of-the-term party

a middle-of-the-road policy

Modifier Noun Proliferation. There's a pitfall for writers in this system of prenoun modifiers: the temptation to string together too many adjectives and/or nouns. It's easy to do. For example, the curriculum committee of the faculty is known as the "faculty curriculum committee." And when the committee meets, it has a "faculty curriculum committee meeting." The minutes of that meeting then become the "faculty curriculum committee meeting minutes." And so on. Such strings are not ungrammatical, but they easily become unreadable.

You can make such noun phrases somewhat easier to read by using an "of" phrase in place of the last modifier in the string:

a meeting of the faculty curriculum committee

the minutes of the curriculum committee meeting

EXERCISE 28

Punctuate the prenoun modifiers in the following sentences with commas and hyphens, if needed. Remember the rule about commas: If you can add *and*, you probably need a comma.

1. The administration's recent clean air proposals have been criticized as inadequate.
2. A high ranking federal employee testified at the hearing on Monday.
3. The stock market reached an all time high last week.
4. There was a splendid old table for sale at the auction.
5. I spoke to a witty delightful man in the cafeteria.
6. A big yellow delivery truck is blocking the driveway.
7. There was not enough fire fighting equipment available this summer for the widespread devastating forest fires in the Northwest.

8. I found an expensive looking copper colored bracelet in the locker room.
9. A commonly held notion among my cynical friends is that big business lobbyists run the country.
10. I have back to back exams on Wednesday.
11. The highly publicized long awaited paper recycling program has finally become a reality on our campus this fall.
12. The British royal family continues to make front page news. According to the London *Daily Mail,* Prince Charles remains a dutiful monarch in waiting despite the revelations of a tell all authorized biography in which he reveals his unhappy childhood and unhappy marriage. Some reviewers have found these extremely personal revelations quite distateful and decidedly unroyal.

The Movable Adjective Phrase. Before looking at the slots that follow the headword, we should note variations in our use of adjectives when they are modified (with a qualifier like *very* or an intensifying adverb like *highly* or *extremely*) or compounded (with a word like *and*). Such expanded adjectives, or adjective phrases, can be shifted either to the slot following the headword or, if the noun phrase being modified is the subject, to the opening position in the sentence:

> Hot and tired, the Boy Scouts trudged the last mile to their campsite.
> The Boy Scouts, hot and tired, trudged the last mile to their campsite.

Both of these variations put added emphasis on the subject slot. The subject would not have that emphasis if the adjectives had stayed in their preheadword position:

> The hot, tired Boy Scouts trudged the last mile to their campsite.

Here's a sentence with the qualified adjective we saw earlier shifted from its preheadword home-base position:

> Highly unusual, the situation called for extraordinary measures.
> The situation, highly unusual, called for extraordinary measures.

Again, you'll notice how this order changes the rhythm.

Prepositional Phrases

The adjectival prepositional phrase, which follows the headword noun, is identical in form to the adverbial prepositional phrase we saw in Chapter 7. In its adjectival role the prepositional phrase identifies the noun headword in relation to time, place, direction, origin, and other such details:

> The people across the hall rarely speak to me.

The security guard in our building knows every tenant personally.
We had delicious fish and chips at the new seafood restaurant near the marina.
The meeting during our lunch hour was a waste of time.
Jack is a man of many talents.
Ed finally found an occasion to meet that beautiful girl in our math class with the long red hair.

Because prepositional phrases are so common, both as adverbials and as adjectivals, they can easily get out of hand. In Chapter 7, you may recall, we pointed out the problem of the proliferating prepositional phrase: the tendency for writers to string them together. Such proliferation can easily obscure the sentence focus. One of the examples in that discussion included a string of four adjectival prepositional phrases at the end of the sentence:

You can undoubtedly find many such sentences in the *pages* of this book about the grammar of English for writers.

The last three of those four prepositional phrases are not only unnecessary, they obscure the focus of the sentence, which was intended to be on "this book." Those three superfluous phrases add nothing but words—no new information at all.

In place of certain adjectival prepositional phrases, the writer may have the option of using a prenoun modifier:

an elderly lady with white hair = an elderly white-haired lady

the old gentleman with the beard = the old bearded gentleman

guests for dinner = dinner guests

the soliloquy in the second act = the second-act soliloquy

the problems with the budget = the budget problems

a friend of Amy's = Amy's friend

the final exam in calculus = the calculus final

And sometimes revision may be just a matter of choosing a more precise word:

a bunch of flowers = a bouquet

the main character of the story = the protagonist

birds that fly south in the winter = migratory birds

Participial Phrases

One of our most versatile adjectivals is the **participial phrase,** a verb phrase headed by the *-ing* or the *-en* form of the verb, known as a **participle.** The noun being modified is the subject of the participle:

The **helicopter** hovering over the roof frightened the dogs.
The **man** sitting by the window is talking to himself.
We were shocked to see all the homeless **people** living on the streets of Los Angeles.

You'll notice that these noun phrases with participial modifiers resemble sentences; the only thing missing is an auxiliary:

the helicopter [is] hovering over the roof

the man [is] sitting by the window

the homeless people [are] living on the streets of Los Angeles

In other words, the noun and the participle that modifies it have a subject—verb relationship. This is an important feature of participial phrases for you to understand, as you will see later in the discussion of dangling participles.

Why do we use participles? Like adjectives and prepositional phrases, participles add information about the noun headword; and because they are verb phrases in form, they add a whole verbal idea, just as the predicate does. In the first example, the subject, *helicopter,* is the subject of two verb phrases: *hovering over the roof* and *frightened the dogs*. The two verb phrases could have been expressed with a compound predicate:

The helicopter hovered over the roof and frightened the dogs.

or with a main clause and a subordinate clause:

The helicopter frightened the dogs as it hovered over the roof.

The participial phrase, however, allows the writer to include both verbal ideas in a more concise way.

Even more important than conciseness is the clear focus of the sentence with a single predicating verb. Here again is one of the sample participles expanded to a full predicate:

The man is sitting by the window; he is talking to himself.
The man is sitting by the window and talking to himself.

In neither of these compound structures is there a clear focus; the result is a kind of flatness or flabbiness. In most contexts a sentence that combines the two ideas in a focused way will be more effective. The idea that should get the main focus will, of course, depend on the context:

What is that noise I hear? The man sitting by the window is talking to himself.

Punctuation of Participial Phrases. The punctuation of a participial phrase depends on its purpose: Does it define the headword or simply comment on it? In other words, does the modifier provide information that is necessary for identifying the referent of the noun?

> The merchants holding the sidewalk sales are hoping for good weather.

Which merchants are we talking about? We wouldn't know without the modifier. Which man is talking to himself?

> The man sitting by the window is talking to himself.

In both of these sentences the purpose of the participial phrase is to make the referent of the noun clear, to define it. You'll notice that the modifier is not set off by commas. We call this a **restrictive modifier:** It restricts the meaning of the noun. In the previous examples, we are restricting the meaning of the words *merchants* and *man* to a particular group or individual that the reader or listener can then identify.

But not all participial phrases are restrictive: Sometimes the referent of the noun is already identified, so a modifier isn't necessary. In such cases, the purpose of the modifier is simply to comment on or to add information about the noun, not to define it. Such modifiers are called **nonrestrictive modifiers:**

> My mother, sitting by the window, is talking to herself.

In this sentence the noun phrase *my mother* is already specific; it has only one possible referent. *Sitting by the window* simply adds a detail of information; its purpose is not the same as in the earlier sentence:

> The man sitting by the window is talking to himself.

Here the participle tells "which man." In the sentence about mother, however, it's not "which mother."

To hear the difference between restrictive and nonrestrictive modifiers, you have only to listen to the sound of your voice when you say them aloud:

> The man sitting by the window is talking to himself.
> My mother, sitting by the window, is talking to herself.

The sentence stress is different. In the first one, the main stress is on *window;* the pitch of your voice rises until it gets to *window,* then falls, in one intonation contour.

> The man sitting by the window is talking to himself.

In the sentence with commas, you'll notice not just one but three patterns, each with a point of stress, probably falling on *mother, window,* and *talking,* with the main focus on the last one.

My mother, sitting by the window, is talking to herself.

Incidentally, if the "mother" sentence sounds strange when you say it, don't be surprised: We rarely use nonrestrictive participial phrases in our speech. In answer to the question "What's that noise I hear?" we'd be most likely to answer, "My mother is talking to herself; she's over there by the window."

You can use this difference in the intonation of the two kinds of modifiers to good advantage. Listen to your sentences after you've written them down; don't include any unwanted implications. For example, read this one without commas:

> My mother sitting by the window is talking to herself.

If you read that sentence with one intonation pattern, with the main stress on *window,* you are implying the existence of another mother, one who is not sitting by the window talking to herself. To write it that way may not mislead your readers—they'll know better than to assume you have multiple mothers—but the error will be obvious.

Here's another sentence to read aloud and listen to:

> My sister living in Atlanta just called.

To say or write this as it is punctuated is to imply the existence of another sister, one who does not live in Atlanta. In other words, if the writer has more than one sister, the modifier *living in Atlanta* is there to define the referent of the noun phrase *my sister.* But if there is no second sister, then the writer has sent an incorrect message to the reader. The modifier needs to be set off by commas.

The participial phrase following a general noun such as *man* (as opposed to a specific noun like *mother*) is not always restrictive; if the reader already knows which man, the purpose of the modifier is different:

> The park was deserted except for a young couple near the fountain. The man, holding an umbrella and a briefcase, looked impatient as he shifted his weight from one foot to the other.

Here the purpose of the participial phrase is not to identify, or define, which man. The reader knows that the man being referred to in the second sentence is the one already mentioned in the first; he's half of the couple. Read the passage without putting in the commas, and you'll be aware of an unwanted implication.

The question to ask yourself about punctuation, then, is related to the purpose of the modifier: Is it simply a comment about the noun, or is it there to identify the referent of the noun?

> Use commas around a nonrestrictive modifier when the modifier is only commenting on the noun rather than defining it—when the reader already knows the referent or if there is only one possible referent.

EXERCISE 29

Decide whether the participial phrases in the following sentences are restrictive (defining) or nonrestrictive (commenting) and punctuate them accordingly.

1. Many coal miners in West Virginia refused to approve two sections of the contract offered by management last week. They maintain that the two sections covering wages and safety represent no improvement over their present contract expiring on Friday at midnight.
2. Franklin Delano Roosevelt took office at a time when the outlook for the nation was bleak indeed. The president elected in 1932 faced decisions that would have overwhelmed the average man.
3. A group of students held a protest rally in front of the administration building yesterday. The students hoping for a meeting with the provost were demonstrating against the tuition hike recently approved by the trustees. The increase expected to take effect in September will raise tuition almost 15 percent.
4. The senator and his wife sitting next to him on the speaker's platform both looked calm as they waited for the mayor to finish the introduction. Then the mayor turning to look directly at the senator shocked both the audience and the listeners on the platform.

The Movable Participle. We can think of the slot following the headword in the noun phrase as the "home base" of the participial phrase, as it is of the adjectival prepositional phrase. Unlike the prepositional phrase, however, the participial phrase can shift to the beginning of the sentence—*but only if it modifies the subject and if it is nonrestrictive:*

Sitting by the window, my mother was talking to herself.
Carrying all of their supplies, the Boy Scouts trudged up the mountain in search of a campsite.
Laughing uproariously, the audience stood and applauded.
Shifting his weight from one foot to the other, the man looked impatient as he waited by the fountain.

Only those participial phrases that are set off by commas can undergo this shift—that is, only those that are nonrestrictive.

That same participial phrase—the nonrestrictive phrase that modifies the subject—can also come at the end of the sentence, especially if the sentence is fairly short:

> The Boy Scouts trudged up the mountain in search of a campsite, carrying all of their supplies on their backs.
> The audience stood and applauded, laughing uproariously.
> The man looked impatient as he waited by the fountain, shifting his weight from one foot to the other.

The reason for choosing one position over another has to do with sentence rhythm and focus. At the end of the sentence the participle gets much more attention than it would at the beginning or in the home-base position.

There is one oddity about the nonrestrictive participle; it is different from other nonrestrictive modifiers in being limited to the subject. Even at the end of the sentence, the participial phrase that is set off by commas modifies the subject of the sentence; it doesn't modify a noun in the predicate. For example, consider the following sentences:

> Bill washed the car standing in the driveway.

> Bill washed the car, standing in the driveway.

As the arrows indicate, in the first sentence the restrictive participial phrase modifies *car;* it's the car that's standing in the driveway. In the second, however, the phrase is nonrestrictive; it modifies *Bill.* And it could be shifted either to the beginning of the sentence or to the slot following *Bill* without any change in meaning.

The Dangling Participle. The nonrestrictive participial phrase provides a good way to change the focus of the sentence, as we have seen in these variations—but it carries an important restriction:

> The nonrestrictive participle can open or close the sentence *only* if it modifies the subject—that is, when the subject of the participle is also the subject of the sentence and is in regular subject position. Otherwise, the participle will dangle.

Remember, a participle modifies its own subject. Simply stated, a dangling participle is a verb without a subject:

> *Carrying all of our supplies for miles, the campground was a welcome sight.

> *Having swung his five iron too far to the left, Joe's ball landed precisely in the middle of a sand trap.

The campground, of course, did not do the carrying, nor did Joe's ball swing the five iron. You can fix such sentences (and avoid them in the first place) by making sure that the subject of the sentence is also the subject of the participle. You'll recognize that this rule about participles is like the rule about adverbial infinitives that you read about in Chapter 7.

Another common source of the dangling participle, and other dangling modifiers as well, is the sentence with a delayed subject—a *there*-transformation, for example, or an *it*-cleft:

> *Having moved all the outdoor furniture into the garage, there was no room left for the car.
> *Knowing how much work I had to do, it was good of you to come and help.

In the second sentence, *you* is the subject of the participle, so it's there in the sentence, but it's not in the usual subject position. Sometimes the most efficient way to revise such sentences is to expand the participial phrase into a complete clause. That expansion will add the missing subject:

> After we moved all the outdoor furniture into the garage, there was no room left for the car.
> It was good of you to come and help when you learned how much work I had to do.

EXERCISE 30

Rewrite the following sentences to eliminate the dangling participles.

1. Having endured rain all week, the miserable weather on Saturday didn't surprise us.
2. Hoping for the sixth win in a row, there was great excitement in the stands when the band finally played "The Star Spangled Banner."
3. Known for her conservative views on taxes and the role of government, we were not at all surprised when the Republican county commissioner announced her candidacy for the General Assembly.
4. Exhausted by the heat and humidity, it was wonderful to do nothing but lie in the shade and drink iced tea.
5. We watched the band members march across the field and form a huge W, wearing their colorful new uniforms.
6. Having spent nearly all day in the kitchen, everyone agreed that my superb gourmet meal was worth the effort.

7. Feeling pressure from the environmentalists, the Clean Air Act was immediately put on the committee's agenda.
8. We drove very carefully on the ice-covered highway, having several notorious curves and steep hills.
9. Obviously intimidated by a long history of defeats in Morgantown, there seems to be no way that our basketball team can beat the West Virginia Mountaineers on their home court.
10. Arriving unexpectedly on a weekend when I had two papers to finish and a big exam coming up, I didn't feel exactly overjoyed at seeing my parents.

The Prenoun Participle. Before leaving the participle, we should note that when it is a single word—the verb with no complements or modifiers—it usually occupies the adjective slot in preheadword position:

> Our snoring visitor kept the household awake.
> The barking dog next door drives us crazy.
> I should replace that broken hinge.
> The old hound growled at every passing stranger.

And, as we saw in the earlier discussion of hyphens, an adverb sometimes modifies the participle:

> a carefully conceived plan
> a well-developed paragraph

Relative Clauses

Another slot in the noun phrase following the noun is filled by the **relative clause,** sometimes called the adjective clause. Because it is a clause—that is, a structure with a subject and a predicate—this adjectival modifier is a powerful tool; it enables the writer to embed a complete subject/predicate idea into a noun phrase.

In many respects, the relative clause and the participial phrase are alike. The participial phrase, in fact, is actually a shortened version of the relative clause. All of the examples we saw earlier could easily be expanded into clauses with no change in their meaning:

> My mother, who is sitting by the window, is talking to herself.
> The man who is sitting by the window is talking to himself.
> My sister who lives in Atlanta just called.
> Bill washed the car that was standing *in the driveway*.
> Franklin Delano Roosevelt, who was elected *president in 1932*, faced problems that would have overwhelmed the average man.

One feature that the participle has that the clause does not is its movability: The clause always stays in the noun phrase, following the noun it modifies.

The Relatives. The relative clause is introduced by either a **relative pronoun** (*that*, *who*, or *which*) or a **relative adverb** (*where*, *when*, or *why*); the relative plays a part in the clause it introduces. In the case of the relative pronoun (the most common introducer), the part will be that of a noun: a subject, direct object, indirect object, subjective complement, object of the preposition, or, as possessive nouns function, a determiner.

The relative pronoun *who*, like the personal pronouns you read about in Chapter 5, has different forms for different cases: *who* (subjective), *whose* (possessive), and *whom* (objective):

> The man who called last night wouldn't leave his name.

Here *who* is the subject in its clause.

> The student whose notes I borrowed was absent today.

Here the possessive relative, *whose*, is the determiner for notes. The clause, in normal left-to-right fashion, is "I borrowed whose notes."

> Our dog, Rusty, whom we all dearly loved, was recently killed by a truck that was going far too fast for road conditions.

Here the objective relative, *whom*, is the object in the clause: "We all dearly loved whom." (Notice too that the noun *truck* is modified by a relative clause introduced by the relative pronoun *that*.)

When the relative pronoun is an object in its clause, it can be deleted if the clause is restrictive—that is, if the clause is not set off by commas. In the previous example, the clause is *non*restrictive, so the relative *whom* cannot be deleted. And you'll notice also that *whom* makes the sentence sound formal, not like something you say. But in the following example, the *whom* can be omitted, and in speech it certainly would be. Most writers would omit it.

> King Edward VIII gave up the throne of England for the woman (whom) he loved.

The relative pronoun *that* always introduces restrictive clauses; it is never set off by commas:

> You choose a color that you like.
> A boy that I knew in junior high called me last week.
> A truck that was going too fast for road conditions hit our dog.

In the first two preceding sentences, *that* can be omitted. Some writers, in fact, would insist on leaving it out in the second one because it refers to a person; some writers insist on *who* and *whom* in reference to people—not *that*. The easiest and smoothest solution is simply to omit the relative:

> A boy <u>I knew in junior high</u> called me last week.

However, the relative cannot be omitted when it functions as the subject in its clause, as in the sentence about the truck. Nor can it be omitted if the clause is nonrestrictive—no matter what role the pronoun fills:

> Rob Miller, <u>whom I knew in junior high</u>, called me last week.

We should note, too, that in speaking this sentence we are more likely to say *who*, even though the objective case of the pronoun is called for; most listeners wouldn't notice the difference. (*Who* actually sounds correct, because it's at the beginning of the clause, where the subjective case is found.)

The relative pronoun *which* is generally reserved for nonrestrictive clauses—those set off by commas:

> My roommate's financial problems, <u>which he finally told me about</u>, have caused him a lot of stress this semester.

The relative adverbs *where*, *when*, and *why* also introduce adjectival clauses, modifiers of nouns denoting place (*where* clauses), time (*when* clauses), and the noun *reason* (*why* clauses):

> In those **countries** of Eastern Europe <u>where the borders were opened for the first time in decades</u>, it was wonderful to see the faces of the people as they experienced freedom at last.
>
> Experts disagree about the **reasons** <u>why the communist regimes of Eastern Europe</u> fell in such quick succession.
>
> Those revolutionary changes came at a **time** <u>when the Soviet Union was experiencing economic problems at home</u>.

Punctuation of Relative Clauses. As we mentioned in connection with participial phrases, in making punctuation decisions, you must take into account (1) what the reader knows (Is the referent of the noun clear without this information?) and (2) what the reader will infer if the modifier is restrictive.

In the punctuation of relative clauses, the relative pronoun provides some clues:

1. The *that* clause is always restrictive; it is never set off by commas.
2. The *which* clause is generally nonrestrictive; it is set off by commas. (For many writers—in this book, for example—the rule is invariable: The *which*

clause is always nonrestrictive.) If you want to figure out if your *which* clause needs commas, try substituting *that*. If you can do so without changing the meaning, then the commas should be omitted.

3. If the relative pronoun can be deleted, the clause is restrictive:
   The bus (that) I ride to work is always late.
   The woman (whom) I work with is always early.

The next two rules of thumb apply to both clauses and phrases:

4. After any proper noun, the modifier will be nonrestrictive:
   Willamette University, which was established seven years before the Gold Rush of 1849, is within walking distance of Oregon's capitol.
   In Alaska, where the distance between some cities is vast, many businesses and individuals own private planes.
5. After any common noun that has only one possible referent, the modifier will be nonrestrictive:
   The highest mountain in the world, which resisted the efforts of climbers until 1953, looks truly forbidding from the air.
   Mike's twin brother, who lives in Austin, has a personality just like Mike's.
   My mother, who is sitting by the window, is talking to herself.

EXERCISE 31

Combine the following groups of sentences into single sentences by embedding some of the ideas as modifiers. You will probably want to use adverbial modifiers as well as adjectivals—participial phrases and relative clauses you have just been studying in this chapter. In some cases you may have to make other changes in the wording as well.

1. In many parts of the country, citizens are mobilizing against crime and drugs.
   They are driving drug dealers out of their neighborhoods.
2. More and more public officials are supporting the legalization of certain drugs.
   They argue that there is no other way to win the drug war.
3. Brian wants nothing to do with computers.
   He refuses to even try a word processor.
   He insists on using his trusty manual typewriter.
4. Burt Lancaster died in 1994 at the age of 80.
   As a young man at New York University, he had a basketball scholarship.
   He dropped out of NYU and joined the circus.

He won an Oscar in 1961 for *Elmer Gantry*.

5. The changes in Soviet–U.S. relations have meant substantial cuts in defense spending.
   Those changes have produced a "peace dividend."
   Many people assume that the changes will make more money available for social programs.
6. The highest incidence of colon cancer in the United States occurs in the Northeast.
   The Northeast also has the highest levels of acid rain.
   Cancer researchers suspect that there is a causal link between the two.
7. The rate of colon cancer is related to the amount of carbon dioxide in the air.
   Carbon dioxide absorbs ultraviolet light.
   Ultraviolet light fuels the body's production of Vitamin D.
8. Influenza, or flu, is a viral infection.
   It begins as an upper respiratory infection and then spreads to other parts of the body.
   Flu causes aches and pains in the joints.
9. Flu viruses mutate constantly.
   We cannot build up our immunity.
   New varieties spread from person to person and from place to place.
10. The sodium intake of the average American is far higher than necessary.
    The recommended level is 400 to 3,300 mg. per day.
    The average American consumes over 4,000 mg. per day.

The Broad-Reference Clause

In the discussion of demonstrative pronouns in Chapter 5, we mentioned the use of *this* and *that* (and *it*) with **"broad reference":**

> I just found out that my roommate is planning to withdraw from school.
> That came as a surprise.

Because the demonstrative *that* is commonly used as a determiner, a noun signaler, the logical way to strengthen this sentence, with its broad-reference *that*, is to provide a noun for *that* to modify:

> That decision came as a surprise.
> or
> That news came as a surprise.

The relative clause introduced by *which* sometimes has the same kind of broad-reference problem. In fact, we can illustrate the problem with a similar sentence:

My roommate told me she is planning to withdraw from school, which came as a surprise.

Remember that the relative pronoun that introduces the relative clause normally has a noun as its antecedent: the headword of the noun phrase that the clause is embedded in:

Joe's car, which he bought last week, looks like a gas guzzler to me.

Here *car* is the antecedent of *which;* the clause says "He bought which [i.e. car] last week." But in the following *which* clause, an example of a broad-reference clause, there is no noun for *which* to stand for:

Joe bought a gas guzzler, which surprised me.

Here it is the idea of the entire main clause, not a specific noun, that is the antecedent of *which*.

Only clauses introduced by *which* fit into the broad-reference category, never those introduced by *who* or *that;* and all are nonrestrictive—that is, they are set off by commas:

Tom cleaned up the garage without being asked, which made me suspect that he wanted to borrow the car.
The summer's heat wave in the Midwest devastated the corn crop, which probably means higher meat prices next year.

Many writers avoid the broad-reference clause, instead using *which* only in the adjectival clause that modifies a specific noun. In inexperienced hands the broad-reference *which* clause often has the vagueness associated with dangling modifiers:

I broke out in a rash, which really bothered me.

In this sentence the referent of *which* is unclear; it could refer to either the rash or the breaking out. There are a number of alternatives in which the meaning is clear:

Breaking out in rash really bothered me.
The rash I got last week really bothered me.

Even though they are not particularly vague, the earlier examples, too, can be revised in ways that avoid the broad-reference *which:*

When Tom cleaned up the garage without being asked, I suspected that he wanted to borrow the car.
Tom's cleaning up the garage without being asked made me suspect that he wanted to borrow the car.

This summer's heat wave in the Midwest, which devastated the corn crop, probably means higher meat prices for next year.

EXERCISE 32

Revise the following sentences to eliminate any instances of the broad-reference *which*.

1. I had to clean the basement this morning, which wasn't very much fun.
2. The first snowstorm of the season in Denver was both early and severe, which was not what the weather service had predicted.
3. The college library has finally converted the central card catalog to a computer system, which took over four years to complete.
4. The president had some harsh words for Congress in his recent press conference, which some observers considered quite inappropriate.
5. Wendell didn't want to stay for the second half of the game, which made Harriet rather unhappy.
6. We're having company for dinner three times this week, which probably means hot dogs for the rest of the month.
7. In his State of the Union message, the president characterized the last two years as a period of "unprecedented prosperity," which one economist immediately labeled "sheer hype and hyperbole."
8. The Brazilian government has grudgingly agreed to consider new policies regarding the rain forests, which should come as good news to everyone concerned about the environment.

Other Nominals

The term ***nominal*** refers to the functions of the noun phrases we've been looking at here, to all of the slots in the sentence patterns that noun phrases fill: subject, direct object, indirect object, objective complement, subjective complement, and object of the preposition. The heading "Other Nominals" refers to structures other than noun phrases that fill those nominal slots. Just as we use verb phrases and clauses as adverbials and adjectivals—that is, to modify verbs and nouns—we use them as nominals too. In this section, then, we will look briefly at verb phrases and clauses in their nominal function.

Verb Phrases

In form, the verb phrases that fill the nominal functions look exactly like the adjectivals and adverbials: They are infinitives (the base form with *to*) as well as *-ing* verbs, known as **gerunds** when they function as nominals.

That young man jogging along the highway looks exhausted. (participial phrase, modifying *man*)
Jogging along the highway can be dangerous. (gerund, as subject)
To lose weight before summer, I am going to take up aerobics. (infinitive, as adverbial)
I plan to lose weight before summer. (infinitive, as direct object)

Obviously these are not unusual sentences, nor are they the kinds of structures that we ordinarily make mistakes with, even in writing. There are, however, two aspects of verb phrases in nominal roles that deserve special mention, both having to do with gerunds.

The Dangling Gerund. You may recall from the discussions of infinitives and participles that when a verb phrase opens the sentence, the subject of the main clause in the sentence is also the subject of the verb in that opening phrase:

To do well in school, **a student** should set aside study time on a regular basis.
Having finished the decorations, **the homecoming committee** celebrated with a keg of root beer.

Remember that an opening verb phrase sets up an expectation in the reader that the subject of that verb will follow. When something else follows, the opening verb phrase will dangle:

***Having finished the decorations,** the ballroom looked beautiful.

The problem is obvious; it sounds as if the ballroom did the decorating. Remember that a participle modifies its own subject. In this sentence the participle has no subject.

This same kind of dangler, this thwarted expectation, can occur when the sentence opens with a prepositional phrase in which the object of the preposition is a gerund:

*After finishing the decorations, the ballroom looked beautiful.
*Since cutting down on fats, my cholesterol level has dropped.

The rule about opening verb phrases is straightforward:

> When a verb phrase opens the sentence (whether an infinitive, a participle, or a gerund in a prepositional phrase), the subject of that verb will be the subject of the sentence.

Shifting the prepositional phrase to the end of the sentence will not solve the problem. The error may not seem quite as obvious, but the dangling nature of the phrase is still there:

*The ballroom looked beautiful after finishing the decorations.
*My cholesterol level has dropped since cutting down on fats.

So whether that verb phrase opens the sentence or simply *could* open the sentence, the subject–verb relationship must be there.

The Subject of the Gerund. Another feature of gerunds that you'll want to be aware of is the form that their subjects sometimes take. In many cases the subject of the gerund will not even appear in the sentence, especially when the gerund names a general activity:

Jogging is good exercise.
Raising orchids requires patience.

However, when the subject of the gerund appears in the gerund phrase itself, it will usually be in the possessive case, especially when the subject is a pronoun:

I objected to **their** arriving in the middle of the meeting.
My objecting didn't make any difference.
There is no point in **your** coming if you're going to be so late.

When the subject is a simple noun, such as a person's name, it too will be possessive:

I was surprised at **Terry's** refusing the job offer.

However, when the noun has modifiers, or when it is compound, then the possessive is not generally used:

I was surprised at **Bill and Terry** turning down that beautiful apartment.

An alternative structure, which may sound more natural, is the use of a clause instead of the gerund:

I was surprised that Bill and Terry turned down that beautiful apartment.

We will look briefly at nominal clauses in the following section.

Nominal Clauses

One of the most common nominal clauses is the one introduced by the expletive *that*, like the preceding example. A clause can fill most of the nominal slots in the sentence, but its most common function is as direct object:

I suspect that our history exam will be hard.
The president recently announced that he will ask Congress for more aid to Haiti.

You'll see that in these examples we have taken a complete sentence and turned it into a part of another sentence:

> Our history exam will be hard.
> He will ask Congress for more aid to Haiti.

Any declarative sentence can be turned into a nominal clause, simply by adding the expletive *that*—and you'll discover that sometimes we don't even need *that:*

> I suspect [______] our history exam will be hard.
> He said [______] he would be late.

In many cases, however, the *that* is a signal to the reader that a clause is coming; its omission may cause the reader momentary confusion.

> Last week I suspected my friend Tom, who never goes to class, was getting himself into academic trouble.
> My uncle knows the stock broker handling his retirement funds never takes unnecessary risks with his clients' money.

Here the expletive *that* would be helpful to signal the reader that *my friend* and *the stock broker* are subjects, not objects.

The expletive *that* also allows us to turn a direct quotation into indirect discourse:

> *Direct:* He said, "For the past two years the economy has experienced impressive growth."
>
> *Indirect:* He said that for the past two years the economy had experienced impressive growth.

The writer can use indirect discourse to summarize or paraphrase:

> The president reported that the economy had been growing during the past two years.

Not all nominal clauses are introduced by the expletive *that*. Many are introduced by interrogative, or question, words:

> I wonder <u>**what** our history exam will cover</u>.
> Congress is now considering <u>**how much** foreign aid it should appropriate for Haiti</u>.

Unlike the expletive, the interrogatives cannot be left out; they provide—or, at least, ask for—information that is part of the nominal clause.

It's important to recognize the structural boundaries of these clauses and to understand how they work so that you will be in control of your sentences, especially their punctuation. It's sometimes tempting to add commas to sentences with nominal clauses simply because they get so long. One fairly common punctuation error occurs when the nominal clause itself has a modifier that could reasonably take a comma:

> *The neighbors said that at the end of the month, they were going to Florida for the winter.

However, we don't separate the expletive *that* from the clause it introduces, as the comma after *month* is doing. The result here is a comma between the verb *said* and its direct object, the nominal clause. If this nominal clause were a full sentence, a comma after *month* would be correct:

> At the end of the month, the neighbors are going to Florida for the winter.

But when we insert this sentence as a nominal clause, we have to omit the comma. One way to solve the problem is to shift the prepositional phrase to the end of the sentence:

> The neighbors said they were going to Florida for the winter at the end of the month.

It's also tempting to add a comma when the sentence has a compound clause in direct object position simply because the sentence is likely to be long. But that, too, sends the wrong message to the reader. You will see examples of such sentences in Chapter 9. In Chapter 11 you will read about "hierarchies of punctuation," a concept that is useful in dealing with embedded structures.

RHETORICAL REMINDERS

Prenoun Modifiers

Have I paid attention to commas and hyphens in the noun phrase?

Have I avoided strings of nouns as modifiers?

Postnoun Modifiers

Do opening and closing participles modify the subject of the sentence?

Have I thought about sentence focus in placing the participles?

Does the punctuation distinguish between restrictive (defining) and nonrestrictive (commenting) phrases and clauses?

Have I made a conscious choice in my use of participles and clauses, selecting the most effective form as modifier?

Have I avoided fuzzy broad-reference *which* clauses?

PUNCTUATION REMINDERS

Use a comma between prenoun modifiers if it's possible to use *and*.

Use commas around a nonrestrictive modifier when the modifier is only commenting on the noun rather than defining it—when the reader already knows its referent or if it has only one possible referent.

Set off a verb phrase that opens the sentence (whether an infinitive, a participle, or a gerund in a prepositional phrase) with a comma. And remember that the subject of that verb will be the subject of the sentence.

Chapter 9

The Long and the Short of Sentences

After studying two chapters about expanding sentences with prepositional phrases and verb phrases and clauses and such, after seeing all the possibilities there are for putting ideas into words, along with the nuances involved in punctuating them, you may need to be reminded of the philosophy underlying this book: that, as an experienced speaker of the language, you are a sentence expert. Those complicated-looking sentences, for the most part, are the same sentences you use every day when you speak—sentences you put together automatically.

Two other aspects of your sentence expertise may sound even more far-fetched: (1) The number of possible sentences you could create is infinite, and (2) there is no such thing as the world's longest sentence—so don't bother to submit your entry for the Guinness book. Sometimes when you read the prose of such writers as William Faulkner and James Joyce, you might think you're reading entries in the world's longest-sentence contest. But even a sentence that goes on for pages and pages can be lengthened: Just add an *and* and keep it going.

In this chapter we'll look at *and,* along with its fellow conjunctions, and we'll consider the effects that long and short sentences have on our readers.

(And how about the world's shortest sentence? That's easy. Think about it. Think!)

Coordination

The technique of **coordination,** of putting together compound structures in sentences, is old hat; you've been doing it all your life. Coordination is a natural part of language, one that develops early in speech. If you pay attention to sentence structure the next time you're within hearing distance of a small child, you'll hear the conjunction *and* used frequently between parts of sentences and between the sentences themselves:

> We built a snow fort <u>and</u> threw snowballs.
> Robbie is mean, <u>and</u> I'm not going to play with him anymore.

Compound structures also show up early and often in writing. Certainly in this book you can't read very far without coming to a conjunction—an *and* or a *but* or an *or*. Your own writing is probably filled with them, too.

So why do we need to study coordination? Because it's so easy!

Any structure or technique that we use as often as we do coordination needs to be under the writer's control. Remember, a written sentence is there to be looked at and pondered, to be read over and over again. We want to be sure not only that every one of those compounds is grammatically correct but also that it's the right structure for the job. And, equally important, we want to use the most efficient and accurate conjunction for that compound structure.

Conjunctions

We use **conjunctions** to connect words and phrases and clauses within sentences and to connect the sentences themselves. Within the sentence our most common connectors are the simple coordinating conjunctions and the correlative conjunctions. For joining sentences we use, in addition, the subordinating conjunctions, also called subordinators, and the conjunctive adverbs. Relative pronouns and relative adverbs also function as connectors, joining clauses to nouns. We discussed subordinating conjunctions in connection with adverbial clauses in Chapter 7, the relatives in connection with adjectival clauses in Chapter 8.

And is one of the **coordinating conjunctions** that we use to put sentences and their parts together. The other major ones are *but* and *or*. In the discussion of coordination within the sentence, you'll see that the punctuation with *but* sometimes varies from that of *and* and *or*.

Another important class for joining both sentences and parts of sentences is that of the **correlative conjunctions:** *either–or, neither–nor, not only–but also*, and *both–and*. The correlatives, which are especially important for adding emphasis and providing focus, are simple but powerful tools for the writer.

Between sentences we can also use the versatile—and movable—**conjunctive adverbs,** such as *however* and *therefore* and *nevertheless*. Understanding how we use the conjunctive adverbs will also help you understand the use of the semicolon.

Punctuation of Coordinate Structures

The earlier example of children's speech illustrates coordination within the sentence:

> We built a snow fort and threw snowballs.

In this sentence the coordinating conjunction *and* joins two predicates:

We < built a snow fort
and
threw snowballs.

You'll notice that there is no comma in this sentence, not because it's short but because the compound structure occurs *within* the sentence. This sentence illustrates a well-established and important punctuation rule:

> Between the parts of a two-part compound structure within the sentence, we use no comma with *and*.

It's often tempting to insert a comma wherever a pause occurs in a long sentence, but that technique will lead to errors: Every pause is not a comma pause. For example, sometimes sentences grow long when one of the sentence slots is itself a clause:

I understand <u>that one section of advanced algebra has been canceled</u>.

Here a clause fills the direct object slot; it names the "something" that "I understand":

I understand <u>something</u>.

And when this long nominal clause is compounded, it is treated as any compound *within* the sentence is treated: It has no comma.

I understand < that one section of advanced algebra has been canceled
and
that another section of trig has been added.

In other words, the *and* in this sentence is connecting a compound direct object, just as it does in this one:

I understand Spanish and Italian.

In contrast, the second example of children's speech consists of two complete sentences—a **compound sentence:**

Robbie is mean
, and
I'm not going to play with him anymore.

Here conventional punctuation calls for a comma with the conjunction. The comma signals the reader that another complete sentence is on the way. So the second punctuation rule in connection with coordination is this:

In a compound sentence, a comma is used with the coordinating conjunction between the two independent clauses.

It's not unusual to see in published works compound sentences without the comma, especially when both **independent clauses** are short. But as a general rule you will want to signal the reader that another full sentence is coming, and the conjunction alone will not do so. The conventional rule calling for the comma with the conjunction in the compound sentence is a good one to follow.

The sentence that is most likely to turn up with a comma error is the one with a compound predicate:

> *Scientists believe that the Amazon basin plays a major role in the global climate, and are worried that the destruction of its forests could lead to climatic chaos.

Here the comma before *and* sends a message to the reader, the message that another complete sentence follows: In this sentence it's the wrong message. What actually follows is another verb phrase, another predicate:

Scientists < believe that the Amazon basin plays . . .
and
are worried that the destruction . . .

Even though the predicates are long ones and even though the reader might pause for breath at the conjunction, there is no place for a comma: The *and* is simply joining a compound structure within the sentence. The comma would be called for only if a subject were added to the second clause:

Scientists believe that the Amazon basin plays . . .
, and
they are worried that the destruction of its forests could lead . . .

Now we need the comma because the *and* connects two independent clauses.

It's important, then, in using *and* to understand exactly what it is you're turning into a compound structure: If it's part of the sentence—that is, a structure within the sentence—then no comma is called for; if it's two complete sentences, then the *and* needs a comma to send a signal to the reader that another sentence is on the way.

Parallel Structure

Using *and* Effectively

One of the most important lessons to be learned about *and*, along with the other coordinating conjunctions, is the concept of **parallel structure.** In Chapter 2 we saw the cohesive effects of parallelism across sentence boundaries. Here we will see the importance of making sure that compound structures within the sentence are parallel.

A coordinate structure will be parallel only when the two parts are of the same *form*. And the parallel structure will be an effective one—and this feature is just as important—only when the *two ideas are equal*, when they belong together. Here, for example, is a compound structure that is unparallel in form:

> *My *new exercise program* **and** *going on a strict diet* will give me a new shape before bikini season.

Here the *and* connects a compound subject:

My new exercise program
and > will give me . . .
going on a strict diet

The first one (*My new exercise program*) is a noun phrase in form; the second (*going on a strict diet*) is a verb phrase, a gerund. In this case the ideas are equal, so in that sense they belong together. But to make the sentence grammatical, you must use the same form for the two subjects:

My new exercise program (noun phrase)
and
a strict diet (noun phrase)

or

Sticking to my exercise program (verb phrase)
and
going on a strict diet (verb phrase)

The problem of unparallel *forms* is not always as obvious and easy to spot as it is in the preceding example. Let's look again at the sentence about the Amazon basin:

Scientists < believe that the Amazon basin plays a major role in the global climate
and
are worried that the destruction of its forests could lead to climactic chaos.

Here the *and* connects two predicates, so technically we could say that the sentence is parallel. The fact that both predicates include *that*-clauses makes it look more parallel than it actually is.

We haven't covered every detail of sentence structure in these chapters, so you can't be expected to pinpoint the precise grammatical problem in sentences like this one. However, looking at the underlying sentence patterns of the predicates will reveal some helpful clues. (You might want to review the sentence patterns in Chapter 1.)

Scientists	**believe**	***something***
(Subject)	*(transitive verb)*	*(direct object)*
Scientists	**are**	**worried (about *something*)**
(Subject)	*(linking* be*)*	*(subjective complement)*

In each case the italicized "something" represents the *that*-clause. As you can see, those two clauses function differently in the two parts of the sentence: The first one is a direct object; the second is a modifier, or complement, of the adjective *worried*. You can see also that the two verbs are of different classes—one transitive and one linking—another common source of fuzzy compound predicates. So it turns out that the sentence isn't actually as parallel as it appeared at first glance. One obvious way to fix it, then, is to get the two *that*-clauses to function in the same way—either as two direct objects or as two adjective complements. Because both clauses name "beliefs," we can construct a compound direct object instead of a compound predicate:

Scientists believe
- that the Amazon basin plays a major role in . . .
- **and**
- that the destruction of its forests could lead to . . .

Another common source of such fuzziness with compound predicates is the sentence in which only one of the two has an auxiliary with its verb:

> Experts in sports medicine emphasize the importance of water intake **and** are recommending a half ounce per day for every pound of body weight.

Or the pair of predicates in which one verb is active, the other passive:

> The 1989 California earthquake was centered in the southern Santa Cruz Mountains **and** measured 7.1 on the Richter scale.

Or a sentence that pairs a linking verb with one of another class:

> The African killer bees are less predictable than European bees **and** tend to attack in vast swarms.

The original Amazon sentence has this same form: a linking verb paired with a transitive verb.

You may be thinking that these sentences seem perfectly normal—like sentences you say every day. And you're right—they do sound normal. We use sentences like these in our conversation all the time—and no one accuses us of being ungrammatical. But writing is different. We want to be as precise and effective as possible. And as writers, we have a second (and third and fourth!) chance to improve our sentences. We don't have to show that first draft to anyone. Sentences with unparallel features like these in their predicates can always be improved.

A related source of fuzziness is the compound sentence—two whole sentences joined by *and*, not just two predicates. All of the examples in the previous discussion could easily be turned into compound sentences with the simple addition of a second subject:

> Experts in sports medicine emphasize the importance of water intake
> **, and**
> they are recommending a half ounce per day for every pound of body weight.

The sentence is now parallel in *form*. But a question remains: Are the two *ideas* parallel? Do they belong together as equal partners? (And remember, that's what the message of *and* is: "These two structures are equal partners.")

If the two ideas were fuzzy partners as predicates—a judgment based on the form of the verbs—then they are just as likely to be fuzzy partners as sentences. The problem is not just that one verb has an auxiliary and the other doesn't (*are recommending* and *emphasize*); it's the underlying reason for that difference. We generally use the simple present tense (*emphasize*) to describe an accepted truth or timeless quality; we use the present progressive tense (*are recommending*) for a present action. It's not that the two ideas don't belong together: They do. But not as equal partners. *And* is simply the wrong connection.

Because the sentence is out of context, we don't know which of the two ideas should be emphasized, but a good guess would be the recommendation:

> Experts in sports medicine, who emphasize the importance of water intake, are recommending a half ounce per day for every pound of body weight.

Here we've used a relative clause for one of the two ideas. Another possibility is the participial phrase. You'll recall that it's movable; it can open the sentence:

> Emphasizing the importance of water intake, experts in sports medicine are recommending a half ounce per day for every pound of body weight.

The other sentences with unparallel verb phrases can also be revised by focusing on one of the two ideas; which one of the two will depend on the context. In the earthquake sentence, we have two kinds of information: place and size.

> The 1989 California earthquake, which measured 7.1 on the Richter scale, was centered in the southern Santa Cruz Mountains.

> The 1989 California earthquake, [which was] centered in the southern Santa Cruz Mountains, measured 7.1 on the Richter scale.

The sentence about the killer bees illustrates another common coordination problem: a fact and a conclusion based on that fact put together as parallel ideas. Our clue that the two predicates don't belong together happens to be a difference in verb classes: linking and transitive. That same mismatch occurs in the Amazon sentence, you'll recall. It, too, has unparallel ideas: a statement about the nature of the place and a prediction about its future.

Again, we need context in order to know which ideas should get the main focus—but here are some possibilities:

> The African killer bees, which are less predictable than European bees, tend to attack in vast swarms.
>
> The African killer bees, which tend to attack in vast swarms, are less predictable than European bees.

The Amazon sentence is a little more challenging:

> Scientists, who believe that the Amazon basin plays a major role in the global climate, are worried that destruction of its forest could lead to climatic chaos.
>
> Scientists are worried that in the Amazon basin, a region they believe plays a major role in the global climate, destruction of the rain forests could lead to climatic chaos.

And there's always the option of two separate sentences.

EXERCISE 33

Revise the following sentences and paragraphs to make the connection between ideas more effective. Be sure to consider the various forms of adverbials, adjectivals, and nominals that you have read about in the preceding chapters.

1. The 1990 census created 635,000 temporary jobs, and it cost $2.6 billion to carry out.
2. In 1933 millions of people were out of work, and the country was on the verge of economic collapse. That year was the height of the Great Depression. It should probably be called the depth rather than the height.
3. Visitors and workers at the Philadelphia Mint must pass throught a metal detector, and it is extremely sensitive. The magnetic strip on a credit card will set it off.
4. Jockey Bill Shoemaker ran his first race in March of 1949, and he ran his last race in February of 1990. He had 8,833 career victories.
5. Buffalo meat is lower in fat and cholesterol and calories than beef and is now starting to become an alternative to beef among diet-conscious Americans. It is now being raised commercially on many Western ranches.

6. Ordinary Japanese consumers pay high prices for everything from gasoline to groceries and have not profited from their country's economic boom.
7. In recent years honeybee populations in the South have been changed by invading Africanized bees. These are the so-called "killer bees." They migrated to the southern United States from Brazil. It is estimated that they have affected three-fourths of the bee populations of Texas, Arizona, and New Mexico. In northern climates the biggest problem for honey producers is a deadly parasitic mite. In 1988 and 1989 Pennsylvania beekeepers lost an estimated 300,000 hives to the deadly mites. Honey production in Brazil has gone up with the Africanized bees. Honey producers in Pennsylvania don't have to worry about the killer bees. They are not adapted to northern winters, and they probably wouldn't survive. Pennsylvania beekeepers are now importing mite-resistant bees from Yugoslavia. These imports have become the industry's saving grace.
8. The chairman of the Township Supervisors refused to allow our citizens' committee to present our petition against rezoning our valley, and he ordered us to leave the meeting. Apton-Kelley Drilling wants to build a limestone quarry in our valley, and they have asked the Supervisors to rezone the land. The land is now zoned "agriculture," and it has to be changed to "industrial" or the quarry cannot be built there. The residents of our valley believe that rezoning would impact negatively on the quality of life in the valley, and we all signed the petition. Our group left the meeting last night, and later we decided that our only recourse is to picket the supervisors at their next meeting. We hope that the local news media will pay attention to our concerns. We are going to notify the local newspapers and the television stations of our plans.

And vs. *But*

There's an important difference between *and* and *but*. While they're both coordinating conjunctions, their meanings are opposite, and their punctuation sometimes reflects that difference:

> I have visited a lot of big cities, *but* never Los Angeles.
> I worked most of the night *but* couldn't finish my project.
> Melanie's new white dress is beautiful, *but* not very practical.

Notice that in two of those sentences we have used a comma, even where the conjunction joins only predicates, not full sentences.

Although we call *but* a *con*junction, its meaning is that of *dis*junction: It introduces a contrast, and that contrast often calls for a comma. The punctuation rule regarding a two-part compound structure within the sentence, then, is different when the conjunction is *but*. When the compound element is connected with *and*, we use no comma; when it's connected with *but*, however, the comma may be appropriate.

At this point we should mention an exception to the comma rule, one that occurs with *and:* When we want to give special emphasis to the last element in a coordinated pair, we can set it off with a comma:

> I didn't believe him, and said so.
> My new white couch is beautiful, and expensive.

The emphasis will be even stronger with a dash instead of a comma:

> I didn't believe him—and said so.
> My new white couch is beautiful—and expensive.

The dash also sends the message that the punctuation was deliberate—not a comma error.

The Ineffective But

Sentence connectors, whether subordinating or coordinating, must be the right tool for the job. If you examine compound sentences with *but,* you'll discover that it's often the wrong tool:

> The prime rate went down two percentage points during the last quarter, but government economists are still worried about high inflation and low productivity.
> The changes had been rumored for months, but the timing came as a surprise.

Because *but* is a coordinating conjunction, just as *and* is, each of these sentences sends the message to the reader that the two ideas are equal. But are they? Probably not.

The problem with *but* sometimes becomes clear when you try to predict what's coming in the second clause. The *but* says that a contrast is coming. Try to predict the second clause in the previous example—without looking back. Here's the first clause:

> The changes had been rumored for months, but—

But what?

> The changes had been rumored for months, but no one believed them.
>
> **or**
>
> The changes had been rumored for months, but the rumors turned out to be untrue.
>
> **or**
>
> The changes had been rumored for months, but they were never implemented.

We don't expect to read,

> The changes had been rumored for months, but the timing came as a surprise.

When you read the original sentence carefully, you'll discover that the first clause is clearly subordinate to the second. The sentence should have only one main focus: the second clause. With the first clause subordinated, that focus is much clearer:

> Although the changes had been rumored for months, the timing came as a surprise.

Here's another compound sentence with *but,* the sentence about sleep that we looked at in Chapter 7 in connection with subordinate clauses. The paragraph preceding this one in the *New York Times* article describes accidents on the job connected with work schedules:

> The biological clock is flexible enough to adjust to slight changes in a person's work schedule, *but* in many industries rotations in shift work are so drastic that they play havoc with body rhythms, leaving employees unable to sleep at home and impairing their productivity at work.

Here the message of *but* is that the two clauses are equal: But look again; you'll see that they're not. The main idea is clearly that of the second clause. The idea in the first clause, although it has not previously appeared in the article, is presented as understood, as information the reader is assumed to know—the known information. The new information is in the second clause. Making the first clause subordinate will help the reader focus on the new idea:

> Although the biological clock is flexible enough to adjust to slight changes in a person's work schedule, in many industries rotations in shift work are so drastic that they play havoc with body rhythms, leaving employees unable to sleep at home and impairing their productivity at work.

Remember that a compound sentence has two points of focus that, in terms of structure, are equal. The compound sentence is effective only when that structure accurately reflects the relationship of the two ideas. If a single point of focus would be more accurate, then a subordinating conjunction should introduce one of the two ideas.

The Serial Comma

In a coordinate structure with more than two components, a series, we use commas to separate the coordinate elements:

> The democratic revolutions in Poland, East Germany, and Hungary surely had a great deal to do with changes in the Soviet Union.

These commas represent the pauses and slight changes of pitch that occur in the production of the series. You can hear the commas in your voice when you compare the series of three with a two-part compound structure:

> The democratic revolutions in Poland and Hungary surely had a great deal to do with changes in the Soviet Union.

You probably noticed a leveling of the pitch in reading the pair, a certain smoothness that the series does not have. In the series with conjunctions instead of commas, you'll notice the same leveling:

> The democratic revolutions in Poland *and* Hungary *and* East Germany surely had a great deal to do with changes in the Soviet Union.

When conjunctions connect all the elements, we use no commas.

In the series of three, some writers—and some publications as a matter of policy—use only one comma, leaving out the serial comma, the one immediately before *and*. The following series of noun phrases, for example, is typical of the punctuation style of *Smithsonian:*

> [Air traffic] Controllers use the analytical talents of a chess grand master, the mental calculations of a mathematician and the terse language of a police dispatcher.
>
> —James R. Chiles

Smithsonian follows an open, or light, style of punctuation, leaving out commas where a boundary is otherwise marked. Here, of course, the conjunction *and* marks the final boundary of the series.

This punctuation style, however, does have a drawback: It may imply a closer connection than actually exists between the last two elements of the series. It also ignores the pitch change, however slight, represented by the comma.

Here is our earlier example without the serial comma:

> The democratic revolutions in Poland, Hungary and East Germany surely had a great deal to do with the changes in the Soviet Union.

In this version "Hungary and East Germany" might be interpreted as a unit—at least, at first glance. The main purpose of punctuation, after all, is to represent graphically the meaningful speech signals—pitch, stress (loudness), and juncture (pauses)—that the written language otherwise lacks. That small pitch change represented by the comma can make a difference in emphasis and meaning.

The Correlative Conjunctions

Like the coordinating conjunctions, the correlatives (*both–and, either–or, neither–nor, not only–but also*) connect both complete sentences and elements within the sentence. Within the sentence, *either–or* and *neither–nor* are used alike:

I will	either	meet you	or	come to
	neither	in the lobby	nor	your room.

As a connector of complete sentences, however, *neither–nor* requires a shift in the subject and the auxiliary of the second clause; *either–or* does not:

> Neither will I meet you in the lobby, nor will I come to your room. (I will neither . . . , nor will I . . .)
> Either I will meet you in the lobby, or I will come to your room.

The correlative pair *not only–but also* is used both within and between sentences:

> Not only the coaches and players but also the fans had high hopes of defeating the Texas Aggies.
> Not only did government economists underestimate the level of inflation that the 1990s would bring, but they also delayed in taking action to bring it under control.

The second sentence would be equally grammatical with either *but* or *also,* rather than both of them. And we have the option of using an adverbial of emphasis other than *also:*

> Not only the coaches and players but the fans too had high hopes. . . .
> Not only the coaches and players but the fans as well had . . .

The correlative *both–and* does not connect complete sentences—only elements within the sentence:

> Franco is a good sport, both on and off the playing field.
> Both Jeannie and Marie worked hard to get their project finished on time.

The problem of unparallel structure with the correlatives is easy to spot and fix; it's a matter of paying attention to the conjunctions you've used. Every time you spot *either,* you know an *or* is coming—and so does your reader. Just be sure that the same form follows both. The writer of the following sentence suffered a lapse in attention:

> *I will **either** take the train **or** the bus.

Here we have a verb phrase (*take the train*) connected to a noun phrase (*the bus*). To correct this unparallel structure, simply move *either:*

> I will take **either** the train **or** the bus.

The correlatives rarely produce structures with unparallel ideas, like those we saw with *and;* generally the ideas belong together. It's the unparallel *form* that's often the problem.

The power of the correlatives lies in their ability to change the rhythm and focus of the sentence in ways that one-word conjunctions cannot—to set up different expectations in the reader:

> Individuals and nations must learn to think about the environment on a worldwide scale.
>
> Both individuals and nations must learn to think about the environment on a worldwide scale.

That change may seem like a small one. But notice what it has done: It has shifted stress to the subject, which normally gets little, if any. Now the reader expects to read on about the response of nations in what follows. Here's another example of the difference that *both–and* can make in contrast to *and* alone: This is a revision of the first sentence in the preceding paragraph:

> The power of the correlatives lies in their ability to change *both* the rhythm and the focus of the sentence in ways that one-word conjunctions cannot.

If you listen carefully, you'll notice that the addition of *both* adds stress to *and*.

The same kind of change in emphasis occurs with *not only–but also* (or *not only–but . . . as well*):

> As citizens of this global village, we must be concerned not only with our own health and safety but with the needs of others as well.
>
> As citizens of this global village, we must be concerned not only with our own health and safety but also with the needs of others.

In reading the two sentences aloud, you'll notice that in the second there is less emphasis on *others;* the peak of stress is on *also*. Note too that both parts of the correlative introduce "with" phrases for parallel structure.

Probably the least common correlative is *neither–nor;* and it's probably accurate to say that inexperienced writers avoid it. But because it is rare, it sends a strong message, one that will affect the reader's response:

> Neither individuals nor nations can afford to ignore what is happening to the environment.

Subject–Verb Agreement

When nouns or noun phrases in the subject slot are joined by *and* or by the correlative *both–and*, the subject is plural:

> My *friends and relatives* are coming to the wedding.

However, the coordinating conjunction *or* and the correlatives *either–or* and *neither–nor* do not have the additive meaning of *and;* with *or* and *nor* the relationship is called disjunctive. In compound subjects with these conjunctions, the verb will be determined by the closer member of the pair:

Neither the speaker nor the listeners were intimidated by the protestors.
Either the class officers or the faculty advisor makes the final decision.

Do the class officers or the faculty advisor make the final decision?
Does the faculty advisor or the class officers make the final decision?

If the correct sentence sounds incorrect or awkward because of the verb form, you can simply reverse the compound pair:

Either the faculty advisor or the class officers make the final decision.

When both members of the pair are alike, of course, there is no question:

Either the president or the vice-president is going to introduce the speaker.
Neither the union members nor the management representatives were willing to compromise.

For most verb forms, you'll recall, there is no decision to be made about subject–verb agreement; the issue arises only when the *-s* form, the present tense, of the verb or auxiliary is involved. In the following sentences, there is no choice:

Either the class officers or the faculty advisor made the final decision.
Either the faculty advisor or the class officers made the final decision.

Another situation that sometimes causes confusion about number—that is, whether the subject is singular or plural—occurs with subjects that include a phrase introduced by *as well as* or *in addition to* or *along with:*

*The sidewalk, in addition to the driveway, need to be repaired.
*The piano player, as well as the rest of the group, usually join in the singing.
*Mike, along with his friend Emilio, often help out at the bakery on weekends.

These additions to the subject are parenthetical; they are not treated as part of the subject. To make the subject compound—to include them—the writer should use a coordinating conjunction, such as *and:*

The sidewalk and the driveway need to be repaired.

The piano player and the rest of the group usually join in the singing.
Mike and his friend Emilio often help out at the bakery on weekends.

EXERCISE 34

A. Experiment with the rhythm and emphasis of the following sentences by substituting correlatives for the coordinating conjunctions.

1. Japanese blue-collar workers work more hours per day than American workers do and typically do so with more dedication and energy.
2. Workers and schoolchildren in Japan put in more time than their American counterparts.
3. Blue-collar workers and students in the United States do not spend as much time at their respective jobs as their Japanese counterparts.
4. In the game against Arizona last night, our center surpassed his previous single-game highs for rebounds and points scored and broke the school's all-time scoring record.
5. Julie got an A in the final exam and an A in the course.
6. When my parents retire, they are planning to sell the house and buy a condo near San Diego or rent the house and buy an RV and travel the back roads.
7. The chairman of the Planning Commission did not allow the citizens' committee to present the petition, and he would not recognize them when they attempted to speak out at the meeting.
8. Aunt Rosa has promised to fix her famous lasagne for my birthday dinner and bake my favorite lemon cake.
9. My history professor would not let me take a make-up exam when I cut his class, and he wouldn't accept my paper because it was late.
10. Day care and education are issues that our elected officials are going to have to address if this country is going to solve its economic and social problems and if they want to get reelected.

B. Revise the following paragraph to take advantage of the added emphasis and rhythm that correlatives can contribute. Consider options for modification and subordination as well.

A surge of voter resentment in the 1994 midterm election put Republicans in control of the Senate and the House of Representatives for the first time in 40 years. The voters' frustration with government affected governorships in addition to Congress. Governor Mario Cuomo of New York and Governor Ann Richards of Texas lost their re-election bids. They were two of the nation's most celebrated governors. In Tennessee, the incumbent Senate Democrat, Jim Sasser, failed to retain his seat, and Tennessee's open Senate seat also went to a Republican. In Pennsylvania, Democrats lost the Governor's race, and incumbent Senator Harris Wofford, who is a Democrat, lost to his Republican opponent. The Democrats celebrated the victories of two important Senate races: Incumbent Charles Robb defeated Oliver North in Virginia, and incumbent Edward Kennedy defeated Mitt Romney in Massachusetts.

—adapted from a report by Steve Daley, *Chicago Tribune*

For Group Discussion

Read the following paragraph, from Chapter One of *Wondrous Times on the Frontier* by Dee Brown, and discuss revisions that might make it more effective. Note especially the author's use of compound structures and the series as he describes the people and their activities. Experiment with those structures by trying correlative conjunctions for greater emphasis. Consider also the effects of the parallel structures you studied in Chapter 2 and look for places where expansions might add drama to the compound structures. Be sure to listen for the peaks of rhythm as you read; consider both end focus and punctuation in your decision-making.

> Anyone traveling westward by wagon, stagecoach, steamboat, horseback, or on foot was not likely to enjoy a painless journey. Yet there were times of pleasure in which the wayfarers defied the daily miseries with merrymaking and a sincere wonder for the awesome land through which they were passing. Most of those traveling overland formed companies for mutual security against the unknown. The rate of movement was not much speedier than that of Geoffrey Chaucer's pilgrims to Canterbury, and there were Chaucerian attitudes among the journeyers who represented the trades and professions of that time—millers, cooks, clerks, merchants, wheelwrights, saddlers, wagonmakers, lawyers, blacksmiths, typesetters, preachers, daguerreotypists, and physicians. Most of the men and women feared God and prayed regularly, but they also enjoyed bawdy comedy and could break into sudden laughter if so moved. During the weeks required to reach their destinations, few secrets were concealed from one another. Over campfire in the long evenings they told each other amusing tales of roguery and romance in which the narrators played leading or supporting roles.

Conjunctive Adverbs

As their name suggests, **conjunctive adverbs** (or adverbial conjunctions, as they are sometimes called) do the job of joining sentences with an adverbial emphasis.

The following list includes single-word conjunctive adverbs along with some prepositional phrases that commonly function as sentence connectors:

Addition: moreover, furthermore, likewise, also, in addition

Time: meanwhile, in the meantime

Contrast: however, instead, on the contrary, on the other hand, in contrast, rather

Result: therefore, so, consequently, as a result, of course

Concession: nevertheless, yet, still, at any rate, after all, of course

Apposition: namely, for example, for instance, that is, in other words

Summary: thus, then, in conclusion

Reinforcement: further, indeed, in particular, above all, in fact

The conjunctive adverbs also differ from other conjunctions in that, like ordinary adverbs, most of them are movable; they need not introduce the clause. That movability is one of their strengths, as you saw in Chapter 3—a feature that makes them especially versatile, enabling the writer to shift the emphasis, to control the sentence rhythm.

We worked hard for the Consumer Party candidates; however, we knew they didn't stand a chance.
We worked hard for the Consumer Party candidates; we knew, however, that they didn't stand a chance.

The campaign contributions we had been counting on simply didn't materialize; in fact, the campaign was broke.
The campaign contributions we had been counting on simply didn't materialize; the campaign, in fact, was broke.

Notice in the second version of the sentences how much more length and stress the reader will give to the verb *knew,* in the first one, and the noun *campaign,* in the second. It's the commas that make the difference—and the conjunctive adverb is always set off by commas. If you'll recall from the discussion of sentence rhythm in Chapter 3, the word preceding a comma will get heavy stress; and because the conjunctive adverbs are movable, you can decide where you want that stress to be. Read the second clause in these two examples without the conjunctive adverb:

We knew they didn't stand a chance.
The campaign was broke.

Given no other signal, the reader will surely give these sentences normal end focus. *However* and *in fact* direct the reader's attention to wherever you want it to be—to the exact word. You can also emphasize end focus by delaying the conjunctive adverb to the end:

. . . ; we knew they didn't stand a chance, however.
. . . ; the campaign was broke, in fact.

Bear in mind, however, that the farther along in the sentence the conjunctive adverb appears, the less importance it will have as a connector. If the reader needs the cohesive signal—such as the message of *however* that a contrast is coming—you will probably want the reader to get to it in timely fashion, not wait until the end of the sentence, especially if the second clause is fairly long.

The Semicolon

One good reason to recognize and understand the various categories of conjunctions—the coordinate, the correlative, and the conjunctive adverbs—is to understand the punctuation conventions that go with them. As connectors of sentences, the coordinate and correlative conjunctions call for a comma, but when the connector is a conjunctive adverb, a comma is simply not strong enough: With the conjunctive adverb, the compound sentence requires a semicolon. In the sentence about the Consumer Party candidates, for instance, a comma as a connector would constitute a "comma splice":

> *We worked hard for the Consumer Party candidates, however, we knew they didn't stand a chance.

Understanding the following punctuation rule will give you the confidence to use semicolons:

> If the compound sentence does *not* have a coordinate or correlative conjunction, we use a semicolon to connect the two clauses.

The Bare Semicolon

While on the subject of semicolons with conjunctive adverbs, we should also consider the compound sentence with a semicolon and no conjunction at all, a very common occurrence:

> No President before Roosevelt ever built such a library; no President since has failed to do so.
>
> —Geoffrey Ward

> A single hot toy can bring in $100 million in retail sales in a single season; a hot toy that unexpectedly goes cold (remember the Cabbage Patch Kids? Teddy Ruxpin?) can help push a company into bankruptcy.
>
> —Doug Stewart

> Handcrafted furniture fits right in with the soft-tech trend in interior design. High tech looks cold; chintz seems overstuffed.
>
> —Maggie Malone

These sentences illustrate one of the most common circumstances for the bare semicolon: the pair of clauses that express parallel ideas. In both cases here the second statement contrasts with the first. Notice the parallel but contrasting subjects:

No President before . . .
no President since . . .

A single hot toy . . .
a hot toy that goes cold . . .

High tech . . .
Chintz . . .

In all three cases, the semicolon is clearly the most effective strategy. With a period, and thus separate sentences, the parallel ideas would lose their cohesiveness. It is the parallel nature of the coordinate clauses in these sentences that obviates the need for the conjunctive adverb.

These sentences don't need the signal that the conjunctive adverb could provide; its connection is already marked by the contrasts expressed in the subjects. To add a signal such as *however* or *on the other hand* would be superfluous. Parallel structure of this kind sends a strong message to the reader: "I've crafted this sentence with care. Pay attention!"

The compound sentence connected by the bare semicolon does not always have that clear parallelism. Sometimes the second clause simply illustrates or further explains or sums up the idea in the first:

> He [Deng Xiaoping] did not know from one moment to another where he could meet his guests; he was no longer master in his own house.
>
> —Harrison E. Salisbury

> Computers now control not only the nation's telephone communications, but everything from traffic lights and microwave ovens to the aircraft over Manhattan; even the average modern automobile contains a half-dozen tiny computers.
>
> —Michael Rogers

And here is one you read earlier in this chapter:

> The technique of coordination, of putting together compound structures in sentences, is old hat; you've been doing it all your life.

In these sentences there is no need for a conjunctive adverb to signal the connection, as there would be if the connection were a contrast or a concession—something the reader would not expect. The writers could also have chosen to use *and*. But if you read the sentences with *and* inserted, you'll understand why the semicolon is a better choice. The semicolon gives the sentences tightness and control. Don't ever think that one little word can't possibly make a difference; it can—especially when that word is a superfluous *and*.

A variation of what we are calling the "bare semicolon" is the semicolon used with a coordinating or correlative conjunction. (In the earlier examples with these conjunctions, you'll recall, the punctuation rule called for a comma with the conjunction.) There are two main circumstances when the semicolon will do the job better than the comma: (1) when the separate clauses are quite long and/or include internal punctuation and (2) when the writer wants to put a stronger emphasis on the second clause:

> Arnold taught us, echoing Camus, that people were not so much good or bad as ignorant. I don't know. I believe in good and evil; and I believe in forgiveness.
>
> —Barbara Grizzuti Harrison

> Although Fang obviously cared deeply about the cause of democracy in China, he was not one to thrust it upon anyone; and although he had been politically persecuted throughout his life, there was no hint of rancor or resentment in his politics.
>
> It was true that he had been forbidden to make political speeches or give interviews to the press, that his phone was bugged, and that his movements were closely watched; but it was also true that he was able to lead a busy life in the capital, teaching, attending scientific meetings, and meeting privately with friends, including some foreigners.
>
> —Orville Schell

> One boat may not catch many turtles; but considering that approximately 7,000 offshore commercial vessels tow for four to five million hours per year, the cumulative impact is serious.
>
> —Jack and Anne Rudlow

In the preceding two examples with *but*, the writers could have used *however:* Both signal that a contrast is coming. The writers apparently preferred the informality of *but*. We also have a conjunctive adverb—*moreover*—that is equal in meaning to *and*—but much more formal and obtrusive.

In the following passage, the first sentence needs the semicolon with the correlative because *but* is missing. With *but* included, a comma would have been strong enough.

> His [Edwin P. Hubbell's] discovery of an expanding universe not only made sense in terms of Newton's theory of gravity and Einstein's relativity; it also proved to be the wellspring for the idea of the Big Bang, now the reigning theory of how the universe began.
>
> —John Noble Wilford

The Bare Conjunctive Adverb

We began the discussion of the conjunctive adverb by pointing out that its usual punctuation partner is the semicolon: Understanding how we use conjunctive adverbs will also help you understand the effective use of semicolons. The previous section, "The Bare Semicolon," describes two common deviations from that pattern: (1) the semicolon connecting the two clauses in a compound sentence without a conjunctive adverb and (2) the semicolon with the coordinating or correlative conjunction. In this section we will see examples of the opposite deviation: the conjunctive adverb without the semicolon. For example, in the following passages from a *Time* cover story on medicine, the connection between the two sentences is signaled by a conjunctive adverb, but they are separate sentences—not coordinate clauses connected by a semicolon:

> As hay fever and other allergy sufferers will testify, the immune system can sometimes react to pollen, animal dander, molds and drugs that are normally harmless. In allergy victims, however, the immune system goes into high gear at the appearance of these substances, or allergens.
>
> Doses of cyclosporine, which works by dampening T-cell attacks on the beta cells, have provided dramatic results: many patients have been able to discontinue their insulin shots for up to a year. Still, by undermining the entire immune system, cyclosporine leaves the diabetic more vulnerable to other diseases.
>
> These extraordinary proteins have a bewildering array of names and functions. There are, for instance, three types of interferon—alpha, beta and gamma.

The conjunctive adverbs are strong rhythm words—no matter what the style of punctuation.

EXERCISE 35

Following are the first six paragraphs of an early draft of a student's essay on the dangers of agricultural chemicals. As you revise it, think about all of the sentence strategies you have been studying in the previous chapters, as well as the principles of coordination in this chapter, including the use of conjunctive adverbs and semicolons. In subsequent revisions the author made a number of changes on the basis of the known–new contract.

> Recommending that anyone wishing to maintain a healthy diet consume sizable quantities of fruits and vegetables is logical advice, given their nutritional value. Now such benefits may be undermined by the risks associated with chemicals that are used to treat our nation's agriculture. Risks have been significantly reduced, but they remain a relevant problem until further

reforms are made in the laws and organizations that are responsible for regulations in the use of these chemicals.

The greatest risk of the use of these chemicals is an increased number of cancer cases. A 1987 study by the National Academy of Sciences reported that 90 percent of all the fungicides used in the United States are capable of causing cancer. In addition, 60 percent of herbicides and 30 percent of all pesticides are also carcinogenic. Use of these chemicals will result in an estimated 1.4 million cancer cases and will slightly increase each American's chance of contracting the disease in their lifetime.

Even more alarming are the risks faced by our nation's children. They are particularly vulnerable because they tend to consume more of the affected foods, and their growing cells may be less equipped to tolerate the chemicals they consume. Specifically, children's neurological, immune, and digestive systems are still forming, and their livers will be less able to metabolize and break down the toxins. These circumstances, in combination with the carcinogenic nature of many chemicals, will cause 5,000 cancer cases among those of preschool age. Cases of mental retardation due to damage to the nervous system can also be anticipated.

These statistics may seem insignificant relative to the total population. While it is true that these statistics could be a great deal worse, they could also be a lot better. Unfortunately, abolishing the use of chemicals is not a viable alternative if we wish to maintain our abundant food supply. But as consumers we ourselves could contribute to a positive improvement through careful washing and removal of the outer peels on produce. These precautions, however, are not sufficient. Alas, the growth regulator used to treat apples that is currently surrounded by controversy, can neither be washed nor processed out.

In recognition of such problems, the Environmental Protection Agency (EPA) was charged with regulating the chemicals used to treat our nation's crops under the Federal Insecticide, Fungicide, and Rodenticide Act of 1972. This is mainly achieved through the determination of tolerance levels. In addition, the Delaney Clause to the Food and Drug Act prohibits the addition to processed foods of any compound found to cause cancer in test animals.

As impressive as these guidelines may seem in print, they are much less effective in practice. The provisions of the Delaney Clause particularly have hindered its effectiveness. For one thing, the clause applies only to processed foods, not to raw agricultural products, where strict standards are often perceived as being counterproductive. While processed foods may pose a more serious threat due to the tendency of pesticides to concentrate once water and oils are removed from raw commodities, 45 percent of the risks associated with chemical treatment stem from foods with no processed form, as is the case with many fruits and vegetables. These cases are beyond the scope of the Delaney Clause.

—Rita Jean Bonessa

(Note: The author's footnotes have not been included.)

The Colon as Sentence Connector

Inexperienced writers often avoid using semicolons simply because they don't understand them; even less understood is the colon as a sentence connector. In Chapter 10 you will read about the colon in its more familiar role—as a signal of appositives:

> Three committees were set up to plan the convention: program, finance, and local arrangements.

In this sentence the message of the colon is "Here it comes, the list of committees I promised."

In the compound sentence, the role of the colon is similar. Like the appositive list in the preceding example, the clause following the colon completes or explains or encapsulates the idea in the first clause:

> The 1988 election confirmed the split-level rule in American politics: The higher the office, the more ideology matters.
>
> —William Schneider

> Rats and rabbits, to those who injected, weighed and dissected them, were little different from cultures in a petri dish: they were just things to manipulate and observe.
>
> —Steven Zak

> It's not that Japanese consumers are eager to throw their money away: to judge by the way shoppers prowl through the neighborhood supermarket and electronics store, they are extremely cost conscious.
>
> —James Fallows

> My mother was not prodigal: she was unnaturally frugal.
>
> —Barbara Grizzuti Harrison

Notice how the first clause sets up an expectation in the reader. The colon says, "Here comes the information you're expecting" or "Here's what I promised." In the last two passages, the *not* in the first clause sets the reader up for a contrast in the second. In general, if you can mentally insert "namely" or "that is" or "in fact," as you can in the preceding examples, you should consider using a colon to connect the sentences.

It's important to recognize that this way of connecting two clauses is quite different from the connection with semicolons we saw earlier. The two clauses connected with the semicolon have parallel ideas. And unless you include a signal to the contrary, your reader will expect the relationship to be an additive one, an "and" connection. If you try to replace the colon with *and*, you'll see that it won't work.

Two other common situations that the colon signals are questions and direct quotations:

> Like millions of her countrymen, [Helen] Suzman now sees South Africa's future hanging on a far more personal question: Can Nelson Mandela live up to the myth that has grown up around him?
>
> —*Newsweek*

> In Sacramento, there is one high-school counselor for every 2,000 students: "I do [college counseling]," said one, "after school, at night, when I can fit it in, for large groups of students and parents."
>
> —Peter Schrag

Another situation that calls for the colon as a signal, which you are probably familiar with, is the block quotation—the long indented quotation.

There is one detail of punctuation in these compound sentences that varies. Except in the case of the direct quotation, you have the choice of using either a capital or a lowercase letter following the colon. (The first word of a direct quotation is always capitalized, whether or not the quotation is a full sentence.) Some publications capitalize all full sentences following colons (the style of this book); others capitalize only questions; some use lowercase for all sentences except direct quotations. Whichever style of punctuation you choose, be consistent.

The Short of Sentences

The title of this chapter suggests that its subject matter will include short sentences as well as long ones. But so far we've focused on the long ones. That focus is understandable, of course, because we've been discussing compound sentences and those with compound structures in them—and they tend to be long. And, besides, you don't need instruction in how to write short sentences. But you may need instruction in using them. Or maybe *encouragement* is a better word: You may need encouragement in using them. Too often inexperienced writers think that writing calls for long sentences rather than short ones—just as they believe that writing calls for fancy words rather than plain ones. Both notions are wrong. The short sentence can send a powerful message. And, in fact, it often serves as the focus of the paragraph.

The purpose of some short sentences and their effect on the reader closely resemble the purpose and effect of short paragraphs. The two- or three-sentence paragraph in an essay of long ones often provides transition to a new focus, shifting gears, redirecting the reader. Experienced writers use the short sentence for that same purpose. In the following paragraph, from an *Atlantic* article on the Japanese economy by James Fallows, the short sentence in the middle changes the focus from the preceding paragraph on the workplace to the following one about schools; in fact, it turns out to be the topic sentence:

> In most Japanese offices people are busy-looking but are often engaged in busywork. Office ladies bustle back and forth carrying tea, groups of men sit through two-hour meetings to resolve a minor point, and of course there are the long evenings in the restaurants and bars. Something similar is true of the schools. The children are at school for more hours each week than American children, but in any given hour they may be horsing around, entertaining themselves while the teachers take one of their (surprisingly frequent) breaks,

conducting "self-improvement" meetings, or scrubbing the floors during dai soji—literally, "big clean-up." (Most schools have no hired janitorial staff.)

The fifth sentence in the following eight-sentence paragraph from a *Smithsonian* article by Michael Parfit has that same gear-shifting purpose; again, it's actually the topic sentence. The four preceding sentences summarize the background and provide transition from the essay's previous paragraphs; the three sentences that follow explain and support this new focus.

> It is not surprising that ranchers continue to destroy forests wherever they can in spite of evidence that many Amazon soils don't support grass for long. Brazil's ranchers carry the moral scythe of manifest destiny. Once that energy belonged to the Soldiers of Rubber and their patraos [bosses]. Now the patraos live in dimly lit rooms among their thoughts of the past and wait for barges that don't come. The momentum is in cattle. In Brazil, where land-protection regulations and enforcement officers often fall off the truck between Brasilia and the forest, momentum is more important than law. Recent studies have shown that rain forest is far more valuable intact than burned, but that doesn't matter to momentum. In the United States in 1875 it would also have been more logical economically to have kept the cows and the alfalfa in Connecticut, and ranched bison on the plains.

The sentences in this paragraph, other than the five-word gear-shifting one, average twenty-four words each. In the paragraph about Japan the two sentences on either side of the middle seven-word sentence have thirty-four and fifty-one words. These short, focused sentences are bound to draw the attention of the reader.

In the following paragraph, from the middle of a *Time* article on earthquake prediction published in the issue following California's 1989 earthquake, again the short sentence refocuses the reader on the new topic:

> Still, there is a vast difference between suggesting that an earthquake is likely to happen and pinpointing when. For now scientists cannot say whether a specific section of the San Andreas fault will snap in one year's time or in a hundred, but they are working on it. Seismic silence is one clue. Soundings taken along the San Andreas over the past 15 years showed that the small earthquakes that are a daily event along other parts of the system were not occurring in the Santa Cruz mountains. Scientists argued over the significance of this blank spot in the data. Then a year ago, activity ominously resumed, and last August brought a damaging earthquake. Such an increase in activity, notes Columbia's Scholz [Christopher Scholz of Columbia University's Lamont-Doherty Geological Observatory], seems to indicate that stress has built up to the point where a major release is imminent.

Frances FitzGerald uses the same technique in her essay about textbooks, "Rewriting American History." In this, the fifth paragraph, the short second sentence is the topic sentence. And she uses another short sentence at the end—as a kind of exclamation point that serves as a lead-in to the following paragraph:

> Of course, when one thinks about it, it is hardly surprising that modern scholarship and modern perspectives have found their way into children's books. Yet the changes remain shocking. Those who in the sixties complained of the bland optimism, the chauvinism, and the materialism of their old civics text did so in the belief that, for all their protests, the texts would never change. The thought must have had something reassuring about it, for that generation never noticed when its complaints began to take effect and the songs about radioactive rainfall and houses made of ticky-tacky began to appear in the textbooks. But this is what happened.

Fiction writers also use short sentences to good advantage, often to evoke the disconnected nature of thoughts and feelings:

> Maybe she misses London. She feels caged, in this country, in this city, in this room. She could start with the room, she could open a window. It's too stuffy in here. . . .
>
> Kat feels her own forehead. She wonders if she's running a temperature. Something ominous is going on behind her back. There haven't been enough phone calls from the magazine; they've been able to muddle on without her, which is bad news. Reigning queens should never go on vacation, or have operations, either. Uneasy lies the head. . . .
>
> She isn't in good shape. She can hardly stand. She stands, despite his offer of a chair. She sees now what she's wanted, what she's been missing. Gerald is what she's been missing: the stable, unfashionable, previous, tight-assed Gerald. Not Ger, not the one she's made in her own image. The other one, before he got ruined.
>
> —Margaret Atwood, "Kat"

In narrative descriptions, too, the short sentence often signals a significant detail:

> Francis got home late from town, and Julia got the sitter while he dressed, and then hurried him out of the house. The party was small and pleasant, and Francis settled down to enjoy himself. A new maid passed the drinks. Her hair was dark, and her face was round and pale and seemed familiar to Francis.
>
> —John Cheever, "The Country Husband"

And short sentences can enhance descriptions of fear and excitement. The following paragraph is from a *Time* essay about China by Theodore H. White:

> For sweep of terror, China under the Cultural Revolution was the equivalent of Nazi Germany. Thugs, Red Guard bands and idealists fought in the

> cities, all rivaling one another to show loyalty to Mao Thought. Stories from the interior convey the sweep of the violence. In Chengdu, capital of Sichuan, the handsome old government palace was blown to bits by Red Guards; in its place they erected a new hall filled only with portraits of Mao. In Chongquin, workers fought each other with machine guns, artillery, armored cars and tanks. In Harbin, the factions used airplanes to bomb each other. In Peking, Red Guards stormed and burned the British Embassy. In Wuhan, center of the great iron and steel complex as well as of several universities, steelworkers shaped up three rival bands, while universities formed rival student bands, all warring within and against one another.

The "sweep of the violence" is reinforced by the five sentences all beginning with "in" prepositional phrases, two of which are only ten words long, in contrast to the last one, which contains thirty-six.

As you can see, short sentences can be powerful. They will call attention to themselves in a paragraph of long sentences. Because the reader will notice them, you'll want to choose carefully the ideas that you put into them.

For Group Discussion

Examine an essay of your own or that of a classmate. Count the number of words in the sentences. Are there any short ones, of eight words or fewer? If so, are they there for a purpose? Do they have that gear-shifting quality that you've seen in the examples, directing the reader's attention to a new focus? Have you used short sentences for your topic sentences? As you revise, be sure to think about the power that short sentences can bring to your prose.

RHETORICAL REMINDERS

Parallelism

Do the coordinate structures within the sentence belong together? (Are the ideas equal? Are the forms the same?)

But

Have I reserved *but* for signaling contrasts?

Correlatives

Have I taken advantage of the strong focus that the correlatives provide: *either–or, neither–nor, both–and, not only–but also?*

Conjunctive Adverbs

Have I used the versatile conjunctive adverbs to good advantage?

Have I placed them where I want the reader to focus?

Colons

Have I used the colon to connect those sentences that set up an expectation in the reader?

Short Sentences

Have I called attention to focusing ideas or shifted gears with short sentences?

PUNCTUATION REMINDERS

Use no comma with *and* between the parts of a two-part compound structure within the sentence.

Use a comma with the coordinating conjunction between the clauses of a compound sentence.

Use a semicolon to connect the two clauses if the compound sentence does not have a coordinate or correlative conjunction.

Chapter 10

The Grammar of Style

Everything we say, we say "with style," in one sense of the word—when the word refers simply to an individual's way of writing. You have your own style of writing, just as you have your own style of speaking and whistling and throwing a Frisbee and wearing your hair. We also use the word *style* to characterize the overall impression of a piece of writing: the plain style, the pompous style, the grand style, the official style. When you follow the advice to be brief and to use simple words, the outcome will be a plain style. Fancy words will probably lead to a pompous style.

The word *style* is also used in connection with variations in sentence structure, with choices that you as a writer have. For example, in the previous paragraph, four verb phrases in a series are connected with three *ands* and no commas:

> speaking <u>and</u> whistling <u>and</u> throwing a Frisbee <u>and</u> wearing your hair

It could have been written with three commas and only one *and:*

> speaking, whistling, throwing a Frisbee, <u>and</u> wearing your hair

Or only commas:

> speaking, whistling, throwing a Frisbee, wearing your hair

These simple changes make a difference in the reader's response.

Such stylistic variations have traditionally occupied an important place in the study of rhetoric. In fact, the Greeks had names for every little deviation from normal word order or usage, and Greek orators practiced using them. Some of the more common ones, you're familiar with—those we call "figures of speech," such as simile, metaphor, and personification. But many of them, you probably don't even notice, such as the shift—in both this sentence and the previous one—of the direct object to opening position. But this deviation has a name too: The Greek rhetoricians called it *anastrophe* (pronounced a-NAS-tro-fee). Such rhetorical "schemes," as they are sometimes called, are, obviously, related to the study of sentence grammar.

In this chapter, then, what you will be doing is using your understanding of grammar to raise your consciousness about style. We will examine how deviations from standard sentence structure and punctuation will affect your style and, more important, will send a message to your reader: "Pay attention! Read this carefully. It's important."

Before looking further at deviations in punctuation and word order, we will take up two further grammatical structures—two important stylistic devices that inexperienced writers rarely use well, if at all: the **appositive** and the **absolute phrase.** Both are tools that you should have under your control, that will make a difference in your writing.

The Appositive

In Chapter 8 you learned the term *nominal*, a word that refers to the function of nouns and noun phrases. By "function of nouns" we mean all of the slots in the sentence that a noun or noun phrase can fill: subject, direct object, indirect object, subjective complement, objective complement, and object of preposition. You'll recall that although nominals are usually nouns or noun phrases, verb phrases and clauses can also fill those slots:

> Randy is an expert at <u>throwing Frisbees</u>. (Here the object of the preposition *at* is a gerund phrase.)
> I decided <u>to leave early</u>. (The direct object is an infinitive phrase.)
> <u>Where you are going</u> is none of my business. (The subject is a clause.)

The appositive, too, is a nominal—but it doesn't *fill* the slot: It *shares* it. The appositive is like a person who says, "Move over. I'm sharing this seat with you"—a nominal companion of sorts.

> Do you know **Ron,** <u>the head butcher at Giant Foods</u>?
> **The security guard in our building,** <u>an ex-Marine who once played professional football</u>, makes us feel very secure indeed.
> The federal Aviation Administration (FAA) takes **people,** <u>many with no aviation background</u>, and filters out two of every five hopefuls in a rigorous screening program in Oklahoma.
>
> —James R. Chiles

Notice that the appositive, the underlined noun phrase, renames the noun or noun phrase that fills the nominal slot. In the first sentence, the appositive renames the direct object; in the second, it renames the subject; in the third, from an article about training air traffic controllers, it renames the direct object. The appositive and the noun phrase it renames have the same referent; in fact, most appositives can substitute for that noun phrase without a change in meaning.

The appositive can be especially useful in helping writers avoid two common problems: choppy sentences and the overuse of *be* as the main verb. Here are two pairs of sentences that would profit from revision:

> Alan B. Shepard was the first American to fly in space. He was launched on a 302-mile suborbital shot over the Atlantic in 1961.
> I'll never forget the birthday present my dad bought me when I was ten. It was a new three-speed bike.

In both of these examples, the writer has used two sentences to identify the topic. And in both cases one of the two has a form of *be* as its predicating verb, followed by a noun phrase as subjective complement. This common situation is the ideal candidate for a combined sentence containing an appositive:

> Alan B. Shepard, the first American to fly in space, was launched on a 302-mile suborbital shot over the Atlantic in 1961.
> I'll never forget the birthday present my dad bought me when I was ten, a new three-speed bike.

In the second sentence you can replace the comma with a dash for greater emphasis:

> I'll never forget the birthday present my dad bought me when I was ten—a new three-speed bike.

In the following passage, *be* acts as the predicating verb of all three sentences:

> There are an estimated 25,000 centenarians in the United States. Centenarians are people aged 100 or over. This is the fastest-growing age group in the U.S. population.

It doesn't take an expert to hear the problem of these three choppy sentences. The best solution in rewriting them will depend on which idea the writer wants to focus on. Here is one possibility:

> The estimated 25,000 centenarians, people aged 100 or over, make up the fastest-growing age group in the U.S. population.

In the earlier examples, too, the context might have called for a different focus:

Alan B. Shepard, launched on a 302-mile suborbital shot over the Atlantic in 1961, was the first American to fly in space.
I'll never forget my first three-speed bike, a birthday present from my dad when I was ten.

In the Shepard sentence we have turned one of the sentences into a participial phrase. (You studied participial phrases in Chapter 8 in connection with the expanded noun phrase.)

We should mention, too, that when the appositive renames the subject, it has a feature in common with the participial phrase: It is movable. It can open or close the sentence. And, like the participial phrase, when it ends the sentence, the appositive will be the point of focus. At the beginning it will tend to put more stress on the subject, which will no longer be an opening valley in the intonation contour. Read these two sentences aloud, and notice how the rhythm changes:

The first American to fly in space, Alan B. Shepard was launched on a 302-mile suborbital shot over the Atlantic in 1961.
Alan B. Shepard was launched on a 302-mile suborbital shot over the Atlantic in 1961, the first American to fly in space.

The reader of the first sentence probably expects to continue reading about Alan Shepard; the next sentence is likely to begin with *He*. The reader of the second would not be surprised to learn, in the following sentence, what happened next in the space program.

Both the opening and the closing appositive—the noun phrase renaming the subject—are fairly unusual structures, unusual enough to call attention to themselves. But they are also dramatic structures, and when well used they send a message to the reader that the writer has taken pains in crafting the sentence. Of the three positions for the appositive, the "home base" position, the slot following the noun, gets the least emphasis. This is what is called the unmarked position; in other words, it is the expected one.

The Introductory Appositive Series

The opening appositive will be even more dramatic when it consists of a series of appositives, not just a single one. The following passage is part of a description of Queen Victoria written by Winston Churchill:

> High devotion to her royal task, domestic virtues, evident sincerity of nature, a piercing and sometimes disconcerting truthfulness—all these qualities of the Queen's had long impressed themselves upon the mind of her subjects.

The subject of the sentence is *all these qualities;* the list of appositives names the qualities. In the following example, the opening series gives details of the "scene":

> Bearded zealots, sitting cross-legged on the ground, wallowing in Haiku poetry, Bhagavad-Gitas and Zen in an atmosphere saturated with the exoticisms of incense, opiates and lanterns—the "scene," in short, smacks of a Dr. Fu Manchu melodrama.
>
> —F. M. Esfandiary

Often the opening noun phrase series is in apposition to a pronoun as subject, in this case *they:*

> Political and religious systems, social customs, loyalties and traditions, they all came tumbling down like so many rotten apples off a tree.
>
> —William Golding

This stylistic device, the opening appositive series, may seem a bit dramatic for your purposes. You might think it would call too much attention to itself if you're writing an essay on politics or economics or history or literature. But it needn't be quite as dramatic as those examples. It can simply be a tight, authoritative way of presenting facts:

> Poland, Hungary, Czechoslovakia, Romania—they all caught the democratic fever that was sweeping across Eastern Europe.

Restrictive vs. Nonrestrictive Appositives

In Chapter 8 we made a distinction between restrictive and nonrestrictive modifiers in the noun phrase. The restrictive modifier can be thought of as necessary to the meaning of the noun—a defining modifier. The modifier added to *sister* in this sentence actually defines the word *sister:*

> My sister living in Atlanta just called.

In other words, without *living in Atlanta* we would not know who called: The absence of commas indicates that the writer has more than one sister. If such were not the case—if the writer has only one sister—then the sentence would need commas; the modifier would be there simply to comment, to add information, not to identify which sister.

The same principle of punctuation applies to appositives. Using commas becomes an issue mainly when a proper name fills the appositive slot. When you read the following pair of sentences—and include the pauses indicated by the commas—you will hear the difference:

> My sister Mary just called.
> My sister, Mary, just called.

The sentence without commas implies the existence of at least one other sister. The appositive *Mary* is there to identify which one.

It's important for you, as a writer, to understand this distinction. Your reader is counting on your punctuation to send the right message.

The Colon with Appositives

In Chapter 9 we saw the colon in its role as a connector of clauses in compound sentences. Here we will see it in its more common role, as a signal for an appositive:

> I'll never forget the birthday present my dad bought me when I was ten: a new three-speed bike.

As we saw earlier, this sentence can be written with a comma or a dash instead of a colon. Like the dash, the colon is a strong signal, putting emphasis on the appositive; you can think of the dash as an informal colon.

One of the most common uses of the colon is to signal a list:

> Three committees were set up to plan the conference: program, finance, and local arrangements.

Here the list is actually a list of appositives renaming the noun *committees*. The colon is a way of saying, "Here it comes, the list I promised." Sometimes the separate structures in the list will have internal punctuation of their own, in which case you will want to separate them with semicolons:

> The study of our grammar system includes three areas: phonology, the study of sounds; morphology, the study of meaningful combinations of sounds; and syntax, the study of sentence structure.

Here each of the three noun phrases in the list has a modifier of its own, set off by a comma; the semicolons signal the reader that the series has three items, not six. This is one of the two occasions in our writing system that call for the semicolon. (The other, you will recall, is the semicolon that joins the clauses in a compound sentence.)

When an appositive in the middle of the sentence is a list, we use a pair of dashes to set it off:

> Three committees—program, finance, and local arrangements—were set up to plan the convention.
>
> All three areas of our grammar system—phonology, morphology, and syntax—will be covered in the grammar course.

If we had used commas instead of dashes, the reader might have been confused:

*All three areas of our grammar system, phonology, morphology, and syntax, will be covered in the grammar course.

We need the two different marks of punctuation—the dashes as well as the commas—to differentiate the two levels of boundaries we are marking. You'll read more about this issue, the hierarchies of punctuation, in Chapter 11. Dashes will also be effective; they will add emphasis, even when the appositive has no internal punctuation. The dashes announce the appositive with a kind of fanfare:

My latest purchase—a personal copier—has made my work much easier.

The main stress of the sentence, however, remains on the predicate.

The list that the colon signals can also consist of independent clauses—complete sentences, rather than simply words or phrases. The boundaries between the clauses in the list will be marked by semicolons. The following example—a complete paragraph from a *Smithsonian* article by Don Stap about an ecological area of Florida called "scrub"—also illustrates another feature of the well-written series: When one of the items in the series is more important or, as in this case, a more complex description, it occupies the last slot. Note also that the sentence directly following the colon is not capitalized, conforming to *Smithsonian* style (in contrast to the style of this book, with its capitalized *When* in the previous sentence).

> The inhabitants of scrub are often as peculiar as they are diminutive: the short-tailed snake has no known relatives and no fossil record; the scrub firefly flies in daylight; and the rare sand skink, a nearly legless lizard, seldom sees the light of day, preferring to spend its time beneath the sand, where it swims fish-fashion in pursuit of its prey—termites and beetle larvae.

Avoiding Punctuation Errors

The use of the colon with appositives is the source of a common punctuation error, but one simple rule can resolve it:

A complete sentence precedes the colon.

Notice in the examples that the structure preceding the colon is a complete sentence pattern, with every slot filled:

Three committees were set up to plan the convention.
The study of our grammar system includes three areas.

Because the colon so often precedes a list, the writer may assume that all lists require colons, but that's not the case. In the following sentences, the colons are misused:

*The committees that were set up to plan the convention are: program, finance, and local arrangements.

*The three areas of the grammar system are: phonology, morphology, and syntax.

Your understanding of the sentence patterns will tell you that a subjective complement is needed to complete a sentence that has a form of *be* (here it's *are*) as the main verb. (You can review the patterns in Chapter 1.)

One common variation for the sentence with a list includes the noun phrase *the following:*

> The committees that were set up to plan the convention are the following: program, finance, and local arrangements.

That noun phrase, *the following,* fills the subjective complement slot, so the sentence is indeed grammatical. But it's not necessarily the most effective version of the sentence. When you read the sentence aloud, you'll hear yourself putting main stress on the word *following*—a word with no information. If you want to use a colon in such a sentence for purposes of emphasis, the earlier version is smoother and more efficient:

> Three committees were set up to plan the convention: program, finance, and local arrangements.

It certainly makes more sense for the word *convention* to be emphasized rather than *following*.

The Sentence Appositive

Another effective—and dramatic—stylistic device is the sentence appositive, a noun phrase that renames or, more accurately, encapsulates the idea in the sentence as a whole. It is usually punctuated with the dash:

> The musical opened to rave reviews and standing-room-only crowds—a smashing success.

Compare that tight sentence with a compound sentence that has the same information:

> The musical opened to rave reviews and standing-room-only crowds; it was a smashing success.

Here are two other examples, in which the reader's attention will be focused on the final sentence appositive:

> A pair of cardinals has set up housekeeping in our pine tree—an unexpected but welcome event.

In September of 1988 Hurricane Gilbert hit Jamaica with winds that clocked 175 mph—the worst natural disaster in the island's modern history.

The sentence appositive is similar to the appositives we saw earlier, except that instead of simply renaming a noun, the sentence appositive offers a conclusion about the sentence as a whole in the form of a noun phrase.

EXERCISE 36

Revise the following passages, using appositives or other modifying structures. Experiment with commas, colons, and dashes.

1. The cost of repairs to the nation's public transportation facilities is an expenditure that cannot be delayed much longer if the system is to survive. Roads, bridges, and railroads are all in need of repair.
2. To many people, the mushroom is a lowly fungus. It has little food value. To other people, it is a gourmet's delight.
3. In the early 1980s the Chinese banned the import of certain American goods, such as cotton, synthetic fibers, and soybeans. The restriction had an adverse effect on the U.S. economy. It especially affected the farmers.
4. The paper nautilus octopus is a rare marine animal. It normally lives in the coastal waters of Japan. It was found recently in the squid nets off Santa Catalina in California.
5. According to fashion experts, the crew cut will be back in style before long. That particular haircut was more or less the hallmark of the 1950s.
6. The ivory-billed woodpecker is one of North America's rarest birds. It is North America's largest woodpecker. It hasn't been sighted with certainty for several decades.
7. Llamas are becoming popular in this country as exotic pets. They are also valuable for their wool. Llamas are peaceable animals. They have been used since ancient times in the Andes as pack animals. They don't like to be petted, but they do like to stand quite close to humans and just stare. Until a few years ago, there were llamas in just a few places in this country. That changed when Dick and Kay Patterson of Sisters, Oregon, who were breeders of Arabian horses, turned their expertise to llamas. Now there are about 6,000 breeders, and there are 70,000 llamas registered with the International Llama Registry. (Adapted from a *New York Times* article by Anne Raver)
8. Potatoes have the reputation of being fattening. A medium potato has only 100 calories. It's the butter and gravy that make the potato fattening. Potatoes are highly nutritious. They contain vitamin C and a number of trace minerals. They are low in sodium, high in potassium, and thus the

ideal food for preventing high blood pressure. The potato is even high in vegetable protein. All in all, the lowly potato is a nutrient bargain. (Information adapted from Jane Brody's *Good Food Book*)

The Absolute Phrase

Among the modifiers that we use to add information to our sentences, the absolute phrase is probably the least used and the least understood. In form, the absolute is a noun phrase—a noun headword with a postnoun modifier; it adds a focusing detail to the idea of the whole sentence:

> There was no bus in sight and Julian, his hands still jammed in his pockets and his head thrust forward, scowled down the empty street.
>
> —Flannery O'Connor, "Everything That Rises Must Converge"

> He smiled a little to himself as he ran, holding the ball lightly in front of him with his two hands, his knees pumping high, his hips twisting in the almost girlish run of a back in a broken field.
>
> —Irwin Shaw, "The Eighty-Yard Run"

> To his right the valley continued in its sleepy beauty, mute and understated, its wildest autumn colors blunted by the distance, placid as a water color by an artist who mixed all his colors with brown.
>
> —Joyce Carol Oates, "The Secret Marriage"

> Silently they ambled down Tenth Street until they reached a stone bench that jutted from the sidewalk near the curb. They stopped there and sat down, their backs to the eyes of the two men in white smocks who were watching them.
>
> —Toni Morrison, *Song of Solomon*

> The man stood laughing, his weapons at his hips.
>
> —Stephen Crane, "The Bride Comes to Yellow Sky"

This technique of focusing on a detail allows the writer to move the reader in for a close-up view, just as a filmmaker uses the camera. The absolute phrase is especially effective in writing description. Notice how the authors of the foregoing passages use the main clause of the sentence as the wide lens and the absolute phrase as the close-up.

In these examples the modifiers following the nouns are participial phrases in the first three and prepositional phrases in the last two. Noun phrases can also be effective in absolutes. In the following sentence from *The Accidental Tourist*, Anne Tyler uses a series of absolute phrases, the first and last of which have noun phrases—"tiny ribbons of light" and "a purple hollow extending to infinity"—as the modifiers; the second has a participial phrase—"curving away at the edges":

> He saw the city spread below like a glittering golden ocean, the streets tiny ribbons of light, the planet curving away at the edges, the sky a purple hollow extending to infinity.

The absolute is an especially useful tool for the fiction writer, as we have seen. But writers of nonfiction prose also make good use of absolutes in their descriptions. The expository and persuasive essays you write in your composition class will include passages of explanation and description where absolutes would be highly appropriate. Notice the close-up detail provided by the absolute phrase in the following passage from an article in *Harper's* by Fred Reed about nuclear subs:

> In the sonar room a half-dozen men sat in near-darkness in front of screens. Luminous green sand drifted slowly down the screens, each grain representing a slight blip of sound.

And in the following passage from an *Atlantic Monthly* article about the economist Lester Thurow, Charles C. Mann describes Professor Thurow teaching his class at M.I.T. Note that the absolute opens its sentence:

> His manner was crisp and confident; Thurow always sounds more certain about nebulous economic concepts than most people feel about anything. The certainty sometimes annoys other, more cautious economists, but students seem to like it. The fact machine in his head unspooling numbers, he began jotting the constituents of the service sector on the blackboard in his scratchy handwriting.

The absolute phrase is essentially a sentence: All that's missing is a form of *be* to turn the modifier into a full predicate:

> The fact machine in his head was unspooling numbers.
> The streets were tiny ribbons of light.
> His hips were twisting in the almost girlish run . . .
> His hands were still jammed in his pockets and his head was thrust forward.
> It wildest autumn colors were blunted by the distance.

The absolute, like the appositive, enables the writer to add what is, in fact, a complete idea, but to do so in the tight, controlled form of a noun phrase. You'll notice, too, that the absolute gets a great deal of stress; in closing position, of course, it will be in line for end focus.

As you revise your sentences, look for those places where you have used a form of *be* either as the main verb or as an auxiliary. If such a sentence is related to the preceding one by giving a focusing detail, it might be a good candidate for an absolute phrase.

EXERCISE 37

Expand the following sentences by adding the modifiers called for. (You might want to review participial phrases and relative clauses in Chapter 8.)

1. Add a *who* clause that tells what one of your relatives is usually like:
   My cousin (aunt, uncle, sister, etc.), who ____________________
   ____________________,
   surprised everyone at the family reunion.

Now add a subordinate clause that explains what your relative did that was so surprising: Now add an absolute phrase at the end of the sentence—a close-up detail.

2. Add a participial phrase that tells what the cyclists were doing:
   From the window we watched the cyclists ____________________
   ____________________.

Now add an appositive at the end of the sentence as a comment on the whole scene.

3. Use an appositive to describe the trucker:
   At the far end of the counter sat a trucker, ____________________
   ____________________.

Now add two prenoun modifiers to explain what sort of counter it is so that the reader will be better able to picture the scene—and an absolute at the end that provides a close-up detail.

4. Start this sentence with an adverbial clause or phrase that tells when:
   ____________________,
   endless cars jammed the freeway.

Now add a series of participial phrases that describe the cars and a sentence appositive that comments on the whole scene.

5. Write a sentence or paragraph describing your classroom or campus. Use the modifiers you have been practicing with.
6. Write a short paragraph describing your teacher, following the pattern of the paragraph about Professor Thurow on page 201.

Word-Order Variation

A number of the classical rhetorical schemes have to do with variation in normal subject-verb-complement word order, as we saw earlier in the examples of *anastrophe*.

Such deviations are especially common in poetry. In reading poetry, we're always on the lookout for subjects and predicates in unexpected places. Here, for example, is the opening of Robert Frost's famous poem "Stopping by Woods on a Snowy Evening":

> Whose woods these are, I think I know.

In this line the opening clause is the direct object of *know*.

> I think I know *something*.

This variation in word order can also be effective in prose, mainly because we're not looking for it. It can put stress on the verb, just as it did in Frost's line. In one of the earlier examples cited from this chapter,

> But many of them, you probably don't even notice,

the verb is in line for end focus. And in the following sentence, Charles Dickens made sure that the reader would hear the contrast between *has* and *has not:*

> Talent, Mr. Micawber has; money, Mr. Micawber has not.

Another variation in word order occurs with certain adverbs in opening position, when a shift of subject and auxiliary is required:

> Never before <u>had I seen</u> such an eerie glow in the night sky.
> Rarely <u>do I hear</u> such words of praise.

You'll notice that the opening adverbial is a peak of stress.

The following sentence, written by Winston Churchill, illustrates yet another kind of shift in word order. Here the very last noun phrase in the sentence is the grammatical subject:

> Against Lee and his great Lieutenant [Stonewall Jackson], united for a year of intense action in a comradeship which recalls that of Marlborough and Eugene, were now to be marshalled the overwhelming forces of the Union.

When you read this sentence aloud, you can hear your voice building to a crescendo on *overwhelming forces*, just as Churchill planned. In fact, it's hard to read the sentence without sounding Churchillian.

In Chapter 8 we saw another variation in the expected word order when we shifted adjective phrases from their usual preheadword position:

> <u>Hot and tired</u>, the Boy Scouts trudged the last mile to their campsite.
> The Boy Scouts, <u>hot and tired</u>, trudged the last mile to their campsite.

Highly unusual, the situation called for extraordinary measures.
The situation, highly unusual, called for extraordinary measures.

These shifts are less dramatic than Churchill's, but they do change the emphasis and call attention to themselves. In both versions, they put the strong stress on the subject, rather than on the predicate, its usual place. The reader of the Boy Scout sentence will not be surprised to read on about the physical condition of the boys. If the writer had not called attention to the adjectives, the reader might have expected to read about the campsite in the next sentence. Likewise, in the other example, both versions put strong stress on the subject. Read them aloud, then compare your reading with this version:

The highly unusual situation called for extraordinary measures.

You probably heard the highest peak of stress on the word *extraordinary* rather than on the subject. The reader of this version will expect to learn more about those measures; in the other two versions the reader probably expects to read more about the situation and what makes it unusual.

All of these word-order variations change the rhythm patterns and thus the messages that the reader will get. As a writer, you will want to construct your sentences with the reader and the reader's expectations in mind.

Ellipsis

Another fairly common stylistic variation is the use of ellipsis, where part of the sentence is simply left out, or "understood." You'll recall elliptical adverbial clauses from Chapter 7. In some the omission is required:

Ed is taller than Bill is [tall].

But in others it's optional:

When [you are] in Rome, do as the Romans do.
While [we were] traveling through Colorado last summer, we visited the Air Force Academy.
Though [I was] disappointed about my grade, I decided not to complain to the instructor.

Another common use of ellipsis occurs in coordinate structures where part of the second clause or phrase is left out to avoid repetition. In the following examples, the verb is left out:

The first day of our vacation was wonderful; the second, miserable.
For breakfast we had eggs; for lunch, eggs; and for dinner, eggs again.

> Some of our games this season were awesome; others, awful.

Note that a comma signals the omission and tells the reader to pause. This use of ellipsis gives the sentence a tight, controlled quality that would be missing if the clauses were complete.

You may be thinking at this point that if you actually used such sentences in your essays your teacher would mark them as sentence fragments and ask you to correct them. But that's not likely. Clearly, these elliptical sentences are not accidental; in fact, the opposite message will come through: "Pay attention. I crafted this sentence carefully."

In the following description of Stonewall Jackson, Churchill uses ellipsis in both sentences. In the first, he left out the linking verb in all but the first clause. The tightness of the sentence actually reflects the qualities of Jackson's character:

> His character was stern, his manner reserved and usually forbidding, his temper Calvinistic, his mode of life strict, frugal, austere.
>
> Black-bearded, pale-faced, with thin, compressed lips, aquiline nose, and dark, piercing eyes, he slouched in his weather-stained uniform a professor-warrior; yet greatly beloved by the few who knew him best, and gifted with that strange power of commanding measureless devotion from the thousands whom he ruled with an iron hand.

Notice also in the last sentence that in the clause after the semicolon both the subjects and the verbs are understood. These elliptical sentences send a strong message to the reader. You can be sure that no one will accuse Churchill of having made a mistake.

The Deliberate Fragment

The sentence fragments used for their stylistic effect are not the kind that teachers mark with a marginal "frag"; those are usually the result of punctuation errors, often a subordinate clause punctuated as a full sentence. But experienced writers know how to use fragments deliberately and effectively—noun phrases or verb phrases that add a detail without a full sentence and invariably call attention to themselves. Here are two examples from the novels of John le Carré:

> They remembered the tinkling of falling glass all right, and the timid brushing noise of the young foliage hitting the road. And the mewing of people too frightened to scream.
>
> —*The Little Drummer Girl*
>
> Our Candidate begins speaking. A deliberate, unimpressive opening.
>
> —*A Perfect Spy*

In the following paragraph from *Love Medicine* by Louise Erdrich, we are hearing fragmented thoughts—ideal candidates for sentence fragments. You'll notice that some are simple noun phrases, some are absolutes—a noun with a modifier following—and some are subordinate clauses. But, obviously, all are deliberate:

> Northern lights. Something in the cold, wet atmosphere brought them out. I grabbed Lipsha's arm. We floated into the field and sank down, crushing green wheat. We chewed the sweet kernels and stared up and were lost. Everything seemed to be one piece. The air, our faces, all cool, moist, and dark, and the ghostly sky. Pale green licks of light pulsed and faded across it. Living lights. Their fires lobbed over, higher, higher, then died out in blackness. At times the whole sky was ringed in shooting points and puckers of light gathering and falling, pulsing, fading, rhythmical as breathing. All of a piece. As if the sky were a pattern of nerves and our thought and memories traveled across it. As if the sky were one gigantic memory for us all. Or a dance hall. And all the world's wandering souls were dancing there. I thought of June. She would be dancing if there was a dance hall in space. She would be dancing a two-step for wandering souls. Her long legs lifting and falling. Her laugh an ace. Her sweet perfume the way all grown-up women were supposed to smell. Her amusement at both the bad and the good. Her defeat. Her reckless victory. Her sons.

The Coordinate Series

Many of the variations that writers use for special effect occur in connection with coordinate structures—pairs and series of sentences and their parts. One of those changes, which we saw in the opening paragraph of this chapter, is a deviation in the use of conjunctions. In a series of three or more structures, we generally use commas between the parts of the series with a conjunction before the final member. Here's the sentence we looked at earlier, with the series punctuated in the conventional way:

> You have your own style of writing, just as you have your own style of speaking, whistling, throwing a Frisbee, and wearing your hair.

Here are two variations; read them aloud and listen to the difference. The first is the way the sentence actually appears on page 191:

> You have your own style of writing, just as you have your own style of speaking and whistling and throwing a Frisbee and wearing your hair.
>
> You have your own style of writing, just as you have your own style of speaking, whistling, throwing a Frisbee, wearing your hair.

The differences are subtle, but meaningful. The first puts emphasis on each verb (the verbs here are gerunds—objects of the preposition *of*) with a fairly equal beat:

/ and / and / and /. It also puts a lilt in your voice. The second variation, the one without conjunctions, has an open-ended quality, as though the list were incomplete. The sentence seems to suggest, "I could go on and on; I could tell you much more."

The first sentence in Churchill's description of Jackson includes that second technique. The phrases themselves have no conjunctions, as a series generally does, nor does the final series of adjectives:

> His character was stern, his manner reserved and usually forbidding, his temper Calvinistic, his mode of life strict, frugal, austere.

The omission of the conjunction contributes to the strictness and frugality of style that echo the words themselves. With conjunctions, the sentence would lose that echo:

> His mode of life was strict and frugal and austere.

In Chapter 9 we saw an example of a series without a conjunction in Margaret Atwood's description of a woman's feelings, which evokes that same kind of austerity—in this case, the feeling of being caged:

> She feels caged, in this country, in this city, in this room.

Repetition

Repetition has come up before in these pages—in both a positive and a negative sense. On the positive side, repetition gives our sentences cohesion: The known–new contract calls for the repetition, if not of words, then of ideas. It is part of the glue that holds sentences together. But we also have a negative label for repetition when it has no purpose, when it gets in the reader's way: Then we call it redundancy. You may recall the discussion of redundancy in connection with flabby prepositional phrases that added nothing but words to the sentence and kept the reader from focusing on the new information.

If you've heard warnings about redundancy, if you've seen "red" in the margins of your essays, you might hesitate to use repetition deliberately. But don't hesitate. It's easy to distinguish redundancy from good repetition, from repetition as a stylistic tool. You saw examples of good repetition in the discussion of parallelism as a cohesive device in Chapter 2.

The Greek rhetoricians had labels for every conceivable kind of good repetition—from the repetition of sounds and syllables to that of words and phrases in various locations in the sentence. We'll confine our discussion to repetition in coordinate structures that will make the reader sit up and take notice.

Consider the Gettysburg Address. Which of Lincoln's words, other than "Fourscore and seven years ago," do you remember? Probably "government of the people, by the people, and for the people." It's hard to imagine those words without the repetition: "Of, by, and for the people" just wouldn't haven't have the same effect. And think about President Kennedy's stirring words, with his repetition of *any:*

> [W]e shall pay any price, bear any burden, meet any hardship, support any friend, oppose any foe to assure the survival and the success of liberty.

(Notice, too, that the conjunction has been omitted before the last member of the series. He seems to be saying, "I could go on and on with my list.")

You don't have to be a president to use that kind of repetition, nor do you have to reserve it for formal occasions. Whenever you use a coordinate structure, there's an opportunity for you to add to its impact with repetition, simply by including words that wouldn't have to be included. The following sentence, from an essay in *Time* by Charles Krauthamer, could have been more concise, but it would have lost its drama:

> There is not a single Western standard, there are two: what we demand of Western countries at peace and what we demand of Western countries at war.

And the sentence by Margaret Atwood that we saw in the last section could certainly have been more concise:

> She feels caged, in this country, in this city, in this room.

Her decision to use *in* three times was obviously deliberate.

In the following sentence, from a *New Yorker* article on the Soviet Union by Jane Kramer, a great deal of the stylistic flair comes from repetition. Note the series of "for" phrases followed by a series of "no" phrases:

> The babel of languages has come to be a metaphor for the cultural confusion, for the lack of community, for the obvious, astonishing fact that five hundred years after the Moscow conquests began in earnest there is still no reason for the Soviet Union to call itself a country—no national dream, no shared "history," no identity that people can agree on to make them responsible to one another.

A series of clauses, too, can be dramatized by repetition. The following sentence by Terrence Rafferty is from a review of the movie *Mountains of the Moon*. It, too, appeared in the *New Yorker:*

> He [Sir Richard Burton] had travelled widely, in Europe, Asia, and Africa; he had mastered a couple of dozen languages; he had written seven books; and he had made a reputation as an intellectual adventurer, a man whose joy was to immerse himself in other cultures, to experience everything—even (or perhaps especially) things that his countrymen loathed and feared.

These uses of repetition, as well as the other stylistic devices we have taken up in this chapter, will invariably call attention to themselves. For that reason, you will reserve these structures for important ideas, for those times when you want your reader to sit up and take notice. But, like the gourmet cook who knows that too many spices can overwhelm a dish, you won't want to overwhelm your reader. You will want to recognize that, like the spice that turns a bland sauce into fine cuisine, these stylistic tools can make the difference between ordinary and powerful prose.

For Group Discussion

The writers of the following passages have used a great many stylistic tools to good advantage. Identify the places where they have sent that special message to the reader: "Pay attention! I've crafted this sentence carefully."

> [George Caleb] Bingham's greatest paintings depend upon an open rhetoric, an uncannily frank relation to their audience. We view his subjects from a perspective that includes us within the painting, and the direct looks we meet there usually recall the openness of Bingham's own disposition, itself characteristically American. Looking at *Fur Traders Descending the Missouri* as if from a canoe or from the Missouri's bank, we are obliged to remember that rivers have mouths and sources. *Fur Traders* can certainly be read as a painting in which the wilderness is brought into the frame of civilization, tending ever downriver. But it is more ambiguous than that, and ambiguity is an important source of its effect. Backlit by the diffuse light of the rising sun, offset by an island still in shadow, barely accented by a line of ducks wheeling over the far shore, these exotic figures are just as redolent of where they have been as of where they are going. And as time moves the viewer farther and farther downstream from the wilderness, it seems more and more as if this painting leads us upstream in imagination to the wilder country from which this man and boy have just descended.
>
> —Verlyn Kilnkenborg, *Smithsonian*

> Firemen are big, brawny, young, and smiling creatures. They sit in the fire hall with its high ceilings and cold concrete floors and dim corners, waiting, ready. Firemen have a perfume of readiness. They wash their shiny trucks and hang the long white hoses from rods to dangle and dry. And when the alarm rings, firemen turn into hurrying bodies that know where to step and what to do, each with a place and duty, without excess motion. Firemen wear heavy coats and big black boots and hard helmets. They can part crowds. They are coalescent and virile like the fire, proud, reticent, and most content when moving; firemen have their own rules, and they break glass, make messes, climb heights, and drive big loud trucks very fast.
>
> —Sallie Tisdale, *Harper's Magazine*

> Now I know that China is still ruled by her three great symbols: the Yellow River, the Great Wall, and the Dragon. The Yellow River is believed to have

given birth to Chinese civilization thousands of years ago in its rich alluvial soil and to have established China as a river country, not an ocean country. She still lives by the yellow river waters, not the blue of ocean seas, turning inward instead of outward, as did the men of the Renaissance and the privateers of Queen Elizabeth. Not yet have the people and their rulers begun to see that the Great Wall keeps the people in, as well as the invaders out; that the walls and courtyards in which they contain themselves, the great magenta walls that surround the Forbidden City and Zhongnanhai, confine minds as well as bodies. And the Dragon is still supreme, China's benevolent dragon that protects the nation, protects the throne, protects the dynasties, protects the people—so long as they do not threaten its order.

—Harrison E. Salisbury, *Tiananmen Diary*

On two occasions, the contractor hired a group of Mexican aliens. They were employed to cut down some trees and haul off debris. In all, there were six men of varying age. The youngest in his late twenties; the oldest (his father?) perhaps sixty years old. They came and they left in a single old truck. Anonymous men. They were never introduced to the other men at the site. Immediately upon their arrival they would follow the contractor's directions, starting working—rarely resting—seemingly driven by a fatalistic sense that work which had to be done was best done as quickly as possible.

I watched them sometimes. Perhaps they watched me. The only time I saw them pay me much notice was one day at lunchtime when I was laughing with the other men. The Mexicans sat apart when they ate, just as they worked by themselves. Quiet. I rarely heard them say much to each other. All I could hear were their voices calling out sharply to one another, giving directions. Otherwise, when they stood briefly resting, they talked among themselves in voices too hard to overhear.

—Richard Rodriguez, *Hunger of Memory*

Yet above all else the spectator of sport desires the poetic moment: The shortstop diving long to his left, stopping a ground ball the eye can't follow, then rising to throw in an impossible gyration and beating the runner by a millisecond (and afterward, adjusting his cap, nonchalant and inscrutable). Or the elegant point guard slashing in from the left who leaves the ball behind his head for the teammate trailing after him, a silky forward who must leap and double-pump his graceful legs, then wait while his off-balance defender descends just half a beat ahead of him, and at the last moment move the ball from right to left to lay it softly off the glass at a high angle—all as if this were an ordinary act he can perform without particular duress. Or the wide receiver going long and longer still, the football apparently just slightly overthrown, and even while we judge from our limited perspective whether the quarterback hasn't given it too much arm, already here is this improbably swift receiver, not only leaping but flinging himself, as if flying from the edge of a precipice, the ball now poised on the tips of three fingers, the opposing team's cornerback arriving at exactly this moment to hurl himself at the receiver's head, and all the while the gravityless receiver just catches the ball, balancing it on his fingertips, then drawing it into his outstretched palm, then clutching it against his side, against his ribs, while the defender pummels him out of bounds, seeking to thrash free the ball from his grip, and still he has the graceful presence to nestle both feet against the neatly drawn sideline before he is slammed full-tilt toward the turf, where rather than curling in contorted pain he performs an amazing, one-handed cartwheel, easily rights himself, slows to a trot, releases the ball from the grip of his right hand, and turns once again in the direction of his teammates with his shirt still neatly tucked inside his pants.

—David Guterson, *Harper's Magazine*

For Group Discussion

Examine the style of an essay that either you or a classmate has written. Look for these features:

- short sentences that grab the reader's attention
- effective repetition
- absolute phrases
- appositives

Also examine the use of punctuation. Has the writer used semicolons and colons and dashes effectively?

RHETORICAL REMINDERS

Appositives

Have I taken advantage of the appositive to replace sentences with the linking *be*?

Have I used colons and dashes to set off appositives with internal punctuation?

Have I taken advantage of opening and closing appositives and of sentence appositives?

Absolute Phrases

Have I used the absolute phrase to focus on a detail?

Other Stylistic Devices

Have I taken advantage of the stylistic possibilities of word-order variation, ellipsis, and repetition?

Have I experimented with the punctuation of coordinate structures?

PUNCTUATION REMINDERS

Make sure that a complete sentence precedes a colon.

Chapter 11

The Rhetoric of Punctuation

In the first ten chapters, you have learned about the structure of sentences: their basic slots and the options we have for expanding and combining them. An important consideration throughout the book has been the effect of those options on the reader—hence the word *rhetorical* in the title. Those rhetorical effects extend also to punctuation, so in addition to the possibilities for constructing sentences, you have learned about both the required and the optional punctuation rules that apply.

As you might expect, the conventions of punctuation have changed through the centuries, just as language itself has changed. Early punctuation practices, designed to assist in the oral reading of medieval manuscripts, eventually evolved into our modern system, based more on structural boundaries than on the oral reader's needs. By the eighteenth and nineteenth centuries, the system we know today was generally in place. However, even though our punctuation rules are well established, they still include a great deal of flexibility. They are open to changing styles. Today we tend toward an "open" or "light" style, omitting commas where they are optional, where the boundaries are apparent without them. For example, modern writers often omit the comma with *and* in a series (known as the "serial comma"), as well as the comma following certain introductory adverbial phrases:

At the grocery store I bought milk, eggs and cheese.

If both optional commas were included, the sentence would have a "heavy," over-punctuated appearance:

At the grocery store, I bought milk, eggs, and cheese.

It's not unusual for writers to sometimes make punctuation decisions in this way, based on aesthetic grounds, on the look of the sentence.

(The writer who prefers both of those commas on principle but wants to avoid the heavy look they create can revise the sentence by putting the opening phrase in closing position. There it will not be set off: "I bought milk, eggs, and cheese at the grocery store.")

In this chapter we will look a little more closely at the punctuation decisions that writers make. First we will examine punctuation as a hierarchy, a description that can sometimes help you make those choices; then we will focus on the underlying purpose of punctuation rules. The last part of this chapter offers a brief glossary of the rules that have been described in the earlier chapters, covering commas, colons, dashes, semicolons, and parentheses, along with a few other issues that writers must deal with in connection with these and other punctuation marks. This section will serve as a handy reference tool.

The Hierarchy of Punctuation

If you were asked to place the parts of the sentence into a hierarchy, starting with "word," the result would look like this:

word
phrase
clause
sentence

The hierarchy of punctuation works in much the same way, usually in reverse order, with "sentence" at the top.

In his book *A Linguistic Study of American Punctuation* (Peter Lang, 1987), Charles F. Meyer describes the hierarchy, the levels of punctuation, according to the kinds of boundaries that a particular punctuation mark encloses. For example, occupying the top level are the period, the question mark, and the exclamation point, all of which define sentence boundaries—and only sentence boundaries.

At the next level are the colon, the dash, and parentheses, all of which can define sentence boundaries, but also define the boundaries of clauses and phrases and words.

The semicolon occupies the next level. It also defines sentence boundaries, but in a much more limited way than the other three; and it has only one other role, that of the coordinate series.

At the bottom level of the hierarchy is the comma, which can define word and phrase and clause boundaries, but not sentence boundaries.[1]

[1]We have a name for the comma when it does define a sentence boundary: It is known as a "comma splice"—and is regarded as a punctuation error. Sometimes, however, writers do use the comma in this way for stylistic effects: "I came, I saw, I conquered." Many of our punctuation conventions get altered for special effects—to call attention to themselves.

Here then is the hierarchy of punctuation marks:

> period, question mark, exclamation point
> colon, dash, parentheses
> semicolon
> comma

The hierarchy is obviously not a measure of importance or of frequency. In fact, the comma, although it occupies the lowest level, is our most frequent punctuation mark; and the exclamation point, one of three marks at the highest level, is the least frequent. The purpose of this scheme, rather, is to recognize the level of the functions that these marks can perform. For example, in Chapter 10 we looked at the following sentence in connection with appositives:

> Three committees—program, finance, and local arrangements—were set up to plan the convention.

The word boundaries here, marked by commas, are subordinate to those of the phrase boundaries; in order to distinguish the two levels, then, we use two different punctuation marks. The dashes mark the higher, or superordinate, level. To use commas for both levels of punctuation would make the sentence difficult to read. In the following version of the sentence, where the word boundaries are taken care of by conjunctions rather than commas, we have used commas for the phrase boundaries:

> Three committees, program and finance and local arrangements, were set up to plan the convention.

However, we could have retained the dashes in this revision, even though the phrase has no internal commas. Dashes would make the series stand out more strongly.

Because commas play so many roles in the sentence—providing boundaries for words and phrases and clauses—a sentence, especially a long one, can sometimes become heavy with commas:

> During the second two-year stretch of a president's term in office, he may find himself on the defensive, even with his own party, and, when, as frequently happens, his party loses a number of Senate and House seats in the midterm election, that second stretch can become even more defensive.

This sentence contains many levels of punctuation, with its coordinate independent clauses. The first clause contains opening and closing adverbial phrases, both of which are set off by commas. The other independent clause includes a subordinate *as*-clause embedded in a subordinate *when*-clause. Yet the only internal punctuation mark used for all of these levels is the comma.

One way to improve the sentence, to make it clearer for the reader, is to consider other punctuation marks that perform at some of these levels. One obvious boundary where we can use different punctuation is at the clause level—that is, to mark the two independent clauses—in place of the comma following *party*. We know that colons, dashes, and semicolons can all mark clause boundaries. In this case the best choice is the semicolon, because of its "and" meaning. (You'll recall that the colon generally connects two sentences with a "namely" or "here it comes" meaning—rather than "and.") Another choice is to begin a new sentence here. The semicolon, however, makes clear the close connection of the two independent clauses.

Next we should look at the comma following *and:* What is its function? It works with a partner, the comma after *election*, to set off the subordinate *when*-clause. Is there any other mark that can do that job? In this position, the answer is probably "no." (On some occasions, dashes or parentheses can enclose subordinate clauses, as we shall see later.) But now that we've substituted a semicolon, it is possible to eliminate *and*. After all, the reason for the *and* was the comma, which we've deleted. (You'll recall the rule about connecting two independent clauses with a comma: It requires a conjunction.)

Already our sentence looks better—and reads much more easily:

> During the second two-year stretch of a president's term in office, he may find himself on the defensive, even with his own party; when, as frequently happens, his party loses a number of Senate and House seats in the midterm election, that second stretch can become even more defensive.

We're also using a comma here to set off the opening prepositional phrase. There's nothing else that can do that job, so that one has to stay. And we're using commas to set off the *as*-clause within the *when*-clause. Have we any other choice? Well, yes. We could mark that boundary with dashes—if we think it deserves the extra attention that dashes provide:

> During the second two-year stretch of a president's term in office, he may find himself on the defensive, even with his own party; when—as frequently happens—his party loses a number of Senate and House seats in the midterm election, that second stretch can become even more defensive.

You may have noticed another place where a dash would fit: after *defensive*, to set off the adverbial *even*-phrase—in this case, only one dash, not a pair. But we probably don't want dashes in both places: They lose their special quality when they're used too often. And twice in one sentence is probably too often. We'll want to try it out in that earlier spot, just to see the difference. But, chances are, we'll leave the dashes where we have them now, where they replace two commas.

Now compare the two versions of that sentence—the original and the last revision. They're both punctuated "correctly." But certainly the difference makes clear how important it is for the writer to understand the various boundaries that require punctuation, to know how the tools of punctuation work.

The Purposes of Punctuation Marks

In his study of punctuation cited earlier, Charles Meyer classifies the purposes of punctuation into three categories: syntactic, prosodic, and semantic. Although you may not recognize these three words, they do in fact describe the punctuation principles you have been studying in the preceding chapters.

> ***Syntax*** refers to the structure of sentences—the main subject matter of this book. When you learned about sentence slots and their relationships and their expansions, you were learning about syntax.
>
> ***Prosody*** is the study of rhythm and intonation, which you remember especially from Chapter 3.
>
> ***Semantics*** is the study of meaning.

Syntax

Linguists generally agree that the purpose underlying most of our punctuation rules is syntactic: In other words, the structure of the sentence determines the punctuation marks it will contain. The sentence we revised in the previous section certainly illustrates that purpose: All of the boundaries were syntactic; none of the commas were there for purposes of rhythm or meaning. Sometimes the other purposes do play a part—for instance, when you add an optional comma to make the sentence easier to read or use a dash for special emphasis.

A good example of a syntactically based punctuation rule is the one you learned in connection with the sentence patterns in Chapter 1: "Do not mark slot boundaries with punctuation." This rule is clearly based on syntax, on sentence structure. In fact, syntax overrides all considerations of rhythm. Even though the reader may have to stop for breath between slots, that pause is not marked by a comma. Here's an example from Chapter 1 of a fairly long sentence, one that requires an extra breath—but has no boundaries that take punctuation:

> The images and information sent back by *Voyager 2* have given space scientists here on Earth enough information about four of our distant planets to keep them busy for years to come.

The predicate contains an indirect object and a direct object with two postnoun modifiers, but not one of those boundaries calls for punctuation.

Prosody

We often revise a sentence in order to change the way that the reader will read it—to change its rhythm pattern. For example, the intonation pattern of the sentence you just read would change if the first two words were reversed:

> Often we revise a sentence . . .

With this word order the reader will probably put more stress on *often*. To guarantee that emphasis, we can follow *often* with a comma. You'll recall from the discussion of sentence rhythm in Chapter 3 that the visual signal of a comma causes the reader to give added length and stress to the preceding word.

> Often, we revise a sentence . . .

This, then, is an example where the purpose of the punctuation mark can be attributed to prosody. There's simply no other reason for that comma.

In Chapter 10 we saw another example in the discussion of the coordinate series, when we compared the rhythm patterns of two punctuation styles:

1. You have your own style of writing, just as you have your own style of speaking and whistling and throwing a Frisbee and wearing your hair.
2. You have your own style of writing, just as you have your own style of speaking, whistling, throwing a Frisbee, wearing your hair.

It is the rhythm of (2) that changes the message: It has an open-ended quality, as if to suggest, "I could go on and on with the list." Again, the purpose of the punctuation is to produce that rhythm. In this case, however, we would have to say that semantics is also involved: The punctuation affects both the rhythm and the meaning.

Semantics

One situation in which semantics, or meaning, determines the need for punctuation is that of the nonrestrictive phrase or clause, as we saw in the discussion of noun modifiers in Chapter 8. Syntax, of course, determines the boundaries of that modifier, but semantic considerations dictate the presence or absence of the commas: Does the modifier define the noun or simply comment on it?

We looked at this pair of sentences to illustrate the distinction:

1. The man sitting by the window is talking to himself.
2. My mother, sitting by the window, is talking to herself.

We can assume in (1) that the scene includes at least one other man and that the purpose of the participial phrase is to identify the referent of the subject noun phrase, *the man*. That kind of identification is unnecessary in (2), where the subject noun phrase, *my mother*, has only one possible referent—no matter how many other women are present. Here the participial phrase merely comments.

The purpose of the punctuation is perhaps even more obviously a semantic one for the writer who has to decide between the following:

1. My sister Mary is coming for a visit.
2. My sister, Mary, is coming for a visit.

The sentence without commas implies that the writer has more than one sister. Clearly, it's the meaning that dictates the use of the comma.

The following pair also makes clear that the purpose of punctuation is sometimes semantic:

1. Call the boss Henry.
2. Call the boss, Henry.

You saw a similar pair in the discussion of the sentence patterns in Chapter 1. These two are different patterns. In (1) *Henry* is an objective complement; in (2) *Henry* is a noun of direct address, known as a vocative.

Meyer cites the following pair of sentences to illustrate another situation where the comma changes the meaning:

1. Earlier negotiations were planned.
2. Earlier, negotiations were planned.

Here the punctuation has actually changed the class of the word *earlier:* In (1) it is an adjective, a modifier of the noun; in (2) it is an adverb, modifying the whole sentence.

In both of these last two examples, where the comma changes the meaning, it has also altered the structure, the syntax, of the sentence. And it has changed the rhythm. So these are probably good examples to illustrate the combination of all three punctuation purposes: syntactic, prosodic, and semantic.

EXERCISE 38

The following paragraphs are reproduced exactly as they were published—with one exception: *All internal punctuation has been removed; only the sentence-end marks have been retained.* Your job is to put the punctuation marks back into the sentences. (Don't forget hyphens and apostrophes!) As you know, punctuation rules are not carved in stone; consequently, in some places your version may differ from the original—and still be right. You can check your versions against those of the authors in the Answers to the Exercises section.

> Management is still taught in most business schools as a bundle of techniques such as budgeting and personnel relations. To be sure management like any other work has its own tools and its own techniques. But just as the essence of medicine is not urinalysis important though that is the essence of

management is not techniques and procedures. The essence of management is to make knowledge productive. Management in other words is a social function. And in its practice management is truly a liberal art.

The old communities family village parish and so on have all but disappeared in the knowledge society. Their place has largely been taken by the new unit of social integration the organization. Where community was fate organization is voluntary membership. Where community claimed the entire person organization is a means to a person's ends a tool. For 200 years a hot debate has been raging especially in the West are communities organic or are they simply extensions of the people of which they are made? Nobody would claim that the new organization is organic. It is clearly an artifact a creation of man a social technology.

—Peter F. Drucker, *The Atlantic Monthly*

The charter school movement is not yet big. Just 11 states beginning with Minnesota in 1991 have passed laws permitting the creation of autonomous public schools like Northland a dozen more have similar laws in the works. Most states have restricted the number of these schools 100 in California 25 in Massachusetts in an attempt to appease teachers unions and other opponents. Nevertheless the charter movement is being heralded as the latest and best hope for a public education system that has failed to deliver for too many children and cannot compete internationally.

A handful of other places notably Baltimore Maryland and Hartford Connecticut are experimenting with a far more radical way to circumvent bureaucracy hiring a for profit company to run the schools.

—Claudia Wallis, *Time*

For Group Discussion

One of Robert Frost's most famous poems is "Stopping by Woods on a Snowy Evening." In some printed versions the last stanza looks like this:

The woods are lovely, dark, and deep,
But I have promises to keep,
And miles to go before I sleep,
And miles to go before I sleep.

In others, the punctuation of the first line follows the poet's original:

The woods are lovely, dark and deep,

Given what you know about the punctuation of the series and of the appositive, do you think that these two versions mean the same thing? If they do, why would anyone object to that extra comma

Glossary of Punctuation

Apostrophe

1. Possessive Case (See also pages 55–56)

A. For Singular Nouns

To show the possessive case, add *s* to singular nouns, both common and proper:

Bob's friend the ocean's blue color

The rule also applies to indefinite pronouns:

someone's book everyone's vote

Note. The one exception to this rule applies to the pronoun *it*, which we turn into possessive without an apostrophe—only the *s*:

The car lost its brakes.

(All other personal pronouns have a separate form for the possessive: I/my; she/her; he/his, you/your; we/our; they/their.)

This exception for the pronoun *it* causes endless errors. It's hard to remember that *it's* always means "it is" or "it has," whereas in the case of all other nouns and the indefinite pronouns, the *s* has three possibilities:

John's here. = John *is* here.
John's been here. = John *has* been here.
John's book is here. = John owns the book (possessive)

When a singular noun ends in *s*, the rule gets a bit fuzzy. A good rule of thumb is related to pronunciation: When you add the sound of *s* in forming the possessive case (Ross's friend), add the letter *s*; however, if you pronounce the possessive *without* adding an *s* sound, do *not* add the letter: Jesus' followers, Texas' laws.

B. For Plural Nouns

To make a regular plural noun possessive, add only the apostrophe:

the cats' tails the students' complaints

For irregular plurals (those formed without adding *s*), add *s*:

the women's movement children's books

2. Plurals of Initials and Words Other Than Nouns

In making initials and non-nouns plural, when the addition of *s* alone would be misleading, add an apostrophe:

A's and B's (but ABCs) p's and q's
do's and don't's

3. Contractions

In writing contractions, use an apostrophe to replace the missing syllable or letter(s):

don't = do not he'll = he will
it's = it is, it has can't = cannot
Pat's = Pat is, Pat has

Brackets

1. Within Parentheses

Use brackets for parenthetical material that is already within parentheses:

The anthropologist who lived with the Iks in northern Uganda (reported by Lewis Thomas in The Lives of a Cell [1974]) apparently detested the tribe he was studying.

2. In Quoted Material

Use brackets for interpolations or explanations within quoted material—to show that it is not part of the quotation:

"Everyone close to the king surmised that she [Mrs. Simpson] would be nothing but trouble for the realm."

Colon

1. Appositives (See pages 196–98)

Use the colon to introduce an appositive or a list of appositives:

The board appointed three committees to plan the convention: finance, program, and local arrangements.

Often such a list is introduced by "as follows" or "the following":

The three committees are as follows: finance, program, and local arrangements.
The board appointed the following committees: finance, program and local arrangements.

Remember that a complete sentence precedes the colon; what follows the colon is an appositive. *Do not* put a colon between a linking verb and the subjective complement:

*The committees that were appointed are: finance, program, and local arrangements.

2. Conjunction of Sentences (See pages 184–86)

Use a colon to join the two independent clauses of a compound sentence, where the second completes the idea, or the promise, of the first. The connection often means "namely" or "that is":

To the rest of the nation, the baseball strike and hockey lockout share one characteristic: they both seem downright stupid.

—*Time*

Only one obstacle lay between us and success: We had to come up with the money.

Note. The convention of capitalizing a complete sentence following the colon is on the fence: Some publishers always capitalize; others capitalize only when what follows is a direct quotation; others capitalize questions and direct quotations; whichever method you follow, as with any optional convention, be sure to follow it consistently.

Comma

1. Compound Sentences (See pages 162–64)

Use a comma along with a coordinating conjunction between the clauses in a compound sentence:

I didn't believe a word Phil said, and I told him so.

Remember that the comma alone produces a "comma splice." (See the footnote on page 214.)

2. Series (See page 171–72)

Use commas when listing a series of three or more sentence elements:

We gossiped, laughed, and sang the old songs at our class reunion.
We hunted in the basement, in the attic, and through all the storage rooms, to no avail.

The serial comma, the one before *and*, is optional.

3. Introductory Subordinate Clauses (See pages 122–23)

Use a comma to set off an introductory subordinate clause:

> When the riot started, the police fired tear gas into the crowd.
> Because the 1993 flood was so devastating, some farmers in the Midwest decided to relocate.

4. Sentence–Ending Clauses (See pages 122–23)

Use a comma to set off a subordinate clause following the main clause if the subordinate clause has no effect on the outcome of the main clause:

> Some people refused to leave their homes, even though the hurricane winds had started.

Note that in the following sentences the idea in the main clause will not be realized without the subordinate clause; therefore, we use no comma:

> I'll pack up and leave if you tell me to.
> We left the area because we were afraid to stay.

In general, *if* and *because* clauses are not set off; those introduced by *although* and *even though* are. If you are in doubt about the punctuation of the clause in post-sentence position, you can shift it to the beginning of the sentence; there it will always be set off.

You should also be aware that the rules regarding subordinate clauses are among the least standardized of our punctuation conventions.

5. Introductory Verb Phrases

Use a comma to set off any introductory phrase that contains a verb:

> After studying all weekend, I felt absolutely prepared for the midterm exam.
> Having worked at MacDonald's for the past four summers, Maxie felt confident when he applied for the job of assistant manager.
> To get in shape for ski season, my roommate has begun working out on the Nordic Track.

Note. In most cases the subject of the sentence must also be the subject of the verb in that introductory phrase; otherwise, the verb phrase "dangles." Exceptions occur with "set phrases":

> Speaking of the weather, let's have a picnic.
> To tell the truth, I have never read *Silas Marner*.

6. Introductory Prepositional Phrases

Use a comma to set off adverbial prepositional phrases of approximately six or more words:

> Toward the end of the semester, everyone in my dorm starts to study seriously.

It is perfectly acceptable to set off shorter prepositional phrases, especially if you think the reader should pause. For example, information of specific dates is sometimes set off:

> In 1994, the Republicans gained strength in the midterm election.

In making the decision about such commas, consider the punctuation in the rest of the sentence: Don't overload the sentence with commas.

Set off any prepositional phrase that might cause a misreading:

> During the summer, vacation plans are our main topic of conversation.

See the next section for prepositional phrases that are parenthetical.

7. Other Sentence Modifiers

Set off words and phrases that modify the whole sentence or that have a parenthetical meaning—at both the beginning and the end of the sentence:

A. Adverbs

> Luckily, we escaped without a scratch.
> We escaped without a scratch, luckily.
> Meanwhile, there was nothing to do but wait.

B. *Yes* and *no:*

> Yes, he's the culprit.
> No, I can't go out tonight.

C. Prepositional phrases

> In fact, there was nothing I could do about her problem.
> In the meantime, I listened to her sad tale.

These parenthetical words and phrases often provide a transitional tie to the previous sentence, which the comma emphasizes. They are also used to slow the reader down or to shift the point of sentence stress. (See Chapter 3.)

D. Absolute phrases (See pages 200–1)

> The rain having stopped, Doug and Deborah decided to go ahead with the picnic.
> Eben and Paula relaxed in front of the fire, their feet propped on the coffee table.

8. Nonrestrictive Modifiers (See pages 143–46)

Use commas to set off "commenting" (nonrestrictive) modifiers in the noun phrase. Remember that an adjectival is nonrestrictive when the referent of the noun it modifies is already clear to the reader or if the noun has only one possible referent:

> My oldest brother, a senior history major, spends every night in the library.

9. Coordinate Adjectives (See page 139)

Use commas in the noun phrase between coordinate adjectives in preheadword position. Coordinate refers to adjectives of the same class—for example, subjective qualities:

a tender, delightful love story
a challenging, educational experience
a tall young man
a huge red ball

A good rule of thumb for making a decision about commas between these prenoun modifiers is this: If you could insert *and* or *but*, use a comma:

A tender and delightful love story

Notice that the two phrases without commas contain adjectives from different classes (height, age, size, color)—so they will not be separated:

*a tall and young man
*a huge and red ball

10. Nouns of Direct Address

Use a comma to set off nouns of direct address in both opening and closing position:

Students, your time is up.
Put your pencils down, everyone.
Help me, dear.

11. Direct Quotations

Use commas to set off direct quotations that fill the direct object slot after verbs such as say and reply:

The waiter said, "Good evening. My name is Pierre."
Harold replied, "I'm Harold, and this is Joyce."

Note. This is actually an exception to the punctuation rule you learned in Chapter 1: "Do not mark the boundaries of the basic sentence slots with commas." When the direct object is a direct quotation, we *do* mark the boundary.
Direct quotations can also be introduced by colons:

Harold replied: "I'm Harold, and this is Joyce."

12. State and Year

Use commas to set off the name of a state when it follows the name of a city:

I was surprised to learn that Cheyenne, Wyoming, isn't a larger city.

Also set off the year in a complete date:

> I remember where I was on November 22, 1963, when I heard the news reports of President Kennedy's assassination.

Notice that we include commas both before and after the state name and the year.

Dash

To type the dash, use two hyphens with no space either before or after.

1. Interruptions Within a Sentence

Use a dash (or pair of dashes) to set off any interrupting structure within the sentence or at the end:

> Tim decided to quit his job—a brave decision, in my opinion—and to look for something new.
>
> Tim decided to quit his job and look for another—a brave decision.

When the interrupter is a complete sentence, it is punctuated as a phrase would be:

> Tim quit his job—he was always a rash young man—to follow Horace Greeley's advice and go West.

2. Appositives (See pages 193–97)

Use dashes to call attention to an appositive:

> The microorganisms that seem to have it in for us in the worst way—the ones that really appear to wish us ill—turn out on close examination to be rather more like bystanders, strays, strangers in from the cold.
>
> —Lewis Thomas

Use a pair of dashes to set off a list of appositives that are themselves separated by commas:

> All of the committees—finance, program, and local arrangements—went to work with real enthusiasm.

The list of appositives set off by a dash can also come at the beginning of the sentence when the subject is a pronoun referring to the list:

> The faculty, the students, the staff—all were opposed to the provost's decision to reinstate the old dormitory regulations.

Namely and *that is*, both of which are signalers of appositives, can be preceded by either a dash or a comma; the dash gives the appositive more emphasis:

Some mammals have no hair—namely, the whales.
The provost's decision brought out over 1,500 student protesters, that is, a third of the student body.

Exclamation Point

1. Exclamatory Sentence

The exclamation point is the terminal punctuation for the exclamatory sentence, a transformation that changes the emphasis of a declarative sentence, usually with a *what* or *how:*

We have a hard-working committee.
What a hard-working committee we have!
It's a gorgeous day.
What a gorgeous day it is!

The exclamation point is actually optional, and in some cases would be inappropriate:

How calm the ocean is today.
What a sweet child you have.

2. Emphasis

The exclamation point is used in sentences that call for added emotions; however, it should be used sparingly. It is rarely used in formal prose.

"Get out!" he shouted. "I never want to see you again!"
The history exam held a real surprise for me: I had studied the wrong chapters!

Hyphen

1. Compound Words or Phrases (See pages 139–40)

The hyphen expresses a compound word or phrase in prenoun position as a unit:

a two-inch board

a silver-plated teapot

a well-designed running shoe

an out-of-work carpenter

Note that when they are not in prenoun position the hyphens are not needed in most cases:

The board is two inches wide.
The shoe was well designed.
The carpenter is out of work.

When the modifier in prenoun position is an *-ly* adverb, the hyphen is not used:

a nicely designed running shoe
a clearly phrased message

Parentheses

1. Interruptions
Parentheses, in many cases, function just as dashes and commas do—to set off explanatory information or, in some cases, the writer's digressions:

I stopped her and put a five-sou piece (a little more than a farthing) into her hand.

—George Orwell

It is hard to remember, when reading the Notebooks, that Camus was a man who had a very interesting life, a life (unlike that of many writers) interesting not only in an interior but also in an outward sense.

—Susan Sontag

Unlike dashes, which call attention to a passage, the parentheses generally add the information as an aside: They say, "By the way," whereas the dash says, "Hey, listen to this!"

2. Technical Information
Parentheses are also used for including technical information within a text:

English poet William Cowper described the experience of tithing in "The Yearly Distress, or Tithing Time at Stock, in Essex" (circa 1780).
For years I never missed an issue of *Astounding* (now published as *Analog*).

(Punctuation Notes)
A. A complete sentence added parenthetically within another sentence has neither an opening capital letter nor end punctuation:

The long winters in North Dakota (newcomers quickly learn that March is a winter month) make spring a time of great joy.

B. When a complete sentence is enclosed in parentheses—one that is not embedded in another sentence—the terminal punctuation is within the parentheses:

I look forward to every month of the year. (February, I will admit, is short on saving graces, but at least it's short.) April is probably my favorite, with its clean spring air and promise of good times to come.

Question Marks

1. Terminal Punctuation

Use the question mark as terminal punctuation in all direct questions:

> Do you have anything to add?
> What can you tell me?
> He said what?

However, polite requests in the form of questions are often punctuated with the period:

> Would you mind opening the window.

2. Quotations

In punctuating quoted questions, include the question mark within the quotation marks:

> John asked, "Do you have anything to add?"

When a quoted statement is embedded at the end of a question, the question mark is outside the quotation marks"

> Who said, "Give me liberty or give me death"?

Note that the period is omitted from the quoted sentence.

When a quoted question is embedded in another question, only one question mark is used—and that one is inside the quotation marks:

> Did he ask you straight out, "Are you a shoplifter?"

Quotation Marks

1. For Direct Quotations

Use double quotation marks to indicate another person's exact words, both spoken and written:

> In 1943 Churchill told Stalin, "In war-time, truth is so precious that she should always be attended by a bodyguard of lies."

Notice that the quotation marks are outside the period. This system applies even when the quotation marks enclose a single word, such as a title:

> I've never seen the movie "Jaws."

However, quotation marks are placed inside semicolons and colons:

She said, "Come to the party"; I had to turn her down.

2. Within Direct Quotations

Use single quotation marks when the quoted material is within a quoted passage:

> Describing the degeneracy of the nation in a letter to Joshua F. Speed, Lincoln wrote that "as a nation we began by declaring that 'all men are created equal.' We now practically read it 'all men are created equal except Negroes.' "

Notice that both the single and the double quotation marks are outside the period.

For quotation marks with questions, see the preceding section under "Question Marks."

Semicolons

1. As a Conjunction (See pages 179–82)

Use a semicolon to connect independent clauses in a compound sentence. You can think of the semicolon as having the connective force of the comma-plus-conjunction:

> The use of the semicolon indicates a close relationship between clauses; it gives the sentence a tight, separate-but-equal bond.

The semicolon can also be used with the conjunction:

> Great indeed is Fear; but it is not, as our military enthusiasts believe and try to make us believe, the only stimulus known for awakening the higher ranges of men's spiritual energy.
>
> —William James

2. In the Separation of a Series (See page 196)

Use semicolons to separate a series of structures that have internal punctuation:

> In this chapter we looked at three purposes underlying our punctuation system: syntactic, related to structure; prosodic, related to sentence rhythm; and semantic, related to meaning.

Glossary of Terms

For further explanation of the terms listed here, check the index for page references.

Absolute phrase. A noun phrase that includes a postnoun modifier and is related to the sentence as a whole, providing a detail or point of focus.

Abstract noun. A noun that refers to a quality, such as peace or happiness, rather than a material, concrete object.

Active voice. A feature of transitive verb sentences in which the subject is generally the agent and the direct object is the goal or objective of the action. *Voice* refers to the relationship of the subject to the verb. See also *Passive voice*.

Adjectival. Any structure, no matter what its form, that functions as a modifier of a noun—that is, that functions as an adjective normally functions. See Chapter 8.

Adjective. One of the four form classes, whose members act as modifiers of nouns; most adjectives can be inflected for comparative and superlative degree (*big, bigger, biggest*); they can be qualified or intensified (*rather big, very big*); they have characteristic derivational affixes such as *-ous (famous)*, *-ish (childish)*, *-ful (graceful)*, and *-ary (complementary)*.

Adverb. One of the four form classes, whose members act as modifiers of verbs, contributing information of time, place, reason, manner, and the like. Like adjectives, certain adverbs can be qualified (*very quickly, rather fast*); some can be inflected for comparative and superlative degree (*more quickly, fastest*); they have characteristic derivational endings such as *-ly (quickly)*, *-wise (lengthwise)*, *-ward (backward)*.

Adverbial. Any structure, no matter what its form, that functions as a modifier of a verb—that is, that functions as an adverb normally functions. See Chapter 7.

Agency. The relationship of the subject and verb. See also *Agent*.

Agent. The initiator of the action in the sentence—the "doer" or "perpetrator" of the action. Usually the agent is the subject in an active sentence: "*John* groomed the dog"; "*The committee* elected Pam." In a passive sentence the agent, if mentioned, will be the object of a preposition: "Pam was elected by *the committee*."

Agreement. (1) Subject–verb. A third-person singular subject in the present tense takes the *-s* form of the verb: "*The dog barks* all night"; "*He bothers* the neighbors." A plural takes the base form: "*The dogs bark*"; "*They bother* the neighbors." (2) Pronoun–antecedent. The number of the pronoun (whether singular or plural) agrees with the number of its antecedent. "*The boys* did *their* chores"; "The *man who* works for us is on vacation." (Note that both *man* and *who* take the *-s* form of their verbs.)

Antecedent. The noun or nominal that a pronoun stands for.

Appositive. A structure, usually a noun phrase, that renames a nominal structure, that shares a nominal slot: "My neighbor, *a butcher at Weis Market*, recently lost his job."

Broad reference. A pronoun that refers to a complete sentence rather than to a specific noun or nominal. The broad-reference clause is introduced by *which*. "Judd told jokes all evening, *which drove us crazy*." The demonstrative pronouns *this* and *that* and the personal pronoun *it* are also sometimes used with broad reference: "Judd told jokes again last night; *that* really drives me crazy." Those sentences with demonstratives can be improved if the pronoun is turned into a determiner: "*That silly behavior of his* drives me crazy."

Case. A feature of nouns and certain pronouns that denotes their function in the sentence. Pronouns have three case distinctions: subjective (*I*, *they*, *who*, etc), possessive (*my*, *their*, *whose*, etc.), and objective (*me*, *them*, *whom*, etc.). Nouns have only one case inflection, the possessive (*John's*, *the cat's*). The case of nouns other than the possessive is sometimes referred to as common case.

Clause. A structure with a subject and a predicate. The sentence patterns are clause patterns.

Cleft sentence. A sentence variation using an *it* clause or *what* clause to shift the sentence focus: "A careless bicyclist caused the accident" → "It was a careless bicyclist who caused the accident"; "What caused the accident was a careless bicyclist."

Cohesion. The connections between sentences. Cohesive ties are furnished by pronouns that have antecedents in previous sentences, by adverbial connections, by known information, and by knowledge shared by the reader.

Collective noun. A noun that refers to a collection of individuals: *group*, *team*, *family*. Collective nouns can be replaced by either singular or plural pronouns, depending on the meaning.

Command. See *Imperative sentence*.

Common noun. A noun with general, rather than unique, reference (in contrast to proper nouns). Common nouns may be countable (*house*, *book*) or noncountable (*water*, *oil*); they may be concrete (*house*, *water*) or abstract (*justice*, *indifference*).

Comparative degree. See *Degree*.

Complement. A structure that "completes" the sentence. The term includes those slots in the predicate that complete the verb: direct object, indirect object, subjective complement, and objective complement. Certain adjectives also have complements—clauses and phrases that pattern with them: "I was *certain that he would come*"; "I was *afraid to go*."

Compound sentence. A sentence with two or more independent clauses.

Conjunction. One of the structure classes, which includes connectors that coordinate structures of many forms (e.g., *and*, *or*), subordinate sentences (e.g., *if*, *because*, *when*), and coordinate sentences with an adverbial emphasis (e.g., *however*, *therefore*).

Conjunctive adverb. A conjunction that connects two independent clauses with an adverbial emphasis, such as *however*, *therefore*, *moreover*, and *nevertheless*.

Contraction. A combination of two words written or spoken as one, in which letters or sounds are omitted. In writing, the omission is marked by an apostrophe: *isn't*, *they're*.

Coordinating conjunction. A conjunction that connects two or more sentences or structures within a sentence as equals: *and*, *but*, *or*, *nor*, *for*, and *yet*.

Coordination. A way of expanding sentences in which two or more structures of the same form function as a unit. All the sentence slots and modifiers in the slots, as well as the sentence itself, can be coordinated.

Correlative conjunction. A two-part conjunction that expresses a relationship between the coordinated structures: *either–or, neither–nor, both–and, not only–but also.*

Countable noun. A noun whose referent can be identified as a separate entity; the countable noun can be signaled by the indefinite article, *a,* and by numbers: *a house; an experience; two eggs; three problems.* See also *Noncountable noun.*

Declarative sentence. A sentence in the form of a statement (in contrast to a command, a question, or an exclamation).

Definite article. The determiner *the,* which generally marks a specific or previously mentioned noun: "*the* man on *the* corner"; "*the* blue coat I want for Christmas."

Degree. The variations in adjectives and some adverbs that indicate the simple quality of a noun, or positive degree ("Bill is a *big* boy"); its comparison to another, the comparative degree ("Bill is *bigger* than Tom"); or its comparison to two or more, the superlative degree ("Bill is the *biggest* person in the whole class"). In most adjectives of two or more syllables, the comparative and superlative degrees are marked by *more* and *most,* respectively.

Demonstrative pronoun. The pronouns *this* (plural *these*) and *that* (plural *those*), which function as nominal substitutes and as determiners. They include the feature of proximity: near (*this, these*) and distant (*that, those*).

Dependent clause. A clause that functions as an adverbial, adjectival, or nominal (in contrast to an independent clause).

Derivational affix. A suffix or prefix that is added to a form-class word, either to change its class (*fame–famous; act–action*) or to change its meaning (*legal–illegal; boy–boyhood*).

Determiner. One of the structure-class words, a signaler of nouns. Determiners include articles (*a, the*), possessive nouns and pronouns (e.g., *Chuck's, his, my*), demonstrative pronouns (*this, that, these, those*), indefinite pronouns (e.g., *many, each, every*), and numbers.

Diction. The selection of words, usually referred to in connection with the correct choice of words in terms of their meaning and the appropriate choice in terms of the audience and purpose.

Direct object. A nominal slot in the predicate of the transitive sentence patterns. The direct object names the objective or goal or the receiver of the verb's action: "We ate *the peanuts*"; "The boy hit *the ball*"; "I enjoy *playing chess.*"

Elliptical clause. A clause in which a part has been left out but is "understood": "Chester is older *than I (am old)*"; "Bev can jog farther *than Otis (can jog)*"; "*When (you are) planning your essay,* be sure to consider the audience."

End focus. The common rhythm pattern in which the prominent peak of stress falls on or near the final sentence slot.

Expletive. A word that enables the writer or speaker to shift the stress in a sentence or to embed one sentence in another: "A fly is in my soup" → "*There* is a fly in my soup"; "I know *that* he loves me." The expletive is sometimes called an "empty word" because it plays a structural rather than a lexical role in the sentence.

Figurative language. Language that expresses meaning in nonliteral terms, characterized by figures of speech, such as metaphors, similes, analogies, and personification.

Flat adverb. A class of adverb that is the same in form as its corresponding adjective: *fast, high, early, late, hard, long,* and so on.

Form classes. The large, open classes of words that provide the lexical content of the language: nouns, verbs, adjectives, and adverbs. Each has characteristic derivational and inflectional affixes that distinguish its forms.

Gerund. An *-ing* verb functioning as a nominal: "I enjoy *jogging*"; "*Running* is good exercise"; "After *getting* my pilot's license, I hope to fly to Lake Tahoe."

Headword. The word that fills the noun slot in the noun phrase: "the little *boy* across (the *street*)"; the verb that heads the verb phrase.

Idiom. A combination of words whose meaning cannot be predicted from the meaning of the individual words. Many phrasal verbs are idioms: *look up* [a word]; *put up with; back down; give in*.

Imperative sentence. The sentence in the form of a command. The imperative sentence includes the base form of the verb and usually an understood subject (*you*): "*Eat* your spinach"; "*Finish* your report as soon as possible"; "You *go* on without me."

Indefinite article. The determiner *a*, which marks an unspecified countable noun. See also *Definite article*.

Indefinite pronoun. A large category that includes quantifiers (e.g., *enough, several, many, much*), universals (*all, both, every, each*), and partitives (e.g., *any, anyone, anybody, either, neither, no, nobody, some, someone*). Many of the indefinite pronouns can function as determiners.

Independent clause. The main clause of the sentence; a compound sentence has more than one independent clause.

Indirect object. The nominal slot following verbs like *give*. The indirect object is the recipient; the direct object is the thing given: "We gave *our friends* a ride home."

Infinitive. The base form of the verb (present tense), usually expressed with *to*, which is called the "sign of the infinitive." The infinitive can function adverbially ("I stayed up all night *to study* for the exam"); adjectivally ("That is no way *to study*"); and nominally ("*To stay up* all night is foolish"). The only verb with an infinitive form separate from the present tense is *be*.

Infinitive phrase. A verb phrase headed by the infinitive that functions as an adjectival, adverbial, or nominal.

Inflections. Suffixes that are added to the form classes (nouns, verbs, adjectives, and adverbs) to change their grammatical role in some way. Nouns have two inflectional suffixes (*-s* plural and *'s* possessive); verbs have four (*-s, -ing, -ed,* and *-en*); adjectives and some adverbs have two (*-er* and *-est*).

Intensive reflexive pronoun. The function of the reflexive pronoun when it serves as an appositive to emphasize a noun or pronoun: "I *myself* prefer chocolate." See also *Reflexive pronoun*.

Intonation pattern. The rhythmic pattern of a spoken sentence, affected by its stress and pitch and pauses.

Intransitive verb. A verb that requires no complement to be complete.

Irregular verb. Any verb in which the *-ed* and *-en* forms are not that of a regular verb; in other words, a verb in which the *-ed* and *-en* forms are not simply the addition of *-d, -ed,* or *-t* to the base form.

It-cleft. See *Cleft sentence*.

Known–new contract. The common feature of sentences in which old, or known, information (information that is repeated from an earlier sentence or paragraph to provide cohesion, often in the form of a pronoun or related word) will appear in the subject slot, with the new information in the predicate.

Lexicon. The store of words—the internalized dictionary—that every speaker of the language has.

Linking verb. A verb that requires a subjective complement to be complete. *Be* is commonly used as a linking verb.

Manner adverb. An adverb that answers the question of "how" or "in what manner" about the verb. Most manner adverbs are derived from adjectives with the addition of *-ly*: *quickly, merrily, candidly*.

Mass noun. See *Noncountable noun*.

Metaphor. The nonliteral use of a word that allows the speaker or writer to attribute qualities of one thing to another for purposes of explanation or persuasion: the *war* on drugs, the *engine* of government, *sunset* legislation, *food* for thought.

Nominal. Any structure that functions as a noun phrase normally functions—as subject, direct object, indirect object, objective complement, subjective complement, object of preposition, appositive.

Nominalization. The process of producing a noun by adding derivational affixes to another word class: *legalize–legalization; regulate–regulation; friendly–friendliness*. Often the sentence will be more effective when the verb is allowed to function as a verb rather than being turned into a noun.

Noncountable noun. A noun referring to what might be called an undifferentiated mass—such as *wood, water, sugar, glass*—or an abstraction—*justice, love, indifference*. Whether or not you can use the indefinite article, *a*, is probably the best test of countability: If you can, the noun is countable.

Nonrestrictive modifier. A modifier in the noun phrase that comments about the noun rather than defines it. Nonrestrictive modifiers following the noun are set off by commas. See also *Restrictive modifier*.

Noun. One of the four form classes, whose members fill the headword slot in the noun phrase. Most nouns can be inflected for plural and possessive (*boy, boys, boy's, boys'*). Nouns have characteristic derivational endings, such as *-ion (action, compensation)*, *-ment (contentment)*, and *-ness (happiness)*.

Noun phrase. The noun headword with all of its attendant pre- and post-noun modifiers. See Chapter 8.

Number. A feature of nouns and pronouns, referring to singular and plural.

Object of preposition. The nominal slot—usually filled by a noun phrase—that follows the preposition to form a prepositional phrase.

Objective case. The role in the sentence of a noun phrase or pronoun when it functions as an object—direct object, indirect object, objective complement, or object of a preposition. Although nouns do not have a special form for objective case, many of the pronouns do: Personal pronouns and the relative pronoun *who* have separate forms when they function as objects.

Objective complement. The slot following the direct object in Pattern 7 sentences, filled by an adjectival or a nominal. The objective complement has two functions: (1) It completes the idea of the verb; and (2) it modifies (if an adjectival) or renames (if a nominal) the direct object: "I found the play *exciting*"; "We consider Pete *a good friend*."

Parallelism. See *Parallel structure*.

Parallel structure. A coordinate structure in which all the coordinate parts are of the same grammatical form: "The stew *smells delicious* and *tastes even better*" (parallel verb phrases); "The entire cast gave *powerful* and *exciting* performances" (parallel adjectives); "I'll take either *a bus* or *a taxi*" (parallel noun phrases).

Participial phrase. An *-ing* or *-en* verb phrase functioning as an adjectival, the modifier of a noun.

Participle. The *-ing* (present participle) or *-en* (past participle) form of the verb. The term *participle* refers both to these forms of the verb and to their function as adjectivals.

Passive voice. A feature of transitive sentences in which the direct object (the objective or goal) is shifted to the subject position. The auxiliary *be* is used with the past participle form of the verb. The term *passive* refers to the relationship between the subject and the verb: "Ed ate the pizza" → "The pizza *was eaten* by Ed." See also *Active voice*.

Past participle. The *-en* form of the verb.

Past tense. The *-ed* form of the verb, usually denoting a specific past action.

Person. A feature of personal pronouns relating to point of view, the relationship of the writer or speaker to the reader or listener: It can refer to writer or speaker (first person), the person addressed (second person), and the person or thing spoken about (third person).

Personal pronoun. A pronoun referring to a specific person or thing: In the subjective case the personal pronouns are *I, you, he, she, we, you, they*, and *it*. The personal pronouns have different forms for objective and possessive case. See Chapter 5.

Personification. A figurative use of language in which a human attribute is applied to a noun that occupies the nonhuman branch of the semantic hierarchy: *blind* justice, *friendly* rain. See Chapter 4.

Phrase. A combination of words that constitutes a unit of the sentence.

Positive degree. See *Degree*.

Possessive case. The inflected form of nouns (*John's, the dog's*) and pronouns (*my, his, your, her, their*, etc.), usually indicating possession or ownership.

Predicate. One of the two principal parts of the sentence, the comment made about the subject. The predicate includes the verb, together with its complements and modifiers.

Preposition. A structure-class word found in pre-position to—that is, preceding—a nominal. Prepositions can be classed according to their form as simple, or single-word (*above, at, in, with, of*, etc.), or phrasal (*according to, along with, instead of*, etc.).

Prepositional phrase. The combination of a preposition and its object. In form, the object of the preposition is usually a noun phrase ("After *my nap*, I'll clean the house"), but it can also be a verb phrase, a gerund ("After *cleaning the house*, I'll take a nap").

Present participle. The *-ing* form of the verb.

Pronoun. A word that substitutes for a noun—or, more accurately, for a nominal—in the sentence. See Chapter 5.

Proper noun. A noun with individual reference to a person, a geographic region or location, building, holiday, historical event, work of art or literature, and other such names. Proper nouns are capitalized.

Prosody. The study of the rhythm and intonation of language, which are determined by pitch, stress (loudness), and juncture (pauses).

Qualifier. A structure-class word that qualifies or intensifies an adjective or adverb: "We worked *rather* slowly"; "We worked *very* hard."

Reader expectation. An awareness by the writer of what the reader is expecting to read.

Reciprocal pronoun. The pronouns *each other* and *one another*, which refer to previously named nouns.

Redundancy. Unnecessary repetition.

Referent. The thing (or person, event, concept, action, etc.)—in other words, the reality—that a word stands for.

Reflexive pronoun. A pronoun formed by adding *-self* or *-selves* to a form of the personal pronoun, used as an object in the sentence to refer to a previously named noun or pronoun.

Regular verb. A verb in which the *-ed* form (the past tense) and the *-en* form (the past participle) are formed by adding *-ed* (or, in some cases, *-d* or *-t*) to the base. These two forms of a regular verb are always identical: "I *walked* home"; "I have *walked* home every day this week."

Relative adverb. The adverbs *where*, *when*, and *why*, which introduce adjectival (relative) clauses.

Relative clause. A clause introduced by a relative pronoun (*who*, *which*, *that*) or a relative adverb (*when*, *where*, *why*) that modifies a noun.

Relative pronoun. The pronouns *who (whose, whom)*, *which*, and *that* in their role as introducers of relative (adjectival) clauses.

Restrictive modifier. A modifier in the noun phrase whose function is to restrict, or define, the meaning of the noun. A modifier is restrictive when it is needed to identify the referent of the headword. The restrictive modifier is not set off by commas. See also *Nonrestrictive modifier*.

Semantics. The study of the meaning of words and sentences.

Sentence. A word or group of words based on one or more subject–predicate, or clause, patterns. The written sentence begins with a capital letter and ends with terminal punctuation—a period, a question mark, or an exclamation point.

Sentence fragment. A part of a sentence—often a noun phrase, verb phrase, or subordinate clause—punctuated as a complete sentence.

Sentence patterns. The simple skeletal sentences, made up of two or three or four required elements, that underlie our sentences, even the most complex among them. The seven patterns listed in Chapter 1 will account for almost all of the possible sentences of English.

Sequence of tenses. The difference in verb tenses that appear in a sentence with more than one clause.

Simile. A comparison that uses *like* or *as*: "My love is *like a red, red rose*" (Robert Burns).

Stative. A quality of nouns, verbs, and adjectives that refers to a relatively permanent state, as opposed to a changing condition. A stative verb is not generally used in the *-ing* form: We would say, "I resemble my mother," not *"I am resembling my mother." A stative noun would not be linked by an *-ing* verb: We would say, "He is a mechanic," not *"He is being a mechanic."

Structure classes. The small, closed classes of words that explain the grammatical or structural relationships of the form classes. The major ones are determiners, auxiliaries, qualifiers, prepositions, conjunctions, and expletives.

Subject. The opening slot in the sentence patterns, filled by a noun phrase or other nominal structure, that functions as the topic of the sentence.

Subjective case. The role in the sentence of a noun phrase or a pronoun when it functions as the subject of the sentence. Personal pronouns have distinctive forms for subjective case: *I*, *he*, *she*, *they*, and so on. And in the subjective complement slot, a pronoun will be in the subjective case.

Subjective complement. The nominal or adjectival that follows a linking verb, renaming or describing the subject ("Pam is *the president*"). In the passive voice the transitive sentence with an objective complement (Pattern 7) will have a subjective complement: "We elected Pam president" → "Pam was elected *president*."

Subjunctive mood. An expression of the verb in which the base form, rather than the inflected form, is used (1) in certain *that* clauses conveying strong suggestions or resolutions or commands ("We suggest that Mary *go* with us"; "I move that the meeting *be* adjourned"; "I demand that you *let* us in") and (2) in the expression of wishes or conditions contrary to fact ("If I *were* you, I'd be careful"; "I wish it *were* summer"). The subjunctive of the verb *be* is expressed by *were*, or *be*, even for subjects that normally take *is* or *was*.

Subordinate clause. A dependent clause introduced by a subordinating conjunction. It is also called an adverbial clause. See also *Subordinating conjunction*.

Subordinating conjunction. A conjunction that introduces an adverbial, or subordinate, clause expressing the relationship of the clause to the main clause: Among the most common are *after, although, as, as long as, as soon as, because, before, even though, if, provided that, since, so that, though, till, until, when, whenever, whereas, while.*

Subordinator. A conjunction that turns a sentence into a dependent clause. See *Subordinating conjunction.*

Superlative degree. See *Degree.*

Syntax. The way in which the words of the language are put together to form the structural units, the phrases and clauses, of the sentence.

Tense. A grammatical feature of verbs and auxiliaries relating to time. Tense is designated by an inflectional change (*walked*), by an auxiliary (*will walk*), or both (*am walking, have walked*).

***There* transformation.** A variation of a basic sentence in which the expletive *there* is added at the beginning and the subject is shifted to a position following *be:* "A fly is in my soup" → "*There is a fly in my soup.*"

Transitive verb. The verbs of Patterns 5, 6, and 7, which require at least one complement, the direct object, to be complete. With only a few exceptions, transitive verbs are those that can be transformed into the passive voice.

Verb. One of the four form classes, traditionally thought of as the action word in the sentence. A better way to recognize the verb, however, is by its form. Every verb, without exception, has an *-s* and an *-ing* form; every verb also has an *-ed* and an *-en* form, although in the case of some irregular verbs these forms are not readily apparent. And every verb, without exception, can be marked by auxiliaries. Many verbs also have characteristic derivational forms, such as *-ify (typify), -ize (criticize),* and *-ate (activate).* See Chapter 6.

Verb phrase. A verb together with its complements and modifiers; the predicate of the sentence is a verb phrase.

Voice. The relationship of the subject to the verb. See also *Active voice and Passive voice.*

What-cleft. See *Cleft sentences.*

Answers to the Exercises

Answers are provided here for the odd-numbered items. In those exercises where you are asked to revise, the sentences given here are simply suggestions; in most cases there is no one "correct" answer.

Chapter 1

Exercise 1, page 6

1. government/relaxed; 3. oil prices/will go up again When; 5. Arkansas/was; 7. issue/was; 9. I/are; 11. I/became; 13. teacher/is; 15. objectives/was.

Exercise 2, page 13

1. *Sometimes* (time [frequency]/adverb); *in his den* (place/prepositional phrase); *for two days* (time [duration]/prepositional phrase); *without leaving* (manner or circumstance/prepositional phrase).
3. *During . . . crisis* (time/prepositional phrase); *in long lines* (manner/prepositional phrase); *at . . . station* (place/prepositional phrase).
5. *in which locker* (place/prepositional phrase).
7. *In 1992* (time/prepositional phrase).
9. *by walking to work* (manner/prepositional phrase); *to work* (place/prepositional phrase).
11. *in . . . language* (manner/prepositional phrase).
13. *because . . . permission* (reason/clause); *without permission* (manner/prepositional phrase).
15. *In Chapter 7* (place/prepositional phrase); *in detail* (manner/prepositional phrase).

Exercise 3, page 15

1. In 1747 / a physician in the British Navy / conducted / an experiment / to discover a cure for scurvy. (Pattern 5)
3. Dr. James Lind / fed / six groups of scurvy victims / six different remedies. (Pattern 6)
5. Although . . . findings, / it / finally / ordered / a daily dose of fresh lemon juice / for every British seaman. (Pattern 6)
7. The British / called / lemons / "limes" / in the eighteenth century. (Pattern 7)

Chapter 2

Exercise 4, page 25

1. Notice that in sentence 4, the main clause in end-focus position—"class attendance becomes difficult"—is known information, a repetition of the previous sentence. One way to revise it is to begin with that clause: "Class attendance becomes difficult when an adult . . . two jobs." This strategy puts the new information at the end of the sentence. However, the revision introduces an awkward repetition of "class attendance." Here's a possible solution:

   One such problem is irregular class attendance. It becomes difficult when an adult . . .

   Another change that would strengthen the paragraph is the substitution of *however* for *though*.

Exercise 5, page 25

1. At the edge of the Mississippi River in St. Louis stands the Gateway Arch, the world's tallest monument. The stainless steel structure, designed by Eero Saarinen, commemorates the Westward Movement.
3. [No change in the first sentence.] It's not unusual for the temperature to reach 110° in Bakersfield, often the hottest spot in the valley. [Note that *summer* in the first sentence makes *June through September* redundant.]
5. [No change in the first sentence.] The Space Shuttle Challenger's crew of five included Sally Ride, American's first woman in space.

Chapter 3

Exercise 6, page 34

There are, of course, no "right" and "wrong" answers for the question of main stress. The answers here are the author's readings of the passages—words that are likely candidates for strong stress:

1. Sentence 1: understand, salesperson; 2: buyer, sellee; 3: want, vacuum, buy; 4: else, selling.
3. Sentence 1: history, particularly, cancer; 2: fight, crusade, killer, victims; 3: culprit; 4: patient; 5: ill, ill, well; 6: disease, enemy, not, lethal, shameful.

Exercise 7, page 39

1. It's chocolate ice cream that Jody loves. / What Jody loves is chocolate ice cream.
3. It was our defense that won the Stanford game in the final three minutes with a crucial interception. / It was in the final three minutes that our defense won the Stanford game with a crucial interception. / It was in the Stanford game that our defense won with a crucial interception in the final three minutes. / There was a crucial interception in the final three minutes that won the Stanford game for us.
5. It was a small slip of the earth eleven miles beneath the ground that started Tuesday's earthquake. / There was a small slip of the earth eleven miles . . . / What started Tuesday's earthquake was a small slip of the earth eleven miles beneath the ground. / It was eleven miles beneath the ground that a small slip occurred, starting Tuesday's earthquake.
7. There was a month of unseasonably warm weather last winter that almost ruined the ski season. / It was last winter that a month of unseasonably warm weather almost ruined the ski season. / What almost ruined the ski season last winter was that month of unseasonably warm weather we had.

Exercise 8, page 41

1. Here is the final draft of David Hamburger's opening paragraph. Has he thought carefully enough about the known–new contract? Perhaps you will think of further revisions.

It is a land where the sun doesn't shine for the entire winter. Warmth is a relative term; temperatures in the fifties constitute a heat wave. Summer can include snowstorms and icy fog. The most abundant form of wildlife seems to be mosquitos, which form dense, black swarms. Inches below the spongy surface lie thousands of feet of permanently frozen ground. Flying overhead, one sees nothing but a great expanse of what appears to be an Arctic wasteland. There are no trees and no signs of habitation, just a never-ending, dingy brown carpet know as the tundra. Why would anyone, other than the 200 or so native inhabitants, be concerned with this place? Why? Because this frozen ground oozes black oil, making the coastal plain of the Arctic National Wildlife Refuge perhaps the most valuable piece of real estate in North America. Money and security are the interests behind those who wish to develop the land, including oil companies, many Alaskans, and the Bush Administration.

Chapter 4

Exercise 9, page 59

For those sentences that are ungrammatical, the corrected form is supplied.

1. The *statement* . . . *was* simply not readable.
3. Apparently the *use* of robots . . . *has* been responsible . . .
5. The government's deregulation *policy* . . . *has* also resulted . . .
7. Correct
9. Carmen's *collection* . . . *was* really impressive.

Exercise 10, page 63

1. grief, grieve, grievous, grievously
3. ability, enable, able, ably
5. quickness, quicken, quick, quickly
7. type, typify, typical, typically
9. critic (criticism/critique), criticize (critique), critical, critically
11. appreciation, appreciate, appreciable, appreciably
13. acceptance, accept, acceptable, acceptably
15. stealth, steal, stealthy, stealthily

Exercise 11, page 64

1. *consideration, changes*: The Senate is considering a bill that would change the way the IRS deals with taxpayers. [Note that the word *change* has the same form as both a noun and a verb.]
3. *preventing, collection*: The bill would prevent the IRS from collecting taxes in ways that would create hardships. [Note that in the original sentence *preventing* is a verb being used as a noun; it is a gerund, not a nominalized verb. In the revision *prevent* is the main verb.]
5. *claim, implementation*: Congressional opponents claim that implementing the law would cost more than $200 million a year. [In this revised version, claim is a verb, not a noun. Note, too, that the nominalized *implementation* has been turned into a verb but that the verb is a gerund—that is, a verb functioning as a noun.]

Exercise 12, page 65

Since 1945, suburbanization has been the most significant fact of American social and political life. The compilers of the 1970 census caught its magnitude by observing that for the first time more people in metropolitan areas lived outside city limits than within them. The 1980 figures confirmed this trend and measured its acceleration. Moreover, the suburban explosion has been accompanied by a marked decline in city populations. The result has been a steady growth of suburban power in American politics. The changing numbers have made its dominance inevitable, but the fact that suburbanites register and vote in much larger percentages than city dwellers has accelerated the shift.

—Richard C. Wade, *The Suburban Roots of the New Federalism*

Chapter 5

Exercise 13, page 70

1. Yesterday I set out to catch the new season, and instead I found an old snakeskin. I was in the sunny February woods by the quarry; the snakeskin was lying in a heap of leaves right next to an aquarium someone had thrown away. I don't know why that someone hauled the aquarium deep into the woods to get rid of it; it had only one broken glass side. The snake found it handy, I imagine; snakes like to rub against something rigid to help them out of their skins, and the broken aquarium looked like the nearest likely object. Together the snakeskin and the aquarium

made an interesting scene on the forest floor. It looked like an exhibit at a trial—circumstantial evidence—of a wild scene, as though a snake had burst through the broken side of the aquarium, burst through his ugly old skin, and disappeared, perhaps straight up in the air, in a rush of freedom and beauty.

The snakeskin had unkeeled scales, so it belonged to a nonpoisonous snake. It was roughly five feet long by the yardstick, but I'm not sure because it was very wrinkled and dry, and every time I tried to stretch it flat it broke. I ended up with seven or eight pieces of it all over the kitchen table in a fine film of forest dust.

Exercise 14, page 75

1. If you are an average American, the energy problem is mainly your monthly fuel bill and the cost of filling up the gas tank. You may also remember that in 1979, and way back in 1974, you had to wait . . . , etc.
3. Here's a version that uses the plural. The changes begin in sentence 2: . . . and there's no reason that educated people shouldn't make a living with their hands. The notion that people who work with their hands aren't also working with their heads is wrong. It's possible to work with your head . . . , etc.

Here's a version that continues the use of second person that Rooney uses in both the beginning and end of the paragraph: . . . and there's no reason that you, as an educated person, shouldn't make a living with your hands. The notion that if you work with your hands, you're not also working with your head is wrong.

Exercise 15, page 84

1. Sentence 2: The use of these chemicals will result in an estimated 1.4 million cancer cases and will slightly increase the chance of Americans to contract the disease in their lifetime.
3. . . . I had no idea that Beth was sick. . . . Our grandmother took one look at her and called the doctor, then drove her to the hospital. That decision turned out to be a good one because Beth's cramps turned out to be appendicitis.

Exercise 16, page 86

1. I recall with great pleasure the good times that we had at our annual family reunions when I was young. With our cousins and younger aunts and uncles, we played volleyball and softball until dark. Those games were a lot of fun.
3. It seemed to my cousin Terry and me that the grownups were different people at those family reunions. Such memories of family reunions may be true for people everywhere.

Chapter 6

Exercise 17, page 98

1. The small band of contras *resisted* the army patrol for several hours, then *surrendered* just before dawn. News reports about the event did not *specify* how many troops were involved.

3. Several economists are saying that they *anticipate* an upturn. . . . Others, however, maintain that interest rates must *stabilize* if . . .
5. The chairman . . . *denounced* the practice. . . . He said that the new rules will *eliminate* all such questionable fund raising. To some observers, such practices *signify* [or *constitute*] bribery. Several senators have promised to *formulate* a new compromise plan.

Exercise 19, page 102

A. Active to Passive:

1. The lead article in today's *Collegian* was written by my roommate.
3. The most expensive houses in town are built by my brother-in-law.
5. Every four years a new tax-collection system is tried out.

B. Passive to Active:

1. The cheerleading squad led the football team onto the field.
3. Someone burglarized Bill's apartment last weekend.
5. We will hold the election of student body officers on Tuesday.

C. Either:

1. We elected John Kennedy president in 1960. (passive to active)
3. The next six chapters should be read before Monday. (active to passive)
5. Good jobs have been found in the Sunbelt by thousands of northern workers. (active to passive)
7. The administration [or someone] is finally repairing the street lights on campus. (passive to active)
9. The plant will be closed for two weeks in July. (active to passive)

Exercise 20, page 106

1. There are two other passives in the Brody passage: (1) *are born* (sentence 1): This is an unusual verb in that it is nearly always used in the passive voice (we do not say, "My mother bore me"); (2) *is not added* (sentence 5): The passive allows for the agent—the specific someone who adds the salt (*they* or *people*)—to remain unspecified. (Note that you might have identified the verb in sentence 3 as a passive: *are unsalted*. However, the verb is simply *are; unsalted* is a subjective complement—an adjective in form. There is no verb "to unsalt.")
3. We know Thomas Jefferson, an exceptionally accomplished and well-educated man, best for writing the Declaration of Independence. . . . A committee developed the substance of the document, but, because of the grace of Jefferson's style, they chose him to do the actual writing. (One difference between the two is that of cohesion. The passive enables the writer to place the old and new information in their logical slots.)

Exercise 21, page 108

1. The woods in the morning seemed both peaceful and lively. Birds sent their shrill messages through the pines and oaks, staking out their territory. Squirrels scampered across the leaves covering the forest floor. In the branches above, the new leaves of the birches and maples, outlined by the sun's rays, rustled to the rhythm of the wind.

Exercise 22, page 110

1. Investors on Wall Street are concerned because the Japanese are buying so many American companies and so much real estate.
3. Analysts of the situation in China agree that opportunities for investment are growing.
5. When Julie applied for a work-study job, she was surprised to learn that her parents would have to submit a detailed financial statement.
7. The overuse of salt in the typical American diet obscures the natural taste of many foods. Nutritionists maintain that if people reduced their dependence on salt they would find their food tastier and more enjoyable.

Chapter 7

Exercise 24, page 123

1. Even though the famous Gateway Arch is in St. Louis, it is Kansas City that claims the title "Gateway to the West."
3. Thomas Jefferson acquired the Ozark Mountains for the United States when he negotiated the Louisiana Purchase with Napoleon in 1803.
5. When the neighbors added a pit bull to their pet population, now numbering three unfriendly four-legged creatures, we decided to fence in our back yard.
7. Fad diets that severely restrict the intake of carbohydrates, the body's prime source of energy, are nearly always ineffective and are often dangerous.
9. When the auto companies offered enticing cash rebates last January, sales of new cars increased dramatically.

Exercise 25, page 127

1. Sift the flour before mixing in the dry ingredients.
3. The police had no doubt about the suspect's guilt after finding his fingerprints at the scene of the crime.
5. If your term project is late, the grade will be lowered ten percent.
7. I was amazed by the generosity of strangers while collecting money for the Women's Resource Center.
9. When you revise and edit your papers, be sure to read the sentences aloud and listen to the stress patterns.

Exercise 26, page 130

1. *To save money* (infinitive, reason); *often* (adverb, frequency); *at my desk* (prepositional phrase, place).
3. *After . . . navy* (clause, time); *from the navy* (prepositional phrase, place).
5. *As soon as the guests left* (clause, time); *in a heap* (prepositional phrase, manner); *on the couch* (prepositional phrase, place).
7. *When October came* (clause, time).
9. *slowly* (adverb, manner); *northward* (adverb, direction).
11. *home* (noun, place); *last night* (noun phrase; time); *because of the snowstorm* (prepositional phrase, reason).

Exercise 27, page 133

1. Ben was so *meticulous*. . . .
3. The foreman gives his orders in a *brusque* manner.
5. It is usually *futile* to argue. . . .
7. The basketball players looked *exhaused [fatigued]*. . . .
9. The choir members were *thrilled [enthusiastic]*. . . .

Chapter 8

Exercise 28, pages 140-41

1. The administration's recent clean-air proposals have been criticized as inadequate.
3. The stock market reached an all-time high last week.
5. I spoke to a witty, delightful man in the cafeteria.
7. There was not enough fire-fighting equipment available this summer for the widespread, devastating forest fires in the Northwest.
9. A commonly held notion among my cynical friends is that big-business lobbyists run the country.
11. The highly publicized, long-awaited paper-recycling program has finally become a reality on our campus this fall.

Exercise 29, page 146

1. Sentence 2: . . . contract, expiring . . .
3. Sentence 2: The students, hoping . . . provost, were demonstrating against a tuition hike recently approved by the trustees. The increase, expected to take effect in September, will . . .

Exercise 30, pages 148–49

1. Having endured rain all week, we weren't surprised by the miserable weather on Saturday. [Another option is: "we weren't surprised when the weather turned miserable on Saturday."]
3. We were not at all surprised when the Republican county commissioner, known for her conservative views . . . , announced her candidacy. . . .
5. Wearing their colorful new uniforms, the band marched across the field and formed a huge *W*.
7. Feeling pressure from the environmentalists, the committee immediately put the Clear Air Act on their agenda.
9. Obviously intimidated by a long history of defeats in Morgantown, our basketball team just can't seem to beat the West Virginia Mountaineers on their home court.

Exercise 31, pages 152–53

1. In many parts of the country, the citizens, mobilizing against crime and drugs, are driving drug dealers out of their neighborhoods.
3. Brian, who wants nothing to do with computers and refuses to even try a word processor, insists on using his trusty manual typewriter.

5. Many people assume that the cuts in defense spending brought about by changes in Soviet-U.S. relations will mean a "peace dividend," which will make more money available for social programs.
7. The amount of carbon dioxide in the air affects the rate of colon cancer because carbon dioxide absorbs ultraviolet light, which fuels the body's production of Vitamin D.
9. We cannot build up our immunity to flu viruses because they mutate constantly, producing new varieties that spread from person to person and from place to place.

Exercise 32, page 155

1. Cleaning the basement this morning wasn't very much fun.
3. Converting the central card catalog in the college library to a computer system took over four years.
5. Harriett was rather unhappy when Wendell didn't want to stay for the second half of the game.
7. When the president characterized the last two years as a period of "unprecedented prosperity" in his State of the Union message, one economist immediately labeled his statement "sheer hype and hyperbole."

Chapter 9

Exercise 33, pages 168–69

1. The 1990 census, which created 635,000 temporary jobs, cost 2.6 billion dollars to carry out.
3. Visitors and workers at the Philadelphia Mint must pass through a metal detector that is so sensitive that the magnet strip on a credit card will set it off.
5. Buffalo meat, which is lower in fat and cholesterol and calories than beef, is starting to become an alternative to beef among diet-conscious Americans. It is now being raised commercially on many Western ranches.
7. In recent years honeybee populations in the southern United States have been changed by invading Africanized bees, the so-called "killer bees" that migrated from Brazil. It is estimated that they have affected three-fourths of the bee populations in Texas, Arizona, and New Mexico. Honey producers in Pennsylvania, however, don't have to worry about the killer bees, which are not adapted to northern winters and would probably not survive. The biggest problem for honey production in the North is a deadly parasitic mite, which infected 300,000 Pennsylvania hives in 1988 and 1989. Pennsylvania beekeepers are now importing mite-resistant bees from Yugoslavia—imports that have become the industry's saving grace.

Exercise 34, pages 176–77

1. Japanese blue-collar workers not only work more hours per day than American workers, they typically do so with more dedication and energy.
3. In the United States neither blue-collar workers nor students spend as much time at their respective jobs as do their Japanese counterparts.
5. Julie earned an A both in the final exam and in the course.
7. Not only did the chairman of the Planning Commission refuse to let the citizens'

committee present their petition, he also refused to recognize them when they attempted to speak out at the meeting.

9. My history professor wouldn't let me take a make-up exam when I cut his class, nor would he accept my late paper.

Chapter 10

Exercise 36, pages 199–200

1. The cost of repairs to the nation's public transportation facilities—roads, bridges, and railroads—is an expenditure that cannot be delayed much longer if the system is to survive.
3. In the early 1980s, a Chinese ban on the import of certain American goods, such as cotton, synthetic fibers, and soybeans, had an adverse effect on the U.S. economy—especially on the farmers.
5. According to fashion experts, the crew cut—the haircut that was more or less the hallmark of the 1950s—will be back in style before long.
7. Llamas, which have been used since ancient times in the Andes as pack animals, are becoming popular in this country as exotic pets. They are peaceable animals, and although they don't like to be petted, they do like to stand quite close to humans and just stare. Until a few years ago, there were llamas in just a few places in this country. That situation changed when Dick and Kay Patterson of Sisters, Oregon, turned their expertise from Arabian horses to llamas. Now there are about 6,000 breeders and 70,000 llamas registered with the International Llama Registry. [Note that the detail about their valuable wool seems out of place; it's not clear if that fact applies to their role in the United States or only in the Andes.]

Exercise 37, page 202

1. My sister, who is one of the most conservative people I know, surprised everyone at the family reunion when she showed up in a 1920s-style dress trimmed with beads and feathers, her normally blonde hair dyed red.
3. At the far end of the diner's chrome and plastic counter sat a trucker, an old man with long grey hair, his leathery face a pattern of creases and scars, his fringed jacket worn nearly through at the elbows.

Chapter 11

Exercise 38, pages 219–20

1. Management is still taught in most business schools as a bundle of techniques, such as budgeting and personnel relations. To be sure, management, like any other work, has its own tools and its own techniques. But just as the essence of medicine is not urinalysis (important though that is), the essence of management is not techniques and procedures. The essence of management is to make knowledge productive. Management, in other words, is a social function. And in its practice management is truly a liberal art.

[Note: If you put a comma after *practice* in the last sentence, you have improved on the original! A comma would make the sentence easier to read.]

2. The charter-school movement is not yet big. Just 11 states, beginning with Minnesota in 1991, have passed laws permitting the creation of autonomous public schools like Northland; a dozen more have similar laws in the works. Most states have restricted the number of these schools (100 in California, 25 in Massachusetts) in an attempt to appease teachers' unions and other opponents. Nevertheless, the charter movement is being heralded as the latest and best hope for a public-education system that has failed to deliver for too many children and cannot compete internationally.

A handful of other places—notably Baltimore, Maryland, and Hartford, Connecticut—are experimenting with a far more radical way to circumvent bureaucracy: hiring a for-profit company to run the schools.

Index